The Leadership of Organizational Change

T0293719

Understanding both leadership and change have been recurrent and popular themes within business, management and organization studies literature. However, our understanding of leadership and organizational change in combination is far more limited. *The Leadership of Organizational Change* offers a critical review of the evolution of leadership and organizational change for the past thirty-five years, taking stock of what we know, identifying what we do not know and establishing how the study of the leadership of change should advance.

In the late seventies and early eighties, as interest in managing and leading change was fuelled by the competitive threat of Asia in general and Japan in particular as perceived by Western businesses and governments, Burns (1978), who was writing in his landmark book *Leadership* at this time, referred to an intellectual crisis:

> The crisis of leadership today is the mediocrity or irresponsibility of so many of the men and women in power, but leadership rarely rises to the full need for it. The fundamental crisis underlying mediocrity is intellectual. If we know all too much about our leaders, we know far too little about leadership.

While the study of managing change has benefitted from sustained critical scrutiny, particularly in the last decade, it is believed that this is to have been at the expense of critical scrutiny of leading change. *The Leadership of Organizational Change* critically reviews how the study of leading change has advanced since 1978 and the crisis of intellectual mediocrity.

Mark Hughes is a Reader in Organizational Change in the Centre for Research on Management and Employment at Brighton Business School, the University of Brighton, UK.

Routledge Studies in Organizational Change & Development

1. **Organizational Change for Corporate Sustainability 3rd Edition**
   By Suzanne Benn, Dexter Dunphy, Andrew Griffiths

2. **Organizational Change, Leadership and Ethics**
   Leading Organizations Toward Sustainability
   Edited by Rune Todnem By, Bernard Burnes

3. **Managing Organizational Change in Public Services**
   International Issues, Challenges and Cases
   Edited by Rune Todnem By, Calum Macleod

4. **Organizational Change for Corporate Sustainability**
   A Guide for Leaders and Change Agents of the Future, 2nd Edition
   By Suzanne Benn, Dexter Dunphy, Andrew Griffiths

5. **The Sustainability and Spread of Organizational Change**
   Modernizing Healthcare
   Edited by David A. Buchanan, Louise Fitzgerald, Diane Ketley

6. **Agency and Change**
   Rethinking Change Agency in Organizations
   By Raymond Caldwell

7. **Reshaping Change**
   A Processual Perspective
   By Patrick Dawson

8. **Organizational Change for Corporate Sustainability**
   A Guide for Leaders and Change Agents of the Future
   By Suzanne Benn, Dexter Dunphy, Andrew Griffiths, Suzanne Benn, Dexter Dunphy, Andrew Griffiths

9. **Change Competence**
   Implementing Effective Change
   By Steven ten Have, Wouter ten Have, Anne-Bregje Huijsmans and Niels van der Eng

10. **Organizational Change and Global Standardization**
    Solutions to Standards and Norms Overwhelming Organizations
    By David M. Boje

11. **Organizational Development and Change Theory**
    Managing Fractal Organizing Processes
    By Tonya L. Henderson and David M. Boje

12. **The Leadership of Organizational Change**
    Mark Hughes

The Leadership of Organizational Change

Mark Hughes

Routledge
Taylor & Francis Group

NEW YORK AND LONDON

First published 2016
by Routledge
711 Third Avenue, New York, NY 10017

and by Routledge
2 Park Square, Milton Park, Abingdon, Oxon OX14 4RN

First issued in paperback 2018

Routledge is an imprint of the Taylor & Francis Group,
an informa business

Library of Congress Cataloging-in-Publication Data
Hughes, Mark, 1962-
    The leadership of organizational change / by Mark Hughes.—First Edition.
        pages cm.—(Routledge studies in organizational change & development ; 12)
    Includes bibliographical references and index.
    1. Organizational change.   2. Leadership/   I. Title.
    HD58.8.H834 2015
    658.4'092—dc23
    2015020619

ISBN 13: 978-1-138-34021-3 (pbk)
ISBN 13: 978-1-138-79177-0 (hbk)

Typeset in Sabon
by Apex CoVantage, LLC

Contents

List of Figures   vii
List of Appendices   ix
Acknowledgments   xi

1   Introduction   1

2   Leadership and Organizational Change: A 35-Year Review   24

3   Understanding Organizational Change   65

4   Leadership Studies   99

5   A Critical Evaluation of Leadership and Organizational Change   144

6   Towards the Leadership of Organizational Change   189

    Appendices   223
    Index   243

Figures

1.1 Levels of disciplines, fields and the sub-field   2
1.2 Fields of leadership studies and organizational change:
     orthodoxy and beyond   8
1.3 Leadership studies isn't working   11
2.1 Mapping the leadership and organizational change
     literature review process and content   26
2.2 The top five most-cited publications as of 2nd of April 2015   28
2.3 Eight leadership transformation errors and eight leadership
     transformation stages   31
2.4 Leading organizational change (Burke, 2009)   44
2.5 Leading change: a process perspective (Hayes, 2014)   48
2.6 Leadership of organizational change papers (Ford and
     Ford, 2012)   51
3.1 35 Years of explaining organizational change   73
3.2 Managing and leading, continuity and change dualisms   83
3.3 Failings of transformation explanations: rethinking
     leadership and organizational change   87
4.1 Major characteristics of the industrial leadership paradigm
     (Rost, 1993)   104
4.2 The mythological leadership studies narrative   110
4.3 Graphic from problems, problems, problems: the social
     construction of leadership. (Grint, 2005b)   112
4.4 Key differences between discursive and psychological lenses
     (Fairhurst, 2008)   113
4.5 Reality construction rules (Fairhurst, 2011)   116
4.6 Leadership framing questions (based on Fairhurst, 2011)   117
4.7 Leadership fourfold typology (Grint, 2005a)   118
4.8 Subordination of followers within industrial-era leadership
     studies (based on Rost, 1993)   122

4.9   The new leadership school view of followers (Rost, 1993 summarised)   123

4.10 Leadership studies—orthodoxy and alternatives (developed from Rost, 1993)   134

5.1   *International Journal of Management Reviews* key principles   145

5.2   Leadership and organizational change background assumptions   149

5.3   Metaphors used to convey too much leadership complacency (Kotter, 1996)   159

5.4   Four leadership discourses (based upon Western, 2013)   161

5.5   Metaphorical narratives framing leaderism (O'Reilly and Reed, 2010)   161

5.6   Explaining leadership and organizational change through the application of a philosophies-based approach (Smith and Graetz, 2011)   163

5.7   Conceptual weaknesses of transformational leadership (Yukl, 1999)   169

5.8   Why Kotter's (1996/2012) transformation explanations of leadership fail   171

5.9   Lewin's (1947) three steps and Kotter's (1996) eight steps   173

5.10 Key findings, themes and insights from chapters two, three and four   176

5.11 Chapter one revisited and chapter five summarised   178

6.1   Emerging explanations of leadership and organizational change   191

6.2   Leadership of organizational change moments lost in translation   202

6.3   Three approaches to leading organizational change   207

Appendices

1. The Most-Cited Transformational Leadership Publications
    (1978–2014)   225
2. The Most-Cited Leadership of Change Publications
    (1978–2014)   227
3. *The Leadership Quarterly* Papers   228
4. The *Journal of Change Management* Papers   238

Acknowledgments

I thank my close family, Derek, Sheila, Stuart, Clair, Rob and Beth for all of their loving kindness. I thank Aidan Berry for his support and encouragement over half a lifetime. I thank Lew Perren for his constructive critiques of draft chapters. It's always difficult asking a friend to critique your work, but I really appreciated his critical yet thoughtful insights.

This book is rooted in my enduring passion (obsession) with critically advancing the field of organizational change studies. It is the best way that I know to make a positive difference in an increasingly negative world. I thank Bernard Burnes for helping and encouraging me in this quest. I have been aware of the *Understanding Organizational Change* series *(now Routledge Studies in Organizational Change & Development)* for many years, yet never imagined that I would have an opportunity to contribute to this series. For this opportunity, I am very grateful. David Varley and his team at Routledge made this publication possible, and I have appreciated their quiet professionalism and serious yet friendly engagement.

As part of this book project, I tested out embryonic ideas at the European Group for Organization Studies Conference and the British Academy of Management Conferences, and I have enjoyed engaging with fellow travellers and benefitting from their insights.

Finally, writing would be a solitary pursuit if it was not for the music that always accompanies me. Modern technology allows whole back catalogues to play in the study on continuous loops. Instrumentals are best for writing and on this project, *System 7*, *Banco de Gaia* and *65 Days of Static* were my writing companions. However, it is *Godspeed You! Black Emperor* that really orchestrated my emotions through encouraging quiet revolutions, quiet refusals and self-determination.

1 Introduction

The leadership of organizational change has been the zeitgeist of recent decades, developed around a narrative of organizational change as the problem and leadership as the solution. Politicians and policy makers, regardless of political allegiance, look hopefully towards leaders who are literally transforming public institutions. Similarly, private sector shareholders look hopefully towards their chief executives to realise their aspirations and radically restructure organizations. The leadership of the organizational change process never seems to fail, with failure instead attributed to the failure of the leader/s. These perceived individual failings are ritualistically and symbolically celebrated through the dismissal and replacement of leaders. Belief in the leadership of organizational change is part of a broader shift from management towards leadership; 'leadership rather than management is currently advocated in the mainstream management literature and organizational policies as the key to effective organizational performance' (Ford and Harding, 2007:475). It is a shift that privileges leadership and simultaneously disparages management. For example, Riggio (2011:120) writes about 'when the field of management began to make the shift from viewing those in positions of power and control as mere "managers" to viewing them as taking on higher-level "leadership" activities. . .' And Grint (2005:15), although sceptical, acknowledges the role subordination implied within leadership and management differentiations with the implication to '. . . get out of management and into leadership!' Gradually and imperceptibly, the word 'leader' has replaced the word 'manager' (Salaman, 2011). This practical interest in the leadership of organizational change has been mirrored by considerable interest in the fields of both leadership studies (Grint, 2005) and organizational change studies (Thomas and Hardy, 2011), with the focus of this critical review narrowing to the sub-field of leadership and organizational change. In Figure 1.1, the leadership and organizational change sub-field is depicted as being informed by both the fields of leadership studies and organizational change studies, with both fields informed by many different disciplines.

The implication of Figure 1.1 is that attempting to understand the sub-field of leadership and organizational change from either a leadership

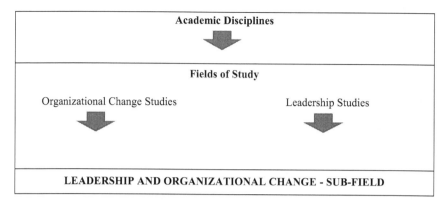

Figure 1.1   Levels of disciplines, fields and the sub-field

studies perspective or an organizational change perspective will be incomplete. However, the academic norm is to specialise within a specific field, which may partially explain why academic progress in understanding the sub-field has been so limited. As Bryman et al (2011:ix) suggest with regards to leadership, '[P]recisely because it is such a productive field, it is difficult for even specialist scholars to keep up with its breadth and it is even more difficult for new scholars to break into it.' Figure 1.1 also suggests that understanding the sub-field of leadership and organizational change will be informed by many competing paradigms, philosophies and perspectives characterising both fields of study, as well as the academic disciplines informing these fields. The leadership of organizational change may be the zeitgeist of recent decades, but that does not equate necessarily to understanding. The understanding of the leadership of organizational change to date may be characterised as a seduction and leadership, as a seduction is nothing new (Calas and Smircich, 1991). In this instance, the leadership of organizational change rhetoric may even exceed/exaggerate the reality.

This critical review of the leadership of organizational change goes back to the future in order to understand the fields of study, academic debates, values, beliefs and assumptions underpinning today's leadership of organizational change. A particular emphasis is placed upon social construction (Berger and Luckmann, 1966) and discourse (Fairhurst, 2008) in the belief that leadership is primarily concerned with managing meaning (Pondy, 1978). As a consequence, the label 'the leadership of organizational change' seeks to reference contemporary discourses and debates, speaking to ongoing contemporary debates regarding both theories and practices. This label even has assumptions embedded within it that leadership will result in successful organizational change, which will be achieved in a rational and linear manner. However, at times, an alternative 'leadership and organizational change' label is used in order to avoid at least some of the progressive assumptions embedded within leadership language. Organizational change may necessitate different forms of leadership, and through organizational change, leaders and leadership may change. The second label is believed to avoid some of the forward-facing linear rationality of the first label.

In this introductory chapter, the historical perspective adopted towards leadership and organizational change is introduced, as well as the process and content of the critical review of leadership and organizational change. The language, landscape, boundaries and map of the book are introduced in terms of defining key terms, what is included and excluded and briefly mapping the content of the subsequent chapters.

FORWARD TO THE PAST OR BACK TO THE FUTURE?

Whereas societal belief in the transformational capabilities of leaders goes back centuries, pragmatically, this critical review focuses on the last 35 years. Burns (1978) believed that leaders in collaboration with followers could transform institutions and societies, and this belief offered the inspirational starting point for this review. Rost (1997:5) reflected back upon Burns's achievement as a way '. . .to redefine leadership around a political frame of reference, and present to his readers a whole new way of looking at leadership as transformational change.' The review concludes at the end of 2014 with economies, societies, organizations and individuals still suffering the consequences of 2008's potentially leadership-related global financial recession.

> . . .some of our dominant theoretical concepts—such as transformational and charismatic leadership—have legitimised an over concentration of decision making power in the hands of a few, with consequences that have been less than socially and economically useful.
>
> (Jackson and Tourish, 2014:4)

Burns (1978) originally appeared to have been attempting to shame leadership studies out of its complacent orthodoxy, describing the study of leadership as suffering from intellectual mediocrity. He constructively offered a lengthy account of how institutions and societies could and should be transformed through ethical leadership, which was more closely aligned with political science, rather than management and organization studies. Burns believed that democratic and egalitarian forms of leadership were capable of transforming institutions and societies. Burns's book was primarily a study of followership, as Burns believed that followers were crucial in terms of democratic/egalitarian changes in societies and institutions. However, unfortunately, scholars have focused too narrowly upon Burns's differentiation between transactional and transformational leaders. His pioneering work on followership, the distinction between reform and revolution and their interplay was 'lost in the translation' into leadership orthodoxy.

The 35-year review window includes increasing engagement with leading change (Kotter, 1996/2012) and transformational leadership (Bass and Riggio, 2006), as Western businesses responded to competition from the East. The 35-year window also includes the 2008 global financial recession, and the opportunities that have arisen to question leadership in general and the leadership of organizational change in particular.

Grint (2008) concluded his own review of leadership studies by critically questioning the tendency of leadership to go forward to the past. He argued that despite the apparently forward-looking developments within leadership studies, these developments reflected and revisited earlier preoccupations. Today's contemporary language of inspirational, transformational, visionary and charismatic leadership revisits the earlier, discredited traits approaches, still encouraging individualistic and heroic conceptions of strong leaders. In the case of the leadership of organizational change, forward-looking rhetoric magnifies what Grint was encountering within leadership studies. Leadership of organizational change language and debates look positively and proactively to imagined futures. As Kotter (1996:186) concluded in *Leading Change*, '. . . [P]eople who are making an effort to embrace the future are a happier lot than those clinging to the past.' One of the dangers of going forward into the past is that potentially the past and earlier learning is lost with those who forget the past condemned to repeat the past (Santayana, 1998). However, looking to one of the key contributors to the debates featured in this critical review, Kotter (1996:142) explicitly expressed his irritation with corporate history in *Leading Change*, writing, '[C]leaning up historical artifacts does create an even longer change agenda, which an exhausted organization will not like. But the purging of unnecessary interconnections can ultimately make transformation much easier.'

Today's strong, individualistic, heroic, masculine notions of leadership (often also associated with organizational change) unfortunately begin to resemble the 'Great Men' leadership theories of earlier centuries and have forgotten the past, which is now being proactively and positively repackaged and revisited upon societies, institutions and individuals. Yet, beneath this enthusiastic, forward-looking rhetoric, gendered leadership inequalities (Alvesson and Billing, 2009) are very prevalent. There is an absence of ethical change leadership (By et al, 2012,2013; By and Burnes, 2013) and a broader movement towards more democratic and egalitarian leadership (Burns, 1978; Rost, 1993) beneficial to wider societies is postponed, possibly indefinitely. As a counterbalance to today's troubling forward-to-the-past trajectory, Grint (2008:116) encouraged going back to the future

> . . .to see how those futures are constructed by the very same decision-makers and consider the persuasive mechanisms that decision-makers use to make situations more tractable to their own preferred form of authority.

Again, this is particularly relevant to the leadership of organizational change and the persuasive, forward-looking discourses that leaders and mainstream academics employ. These accounts go back further and are far wider than organizational change: '. . . [W]e are told wonderful stories about the role that great leaders have played in making history and initiating the changes that have created the world as we know it' (Haslam et al, 2011:1). Whereas the leadership of organizational change captures the organizational imagination today, early forms of leading change within societies and within institutions go back centuries, informing both the early and more recent development of civilisations. In a similar manner, textbook orthodoxy reassuringly depicts leadership studies historically developing over the past century, implying the successful advance of knowledge (see Cummings, 2002 for a critique). Grint's (2008) overview of leadership literature focused upon a more recent epoch between 1965 and 2006. Initially, Grint revisited the 1800s and the 'Great Men' accounts of leadership prior to 1965, which depicted leadership as masculine, heroic, individualist and normative, a depiction that prevailed into the 1900s and unfortunately still exists to this day. Grint critically reviewed management and organizational studies developments through the 1900s, bringing the story up to date with the contemporary arrival of transformational and inspirational leadership. Grint (2008) feared that despite all the inspiring visions and missions, there had been a return to earlier normative trait approaches and that we had gone forward to the past. In critically understanding leadership and organizational change, such inspirational missions have a shadow side:

> . . .[K]nowledge—what counts as "true"—is the property of particular communities and thus that knowledge is never neutral or divorced from ideology.
>
> (Grint, 2008:109)

A further advantage of this 35-year window is that it allows for the consideration of early conceptualisations of the leadership of organizational change, which used to feature strong leaders making tough decisions. Bennis (2000:114) parodies such enduring conceptualisations:

> But even as the lone hero continues to gallop through our imaginations, shattering obstacles with silver bullets, leaping tall buildings with a single bound, we know that's a false lulling fantasy and not the way real change, enduring change, takes place. We know there is an alternative reality.

Once again, the shortcomings of leadership orthodoxy are highlighted, although unfortunately, the lone hero still to this day gallops through many people's imaginations, with gunfights still to be won and cowgirls (and cowboys) still to be saved. More importantly, the criticism of leadership that Bennis implies helps make sense of the recent attempts to rethink leadership. Acknowledging the centrality of followers (Grint, 2005), gender and leadership differences (Alvesson and Billing, 2009) and the goal of leading change ethically (By and Burnes, 2013) all make greater sense when understood as attempts to address earlier leadership deficiencies, rather than as extensions of earlier leadership thinking. As well as being proactive attempts to lead organizational change in a more moral and inclusive manner, they offer critiques of the past conceptualisations of leading organizational change.

In critically reflecting back on the past 35 years, this review takes in the eighties and early attempts to manage organizational change, particularly cultural change, which failed to meet the unrealistic expectations placed upon such change initiatives (see Deal and Kennedy, 1999 for a critique by the original proponents of cultural change). Whereas the failures in delivering on these unrealistic expectations are not disputed, the rational, linear and unambiguous managing-change mindsets informing theory and practice are disputed, and will be discussed in terms of the competing perspectives, paradigms and philosophies of organizational change (see Chapter Three).

In looking back to the nineties, leading change became the new managing change with a tangible shift from managing organizational change towards leading organizational change. It will be necessary to revisit this shift with the benefit of hindsight, as this shift informs today's leadership of organizational change discourse (see Chapter Four for further discussion). In the interim, as this perceived shift was a major driver for writing this book, it was surprising to learn that two American billionaires (Ross Perot and J.D. Rockefeller) played an explicit role in encouraging the shift, with their wishes subsequently championed by Harvard Business School professors. Influential publications relating to management and leadership differentiations were reviewed and perversely, the anticipated evidence base informing the significant shift from managing change to leading change integral to this story does not exist (discussed further in Chapter Four and Six). Rather, it remains another of the assumptions characterising the sub-field of leadership and organizational change. Even Kotter (1990, 1996), one of the most famous advocates for a greater emphasis on leadership, acknowledged that management was an equally essential activity within organizations, but again, his caveats appear to have been lost in the stampede from management to leadership.

In the nineties, unrealistic expectations were cultivated about leading organizational change, facilitated through the apparent superhuman capabilities and competencies of new transformational leaders and change leaders. Kotter (1995) famously warned that corporate transformation efforts were failing and followed up this warning with reassurance about how to lead transformations (Kotter, 1996). Kotter's influential contributions will be critically evaluated (Chapter Five). However, a larger concern relates to the leadership orthodoxy Kotter typified, depicting leadership as a rational, linear and an unambiguous process. These views have to date not been superseded; if anything, they have become more deeply embedded within academic as well as practitioner thinking. As Storey (2011:3) warned, '[V]irtually every sector and all levels of staff appear to be represented and engaged in the search for leadership. Everyone, it seems, is being invited to join in.' Storey regarded eighties change management as one of the catalysts for this increasing interest in leadership:

"Change management" became the urgent requirement; "leadership" offered a widely appealing response. The case "for leadership" is thus seemingly easily made. The agenda in the reports quickly turns to how to meet the need.

(Storey, 2011:8).

Paraphrasing the science fiction television series *The X-Files*, 'We want to believe.' The belief is that through heroic change leadership, our schools, hospitals, factories or banks, whatever organizations we care about, will successfully change. This societal belief has become difficult to abandon and now pervades our work (factories, banks and supermarkets), rest (hospitals and care homes) and play (football teams). But despite such pervasiveness, is belief in the leadership of organizational change sufficient to make change happen? Organizations keep the aspiration alive by investing heavily in leadership development programmes (Loew and O'Leonard, 2012), and they keep on investing, despite critical questioning (Edwards et al, 2013). Politicians and shareholders suggest that leaders and super-leaders will change or turn around failing organizations, new university leadership courses appear, new leadership journals and more and more books (including this one) are written. In breathlessly celebrating the leadership of organizational change the contentious nature of leadership may be overlooked, as well as the philosophical challenges of explaining and predicting unknown futures as organizations change. The variability and context-dependent nature of both leadership and organizational change may be overlooked, as well as the problematic nature of critically evaluating leadership and organizational change success and failure (Hughes 2011). Prepare to be underwhelmed.

CRITICALLY REVIEWING LEADERSHIP AND ORGANIZATIONAL CHANGE: BEYOND THE ORTHODOXY

Critical evaluations of both leadership studies and organizational change are troubling for people working in these fields, as they potentially diminish the academic legitimacy and credibility of the theories, models and concepts being promoted. An understandable aspiration is for the rational and progressive development of the fields, in which more and more knowledge is acquired.

A striking and appealing feature of the rational philosophy resides with its assurance that mapping out change can be done in advance. For change agents seeking control in uncertain contexts, the rational philosophy offers a compelling and risk-averse framework.

(Smith and Graetz, 2011:46)

However, the advantage of a critical historiography is that by highlighting the taken-for-granted orthodoxies, assumptions and mindsets, the current orthodox thinking is disrupted and rethinking is encouraged. Figure 1.2 elaborates upon Figure 1.1, which featured leadership and organizational change as a sub-field informed by the fields of leadership studies and organizational change studies, as well as being informed by different academic disciplines.

In this section, the implications of Figure 1.2 for understanding leadership and organizational change as well as for this critical literature review are discussed. In Figure 1.2, the fields of both leadership studies and organizational change studies feature prominently. The majority of the literature informing both of these fields tends to be orthodox, favouring

Academic Disciplines	Academic Fields of Study	Field Characteristics	Sub-Fields	Sub-Field Characteristics
Disciplines informing leadership studies such as:	Orthodox leadership studies	Consensus, Convergence, Synthesis and Accumulation of Knowledge	Leadership of organizational change	Leadership resulting in organizational change, Both fields important
Psychology, History, Political Science, Sociology	Critical leadership studies	Dissensus, Divergence, Discourses	Leadership & organizational change	Knowledge construction not accumulation
Disciplines informing organizational change studies such as:	Orthodox organizational change studies	Consensus, Convergence, Synthesis and Accumulation of Knowledge	Leadership of organizational change	Organizational change through leadership, Both fields important
Sociology, Economics, Psychology, Cultural Studies	Critical organizational change studies	Dissensus, Divergence, Discourses	Leadership & organizational change	Knowledge construction not accumulation

Figure 1.2   Fields of leadership studies and organizational change: Orthodoxy and beyond

rationalist and functionalist explanations of both leadership as well as organizational change. The mainstream orthodoxy of leadership studies and organizational change studies both reassures and prescribes. It is probably for these reasons that orthodox treatments account for the majority of the publications within these fields. However, the quantity of literature is no indicator of the quality of what is currently being espoused. Theories and practices in both fields, when reassuringly presented as rational, linear and unambiguous, become self-sustaining. In *The Dark Side of Transformational Leadership: A Critical Perspective*, difficult themes being developed within this introductory chapter are introduced using different terminology.

> . . .[T]he need to question and challenge will not go away. This book encourages its readers to resist the status quo, question authority and always approach the practice of leadership and its claims with a healthy feeling of scepticism.
>
> (Tourish, 2013:12)

Unfortunately, this is not the party line for most business school leadership and/or organizational change university courses, which encourage and prepare future managers/leaders to maintain the status quo. Explanations that present leadership and organizational change as rational, linear and unambiguous will always be favoured over explanations that depict leadership as socially constructed, organizational change as ambiguous and people as acting irrationally. This orthodoxy by definition favours consensus, convergence, synthesis and the accumulation of knowledge. If you are an orthodox leadership studies scholar, your favoured explanation of leadership and organizational change is likely to emphasise leadership resulting in organizational change, whereas if you are an orthodox organizational change studies scholar, your favoured explanation is likely to emphasise organizational change enabled through leadership. As both fields are informed by competing academic disciplines even within orthodoxy, a range of paradigms, philosophies and perspectives surfaces (see Deetz, 1996; Hughes, 2013 for further discussion).

The implication of Figure 1.2 for undertaking this literature review is the need to initially be as open as possible to whatever explanations have been offered for the interrelationships between leadership and organizational change. In this spirit, Chapter Two answers three questions:

1) Which leadership and organizational change explanations have academics cited the most?
2) Which aspects of leadership and organizational change have academics focused on in their journal papers?
3) How do academics currently explain leadership and organizational change?

These questions are discussed further in the next chapter, but may be introduced at this stage as follows: The first question is concerned with using citations as a means of establishing the most influential accounts of leadership and organizational change offered between 1978 and 2014. The second question focuses on papers published in two focused journals, from when each journal was founded until the end of 2014. These are the organizational change and transformation papers in *The Leadership Quarterly*, and the leadership papers in the *Journal of Change Management*. The third question identifies the meta-level explanations of leadership and organizational change offered in recent years. The tone and style of Chapter Two is intentionally neutral, largely reflecting the functionalist orthodoxy of leadership and organizational change that was encountered. Subsequently, however, this book, in order to advance understanding about leadership and organizational change, critically questions this orthodoxy.

Looking critically for a moment at the leadership of organizational change, it becomes apparent that difficult academic questions do not merely remain unanswered; they are not even being asked. Rhetoric is repeatedly employed to discourage questioning; phrases such as 'resistant to change,' 'organizational terrorist,' 'saboteur,' 'cynic' and 'sceptic' are used (see Hughes, 2010 for further discussion about the pejorative semantics of resistance to change language). Advancing an academic field of study by questioning taken-for-granted myths, assumptions and orthodoxies has real value. Writing specifically with reference to leadership and organizational change, Ladkin (2010) acknowledged that within traditional conceptualisations of leadership, leaders provide the vision of a new and different future. However, drawing upon process philosophy and hermeneutics in her concluding chapter, she encouraged asking the right questions in order to inform organizational members' meaning-making and understanding about how work contributed to the organization's or community's purpose.

In beginning to critically review the literature over 35 years, enduring thinking patterns become apparent, which may not have been so apparent if the focus had been on the present. For example, the mythological leadership studies narrative (Rost, 1993) encourages concentrating on the latest leadership literature, in the belief that we are becoming more and more knowledgeable, whereas critically reviewing leadership studies over 35 years reveals repeated red flags about the state of leadership knowledge (see Figure 1.3).

Burns's annoyance with leadership was not an isolated critique. Rost, Grint and Salaman (see Figure 1.3) feature in later chapters and reached similar conclusions over subsequent decades that were informed by their own critical literature reviewing. For Van de Ven and Poole (1995), a central and ongoing quest of scholars in management and other disciplines has been explaining how and why organizations change. Accounts of organizational

The fundamental crisis underlying mediocrity is intellectual. If we know all
   too much about our leaders, we know far too little about leadership. (Burns,
   1978:1)

They (critiques cited) destroy the notion that the leadership literature adds up and
   makes sense. It does not. (Rost, 1993:22)

Although leadership research seems to be increasing exponentially we have
   yet to establish what it is, never mind whether we can teach it or predict its
   importance. (Grint, 2005:1)

The practical encouragement and emphasis on leadership has been matched by an
   enormous increase in a largely uncritical focus on leadership at the academic
   level—both through courses and programmes and through research and writing.
   (Salaman, 2011:56/57)

(Editorial of the journal *Leadership*) . . .[Y]et another problem in the field—its
   unrelenting triviality. (Tourish, 2015:138)

Figure 1.3   Leadership studies isn't working

change were critically questioned as far back as 1974, with Kahn provocatively characterizing organizational change as follows:

> A few theoretical propositions. . .repeated without additional data or
> development; a few bits of homey advice. . .reiterated without proof or
> disproof; and a few sturdy empirical observations quoted with rever-
> ence but without refinement or explication.
>
> (Kahn, 1974:487)

Thirty years later, the subsequent editor of the *Journal of Change Management* again took critical stock of organizational change management,
concluding that '. . .what is currently available is a wide range of contradictory and confusing theories and approaches, which are mostly lacking
empirical evidence and often based on unchallenged hypotheses regarding the nature of contemporary organizational change management' (By,
2005:378). The implication here is that whereas belief in the orthodoxy of
the sub-field and its underpinning fields may reassure and be prevalent, it
provides a very shaky foundation upon which to build understanding. Jackson and Tourish (2014:4), in their first editorial of *Leadership*, emphasised
the importance of challenging the leadership studies status quo.

> Our field is too complex to rely on only one explanation, or to be
> explored via only a small coterie of methodologies. We therefore reaf-
> firm that we see the journal as offering an outlet for a broad range of
> theoretical perspectives and multifarious methodologies. But it is above
> all receptive to ideas that challenge the status quo.

Despite the persistence of orthodoxies, academic concerns still surface about the utility of the ontologies and epistemologies that convergent and consensus-based orthodoxies imply. Academic explanations of both leadership and organizational change are contested terrains, with multiple explanations competing for our attention. Chapters Three to Six embrace this spirit of challenging the status quo. Again referring to Figure 1.2, instead of the consensus, convergence, synthesis and accumulation of knowledge of orthodoxy, critical studies emphasise dissensus, divergence, discourses and knowledge construction.

Issues of dissensus, divergence, discourses and knowledge construction are equally applicable to the fields of both leadership studies and organizational change studies, but the intention is not to duplicate these discussions. Chapter Three focuses on the disciplines and the field of organizational change studies, highlighting how advances in this field have been characterised by dissensus and divergence rather than consensus and convergence, with such dissensus and divergence equally applicable to leadership studies. In Chapter Four, the focus turns to the social construction, framing and discourses of leadership in order to highlight how understanding is more about social construction than knowledge accumulation, which is again equally applicable to organizational change studies. In seeking to understand the interrelationships between leadership and organizational change, it is necessary to draw upon the field-specific literature cited in Chapters Three and Four, but also the equally applicable concepts of dissensus, divergence, discourses and knowledge construction. In combination, such resources inform the critical evaluation featured in Chapter Five and the explanations offered in Chapter Six.

In challenging the consensus, convergence, synthesis and accumulation of knowledge of orthodoxy by favouring dissensus, divergence, discourses and knowledge construction, our belief in science and its applicability to society is questioned. A science of leadership and organizational change that might be anticipated does not exist. At times, the discussions about transformational leadership and papers published in, for example, *The Leadership Quarterly*, imply a reassuring science of leadership, but the application of natural science principles to organizations and societies will never fully explain the subtleties and complexities of societies, organizations and individuals. Instead, leadership and organizational change have to be interpreted in a manner similar to an artist painting an interpretation of what they see. Language, social construction and discourse play significant roles within leadership (Fairhurst and Grant, 2010; Kelly, 2014) as well as processes of change (Doolin et al, 2013). In implying discovery, the leadership of organizational change takes us back into the realms of the natural sciences and profoundly significant discoveries, such as the discovery of penicillin. The quest intrigues with leadership studies and organizational change studies framed in terms of a journey towards discovering the essence of this union between leadership and organizational change. But such one-size-fits-all approaches inappropriately impose natural science methodologies onto the diversity of social sciences.

> . . .[W]e should be clear from the start that leadership is not a science but an art; it is a performance not a recipe; it is an invention not a discovery. If it was a science, we could reduce the essence down to a parsimonious set of rules and apply the result with confidence. Unfortunately, this is not the case.
>
> (Grint, 2000:417)

Grint's (2000) salutary warnings offered towards the end of his account of famous and infamous leaders throughout history equally serves as a cautionary note to begin this critical history of 35 years of researching, studying and theorising leadership and organizational change. Grint's (2000) position was informed by the philosophies, beliefs and assumptions that he favoured. Understanding leadership and organizational change equally is informed by favoured philosophies, beliefs and assumptions with regards to both the study of leadership and the study of organizational change. The warning here is that belief in causal theories arising out of a science of leadership and organization change, which many people believe already exists or will soon be discovered, is an illusion.

The existence of a mythological leadership studies narrative perceptively highlighted by Rost (1993) will be discussed further in Chapter Four, but by way of introduction, it implies that research has been successful, leadership scholars have increased our understanding of leadership, and scholars and practitioners can rest assured that they have an increasingly sophisticated understanding of leadership. Similar narratives surround organizational change understanding, paraphrased as, 'We are almost there!' The existence of such reassuring narratives is understandable; most social scientists require the encouragement that a natural science discovery quest offers. It is not motivating to expend large amounts of time and energy attempting to resolve a socially constructed conundrum that will never satisfactorily be resolved.

A critical theme that will be developed in this review is the leadership of organizational change, paradoxically maintaining the status quo: '. . .[T]he more things change, the more they remain the same' (Calas and Smircich, 1991:568). In subsequent chapters, the considerable dissensus characterising both the fields of leadership studies and organizational change will be highlighted and more troublingly, the lack of empirical evidence (see Ford and Ford, 2012; Parry, 2011) informing leadership and organizational change. By way of a preface to these debates, a quotation from *The SAGE Handbook of Leadership*, which is edited and authored by respected leadership academics, is informative:

> Leadership and organizational change are inextricably intertwined. However, "organizational change" has become an interest for organizational

consultants more so than for empirical researchers. There are many more books and articles on practitioner or conceptual scholarship than on theoretical or empirical scholarship. Much of the practitioner work is case study-based, and anecdotal and not rigorous in its conduct.

(Parry, 2011:57)

Independently of Professor Parry, the same conclusion was being drawn whilst writing this book, so at the very least, there are two non-believers. This critical review will seek to persuade readers about the taken-for-granted assumptions underpinning dominant discourses about the leadership of organizational change, with Parry's quotation revisited again as a critical touchstone.

LANGUAGE, LANDSCAPE, BOUNDARIES AND THE MAP

In this final section, the language, landscape, definitional boundaries and a map of the five subsequent chapters are introduced. If we survey the leadership of organizational change landscape, what is evident? Understanding the landscape of leadership and organizational change requires engagement with definitional boundaries, in particular, defining leadership and organizational change as well as related concepts. Whereas singular, universal definitions may be criticised for misrepresenting the fragmented, discursive and contradictory nature of these ambiguous and contradictory fields, definitions help to convey the focus of the review. In deference to Rost's (1993, 1997) contribution to leadership studies, the following definition of leadership is favoured: '[L]eadership is an influence relationship among leaders and collaborators who intend real changes that reflect their mutual purposes' (Rost, 1997:11).

Rost (1993) originally favoured 'followers' in his definition, but became increasingly disillusioned with the semantic implications of 'followers' and subsequently replaced it with the term 'collaborators' (discussed further in Chapter Four). This definition emphasises the relational nature of leadership achieved through participative processes. Its emphasis upon real, intended changes is very pertinent to this critical review, with Rost believing that change does not have to happen, but that change must be the intention and must be grounded in mutual purposes, rather than just the leader's will. This definition is radically different from normal conceptualisations of leadership celebrating the agency and will of exceptional leaders and by implication, the insignificance and subservience of collaborators (followers). Leaders frequently depict themselves as playing the most important facilitative role in making change happen, thus fuelling, rather than informing, such beliefs (see Collins, 2000 and Huczynski, 2006 for a critical overview of such hagiographies).

The leadership definition raises another issue that will be revisited in subsequent chapters—are leadership and organizational change separate activities, or is the facilitation of organizational change really always an integral aspect of leadership? Rost's definition is favoured, but it cannot be universally applied to all leadership literature. However, it will be revisited in the concluding chapter in terms of beginning to rethink the leadership of organizational change. The boundaries of organizational change prove equally difficult to definitively define.

> Organizational change literature encompasses a vast and diverse body of work that encompasses micro and macro views of the firm, as well as varying foci (scale of change, type of change, interventions in change and people in change).
>
> (Frahm, 2007:946)

The word 'change' itself has been characterised as a container concept, with the search for the words underlying values resulting in a whole range of meanings (De Caluwe and Vermaak, 2003). Academically engaging with change reveals change that takes on many different guises, including 'transformation, development, metamorphosis, transmutation, evolution, regeneration, innovation, revolution and transition . . .' (Stickland, 1998:14). In seeking to explain and understand leadership and organizational change in combination, the diversity of understandings and definitions is exceptionally slippery. This slipperiness is compounded by the terminology that is in everyday use, with everyone having their own slightly different grounded understanding.

In the next chapter, the most cited leadership and organizational change publications will feature, with the most cited contribution (as gauged by the citation rankings) being Kotter's (1996) *Leading Change*. This contribution illustrates a semantic problem central to this critical review. The title of Kotter's practitioner-orientated book refers to 'change;' however, within the book, Kotter mainly refers to transformation. Unfortunately, he never clarified/defined what he was writing about, although in the preface to a follow-up book, he offered his readers some clarification.

> By transform I mean the adoption of new technologies, major strategic shifts, process reengineering, mergers and acquisitions, restructuring into different sorts of business units, attempts to significantly improve innovation, and cultural change.
>
> (Kotter and Cohen, 2002:ix)

In the citation rankings, *Transformational Leadership* (Bass and Riggio, 2006) received the third-highest number of citations. In seeking to understand the boundaries of the sub-field of leadership and organizational change, the expectation would be that two of the most-cited authors would make reference to each other's work in advancing understanding, either positively or negatively, but this does not happen. Kotter (1996:x) openly acknowledged, 'I have neither drawn examples or major ideas from any published source except my own writing nor tried to cite evidence from other sources to bolster my conclusions.' Bass and Riggio (2006) did refer to Kotter (1982) and Kotter and Heskett (1992), but these books were primarily neither about 'change' nor 'transformation.'

Bass and Riggio (2006:225) believed that 'transformational leadership is, at its core, about issues around the processes of transformation and change.' This is promising, but the anticipated engagement with organizational change remains elusive. The authors acknowledged a common criticism and misconception of transformational leadership as 'smoke and mirrors' and in mitigation, their book cites literature supporting their thesis as well as literature critical of their thesis. Equally, they cite empirical evidence supporting their conceptualisations of transformational leadership, transactional leadership, the full range of leadership model and the Multifactor Leadership Questionnaire (discussed in Chapter Two). As Bass and Riggio (2006:55) acknowledged, transformational leadership (particularly charismatic) had been associated with producing change in groups and organizations; however, they conceded that 'unfortunately, there has been relatively little research directly examining how transformational leadership affects change in organizations.' This honest concession by leading proponents of transformational leadership again highlights the semantic challenges of relating leadership and organizational change. The unifying belief of Bernard Bass and other transformational leadership scholars was that a transformational leader transforms followers' attitudes and motivations, with an implication that their subsequent behaviours would result in subsequent organizational developments and changes. Whilst both John Kotter and Bernard Bass were highly cited and both referred to 'transformation,' they conceived 'transformation' in completely different ways.

Transformation as part of today's leadership of organizational change zeitgeist results in buildings no longer being refurbished; instead, they are transformed. Teaching is no longer enhanced by the addition of access to an intranet; instead, teaching is digitally transformed. I even learnt recently about a student spending a placement year working on an invoicing transformation project. When the supervisor queried this focus, the reply was that the manager liked to refer to every project as a transformation. The fashionable language of transformation only complicates critical literature reviewing. By way of a scholarly antidote, in their classic paper, Dunphy and Stace (1988) acknowledged organizational change arguments both for incrementalism and arguments for radical organizational transformation. They regarded incremental organizational change as characterised by organization development being the norm, but that the discontinuities of the environments of the 1970s and 1980s were perceived as requiring more radical transformations. Dunphy and Stace (1988) themselves argued that approaches to organizational change needed to embrace both incrementalism and transformation, identifying four ideal types of change strategy: Participative evolution, charismatic transformation, forced evolution and dictatorial transformation. They differentiated change strategies in terms of their degrees of collaboration/coercion and their degrees of incrementalism/ transformation. In this review, both the leadership of transformation and the leadership of organizational change are explored, although with the caveat that consistent differentiations between 'transformation' and 'change' within this sub-field are not employed. Equally, leading organizational transformation and change is not the only progressive agenda in town; technological, innovation management, project management, organizational development, human resource development and human resource management in engaging with leadership compete for our attention, although they are outside the scope of this particular review.

As transformational leadership may eventually result in organizational change and as it developed directly in response to Burns's (1978) work, it will feature in the next chapter. However, as Haslam et al (2011:41) warned, '. . .[W]ould-be-leaders often resort to a literal interpretation of the term "transformational" and seek to demonstrate their leadership credentials by restructuring their organization at the first available opportunity.' The belief that good leaders have to subject organizations to radical transformation remains a very negative legacy of this common misunderstanding of transformational leadership (Haslam et al, 2011). In a knowledgeable reflection upon temporality and organizational change, Dawson (2014) highlighted the assumptions and anomalies that are impeding understanding.

> It is understandable that when the common phenomenon of interest is how best to represent change, that models incorporate some element of movement (temporality) in progressing from point T1 to point T2.
> (Dawson, 2014:293)

He highlighted theorists depicting change as an ongoing, ceaseless process or a series of clearly marked episodes, depicting change within a unidirectional time framework or a multidirectional time framework. In this critical review, organizational change is defined as '. . .the process by which organizations move from their present state to some desired future state to increase their effectiveness' (Jones, 2010:31). There are subtler and more sophisticated explanations of change (such as Dawson's), but in seeking to critically advance the sub-field of leadership and organizational change, the pragmatism of a broad definition accommodates discussion and informs pluralistic understanding.

There are unlikely to be consensus definitions of either leadership or organizational change, and perhaps there never should be, given the different paradigms, philosophies and perspectives informing the respective fields. However, in academically seeking to explain leadership and organizational change, this diversity of definitions obscures, rather than clarifies, understanding. Palmer and Dunford (2008:S27) highlighted the problematic nature of the existence of different ontological assumptions about managing change when they wrote, '[T]he critical starting point is to recognise that 'managing change' is not an unambiguous term because no one common ontological assumption underlies either the notion of 'managing' or that of 'change." These ontological problems will inevitably be replicated in studies of leadership and organizational change.

In mapping this book, it is informative first to concisely explain the book's overall structure and then to elaborate upon the key themes within the subsequent chapters. The next chapter identifies the existing explanations for leadership and organizational change (Chapter Two), followed by two chapters that explain the understanding of organizational change (Chapter Three) and leadership studies (Chapter Four). The fifth chapter critically evaluates the explanations presented in Chapter Two using the theories, models and concepts introduced in Chapters Three and Four. The final chapter constructively highlights the competing explanations of leadership and organizational change.

Leadership and organizational change: A 35-year review (Chapter Two). This chapter adopts a 35-year time frame of reference in order to highlight the explanations that have been offered for leadership and organizational change. In light of the large amount of publications written between 1978 and 2014, citation rankings were used to identify the twenty most-cited publications. In order to identify empirically based leadership and organizational change themes, contributions to two refereed journals were reviewed. Specifically, these were the leadership-related papers in the *Journal of Change Management* and the change/transformation papers in *The Leadership Quarterly*. The downside of citation counts and emerging themes is that they compartmentalise what is known about leadership and organizational change. Consequently, overarching explanations synthesising what was known were identified. In terms of gauging the current state of knowledge, two different types of academic publication were reviewed: Academic handbooks that have come into vogue in recent years, as well as university textbooks that potentially offer insights into how leadership and organizational change is currently taught.

Understanding organizational change (Chapter Three). This chapter takes critical stock of understanding organizational change, as academic explanations of leadership and organizational change draw upon (or should draw upon) what is known about organizational change. Organizational change as a field is differentiated from an academic discipline such as physics. Whereas Kuhn (1962) regarded physics as being convergent, organizational change is far more divergent. Progressive and linear histories of organizational change are questioned in favour of historiography. Dominant interests privilege selective accounts of history, whilst marginalizing alternative conceptualisations. Mindful of this caveat, seven influential explanations of organizational change drawn from the last 35 years were reviewed. These competing explanations demonstrate the pluralism of the field and the different beliefs, assumptions and philosophies underpinning these explanations. What emerges is closer to an ever-changing image as viewed through a kaleidoscope (Hope Hailey and Balogun, 2002) rather than a singular and uniform image as viewed through a telescope, which orthodoxy inevitably encourages. Whilst each explanation has its merits, Smith and Graetz's (2011) philosophies and dualities of organizational change feature prominently due to their applicability for explaining relationships between leadership and organizational change. In rethinking leadership and organizational change, empirical/theoretical advances relating to resistance, ethics, power and politics, process thinking, learning, agency and discourse, context and evaluation are discussed, and are gathered together using a mnemonic—REPLACE. The chapter concludes with an acknowledgement that organizational change is characterised as being critical and contested, with implications for how this body of divergent knowledge is related to leadership.

Leadership studies (Chapter Four). In parallel to Chapter Three, this chapter looks to the field of leadership studies with regards to explaining leadership and organizational change. The chapter draws upon Rost's (1993) critical review of leadership studies, in which he differentiated a twentieth-century industrial paradigm of leadership studies from a twenty-first-century post-industrial paradigm of leadership studies. This differentiation helps highlight the orthodoxy of mainstream leadership studies, still believed to be impeding understanding of leadership today, but also gives impetus to alternative conceptualisations of leadership. In particular, social construction, myths and discourses of leadership with implications for framing thinking are discussed. Grint (2005), in *The Limits and Possibilities of Leadership*, illustrates the application of these concepts. In critically rethinking leadership, the neglect of collaborators in the mainstream accounts of leadership is highlighted and is believed to be particularly pertinent to the focus on leadership and organizational change. The chapter critically revisits theoretical milestones that signal a perceived shift from managing change towards leading change. The chapter concludes positively by suggesting that despite the many criticisms of leadership studies as it is currently configured, critiques potentially offer a more meaningful understanding of leadership that may eventually benefit leadership practice.

A critical evaluation of leadership and organizational change (Chapter Five). This chapter addresses the key principles of literature reviewing as encouraged by the *International Journal of Management Reviews*, with each section addressing a particular key principle. The principles addressed may be introduced here as follows: Firstly, the boundary of the sub-field of leadership and organizational change is considered, and what is included and excluded. Secondly, the maturity of the sub-field is critically evaluated. Thirdly, the role research has played in terms of informing the sub-field's development is evaluated. Fourthly, the research methodologies employed are compared and contrasted. These evaluations inform the fifth section, which considers the accumulated state of knowledge that informs the sub-field of leadership and organizational change. The chapter concludes with a discussion about the divergence, dissensus, discourses and disappearance of the sub-field of leadership and organizational change.

Towards the leadership of organizational change (Chapter Six). This chapter presents eight explanations of leadership and organizational change. The fields of leadership studies and organizational change, which are characterised by divergence and dissensus, result in competing philosophies, paradigms and perspectives that encourage a range of explanations of the nature of the sub-field of leadership and organizational change. The leadership of organizational change may be explained as problematic assumptions, the gap between literatures, a socially constructed mythology, leading change rather than managing stability, opportunities lost in translation, the show that never ends, the practice of leading organizational change and collaborative change leadership. In conclusion, it is time to reconceptualise leadership and organizational change as collaborative, participative, democratic and egalitarian.

REFERENCES

Alvesson, M., and Y.D. Billing. 2009. *Understanding Gender and Organizations.* London: Sage Publications Ltd.

Bass, B. M., and R. E. Riggio. 2006. *Transformational Leadership*, 2nd ed. Mahwah, NJ: Lawrence Erlbaum Associates Inc/Psychology Press.

Bennis, W. 2000. "Leadership of Change." In *Breaking the Code of Change*, eds. M. Beer and N. Nohria, 113–22. Boston: Harvard Business School Press.

Berger, P.L., and T. Luckmann. 1966. *The Social Construction of Reality: A Treatise in the Sociology of Knowledge.* Garden City (NY): Anchor Books.

Bryman, A., D. Collinson, K. Grint, B. Jackson and M. Uhl-Bien, eds. 2011. *The SAGE Handbook of Leadership.* London: Sage Publications Ltd.

Burns, J.M. 1978. *Leadership.* New York: Harper Row Publishers.

By, R.T. 2005. "Organizational Change Management: A Critical Review". *Journal of Change Management* 5 (4): 369–380.

By, R.T., and B. Burnes, eds. 2013. *Organizational Change, Leadership and Ethics: Leading Organizations Towards Sustainability.* London: Routledge.

By, R.T., B. Burnes and C. Oswick. 2012. "Change Management: Leadership, Values and Ethics". *Journal of Change Management* 12 (1): 1–5.

By, R.T., B. Burnes and C. Oswick. 2013. "Creating a Leading Journal and Maintaining Academic Freedom". *Journal of Change Management* 13 (1): 1–8.

Calas, M.B., and L. Smircich. 1991. "Voicing Seduction to Silence Leadership". *Organization Studies* 12 (4): 567–602.

Collins, D. 2000. *Management Fads and Buzzwords: Critical—Practical Perspectives*. London: Routledge.

Cummings, S. 2002. *Recreating Strategy*. London: Sage Publications Ltd.

Dawson, P. 2014. "Reflections: On Time Temporality and Change in Organizations". *Journal of Change Management* 14 (3): 285–308.

Deal, T.E., and A.A. Kennedy. 1999. *The New Corporate Cultures: Revitalizing the Workplace after Downsizing, Mergers and Reengineering*. London: Orion Business.

De Caluwe, L., and H.Vermaak. 2003. *Learning to Change: A Guide for Organization Change Agents*. London: Sage Publications.

Deetz, S. 1996. "Crossroads—Describing Differences in Approaches to Organization Science: Rethinking Burrell and Morgan and Their Legacy". *Organization Science* 7 (2): 191–207.

Doolin, B., D. Grant and R. Thomas. 2013. "Translating Translation and Change: Discourse-based Approaches". *Journal of Change Management* 13 (3): 251–265.

Dunphy, D., and D. Stace. 1988. "Transformational and Coercive Strategies for Planned Organizational Change: Beyond the OD Model". *Organization Studies* 9 (3): 317–334.

Edwards, G., C. Elliott, M. Iszatt-White and D. Schedlitzki. 2013. "Critical and Alternative Approaches to Leadership Learning and Development". *Management Learning* 44 (1): 3–10.

Fairhurst, G.T. 2008. "Discursive Leadership: A Communication Alternative to Leadership Psychology". *Management Communication Quarterly* 21 (4): 510–521.

Fairhurst, G.T., and D. Grant. 2010. "The Social Construction of Leadership: A Sailing Guide." *Management Communication Quarterly* 24 (2): 171–210.

Ford, J.D. and L.W. Ford. 2012. "The Leadership of Organization Change: A View from Recent Empirical Evidence". In *Research in Organizational Change and Development (Research in Organizational Change and Development, Volume 20)*, eds. In Abraham B. (Rami) Shani, William A. Pasmore, Richard W. Woodman (eds.) 1–36. Emerald Group Publishing Limited.

Ford, J.D., and N. Harding. 2007. "Move over Management: We Are All Leaders Now". *Management Learning* 38 (5): 475–493.

Frahm, J. 2007. "Organizational Change: Approaching the Frontier, Some Faster Than Others" (combined review of five books). *Organization* 14 (6): 945–955.

Grint, K. 2000. *The Arts of Leadership*. Oxford: Oxford University Press.

Grint, K. 2005. *Leadership: Limits and Possibilities*. Houndmills: Palgrave Macmillan.

Grint, K. 2008. "Forward to the Past or Back to the Future? Leadership, 1965–2006". In *Mapping the Management Journey: Practice, Theory and Context*, eds. S. Dopson, M. Earl and P. Snow, 104–18. Oxford: Oxford University Press.

Haslam, S.A., S.D. Reicher and M.J. Platow. 2011. *The New Psychology of Leadership: Identity, Influence and Power*. Hove: Psychology Press.

Hope Hailey, V., and J. Balogun. 2002. "Devising Context Sensitive Approaches to Change: The Example of Glaxo Wellcome". *Long Range Planning* 35 (2): 153–178.

Huczynski, A. 2006. *Management Gurus*, rev ed. London: Routledge.

Hughes, M. 2010. *Managing Change: A Critical Perspective*. London: CIPD Publishing.

Hughes, M. 2011. "Do 70 Per Cent of All Organizational Change Initiatives Really Fail?" *Journal of Change Management* 11 (4): 451–464.

Hughes, M. 2013. "Book Review Essay: The Territorial Nature of Organizational Studies." *Culture and Organization* 19 (3): 261–274.

Jackson, B., and D. Tourish. 2014. "Reflections on the Future of the Journal". *Leadership* 10 (1): 3–6.

Jones, G. 2010. *Organizational Theory, Design and Change*, 6th ed. Boston: Pearson Global Edition.

Kahn, R.L. 1974. "Organizational Development: Some Problems and Proposals". *Journal of Applied Behavioural Science* 10 (4): 485–502.

Kelley, S. 2014. "Towards a Negative Ontology of Leadership". *Human Relations* 67 (8): 905–922.

Kotter, J.P. 1982. *The General Managers*. New York: The Free Press.

Kotter, J.P. 1990. *A Force for Change: How Leadership Differs from Management*. New York: The Free Press.

Kotter, J.P. 1995. Leading Change: Why Transformation Efforts Fail. *Harvard Business Review* 73 (2): 44–56

Kotter, J.P. 1996 and 2012. *Leading Change*. Boston: Harvard Business School Press.

Kotter, J.P., and D.S. Cohen. 2002. *The Heart of Change: Real-Life Stories of How People Change Their Organizations*. Boston: Harvard Business School Press.

Kotter, J.P., and J.L. Heskett. 1992. *Corporate Culture and Performance*. New York: The Free Press.

Kuhn, T.S. 1962. *The Structure of Scientific Revolutions*. Chicago: The University of Chicago Press.

Ladkin, D., M. Wood and J. Pillay. 2010. "How Do Leaders Lead Change?" In *Rethinking Leadership: A New Look at Old Leadership Questions*, ed. D. Ladkin, 127–52. Cheltenham: Edward Elgar.

Loew, L., and K. O'Leonard. 2012. *Leadership Development Factbook 2012: Benchmarks and Trends on U.S. Leadership Development*. Bersin by Deloitte, www.Home.bersin.com.

Palmer, I., and R. Dunford. 2008. "Organizational Change and the Importance of Embedded Assumptions". *British Journal of Management* 19 Special Issue: S20–S32.

Parry, K.W. 2011. "Leadership and Organization Theory". In *The SAGE Handbook of Leadership*, eds. A. Bryman., D. Collinson, K. Grint, B. Jackson and M. Uhl-Bien, 53–70. London: Sage Publications Ltd.

Pondy, L.R. 1978. "Leadership Is a Language Game". In *Readings in Managerial Psychology*, eds. H.J. Leavitt, L.R. Pondy and D.M. Boje, 224–233, 1989. Chicago: University of Chicago Press.

Riggio, R.E. 2011. "The Management Perspective: Engineering Effective Leadership in Organizations". In *Leadership Studies: The Dialogue of Disciplines*, eds. M. Harvey, and R.E. Riggio, 119–128. Cheltenham: Edward Elgar.

Rost, J.C. 1993. *Leadership for the Twenty-First Century*. Westport: Praeger Publishers.

Rost, J.C. 1997. "Moving from Individual to Relationship: A Post-Industrial Paradigm of Leadership". *The Journal of Leadership Studies* 4 (4): 3–16.

Salaman, G. 2011. "Understanding the Crises of Leadership." In *Leadership in Organizations: Current Issues and Key Trends*, ed. J. Storey, 56–68. London: Routledge.

Santayana, G. 1998. *The Life of Reason*. London: Prometheus Books.

Smith, A.C.T., and F.M. Graetz. 2011. *Philosophies of Organizational Change*. Cheltenham: Edward Elgar Publishing Ltd.

Stickland, F. 1998. *The Dynamics of Change*. London: Routledge.

Storey, J. ed. 2011. *Leadership in Organizations: Current Issues and Key Trends*. London: Routledge.

Thomas, R., and C. Hardy. 2011. "Reframing Resistance to Organizational Change". *Scandinavian Journal of Management* 27 (3): 322–331.

Tourish, D. 2013. *The Dark Side of Transformational Leadership*. London: Routledge.

Tourish, D. 2015. "Some Announcements, Reaffirming the Critical Ethos of Leadership, and What We Look for in Submissions". *Leadership* 11 (2): 135–141.

Van De Ven, A.H., and M.S. Poole. 1995. "Explaining Development and Change in Organizations". *Academy of Management Review* 20 (3): 510–540.

2 Leadership and Organizational Change

A 35-Year Review

INTRODUCTION

This chapter reports upon the leadership and organizational change literature reviewed. The literature identified is highlighted and documented as neutrally as possible, with the critique developed in the subsequent chapters. Whereas, Chapter One acknowledged practitioner interest in the leadership of organizational change, previous reviews have highlighted the limitations of the empirical evidence supporting this interest (Ford and Ford, 2012; Parry, 2011). In the literature review, both academic and practitioner explanations feature, as exclusively academic accounts may neglect the highly applied and practice-orientated nature of this sub-field. It has also been necessary to creatively seek out insights in atypical sources such as academic handbooks and university textbooks in order to establish the current meta-level understanding about the sub-field of leadership and organizational change.

The milestone commencing the 35-year (1978–2014) literature review window was Burns's (1978) critique of leadership studies as suffering from intellectual mediocrity. The timeframe was chosen as an antidote to the progressive linearity of knowledge accumulation typified by the forward-to-the-past (Grint, 2008) thinking discussed in Chapter One. It is feasible that profound insights were made in earlier decades, yet lost through the passage of time. In reviewing leadership and organizational change over 35 years many contextual boundaries, including national, sectorial, temporal, political and economic boundaries, have been crossed. Two American academics feature prominently in shaping the sub-field: Professor Bernard Bass and Professor John Kotter. More generally, the most-cited publications do have a distinctly Anglo-American feel. In terms of sector focus, it was the health and education sectors that featured the most prominently, particularly from the nineties onwards. However, theories and practices are likely to vary considerably between sectors.

The literature reviewing featured in this chapter generated a large volume of references of variable quality and relevance. Consequently, appendices (see the end of the book) are used extensively to support this chapter and maintain the narrative flow of what is inevitably a dense and discursive chapter. Given the scale and dissensus of both the fields of leadership studies and organizational change studies, both of which draw upon different academic disciplines and competing philosophies, this overview cannot claim to be definitive. However, it is hoped that through sharing as thoroughly as possible those publications identified, this review may inform the work of other scholars, advancing understanding with regards to the sub-field of leadership and organizational change. As a final caveat, Grint's (2000) belief that leadership is primarily rooted in and a product of the imagination is relevant. The social construction of leadership is discussed in Chapter Four, but for now, there were times when reviewing the combination of the ambiguous leadership literature with the equally ambiguous organizational change literature frustratingly felt like a quest to make the intangible tangible.

Figure 2.1 maps how the literature review was undertaken and also highlights the major sections of this chapter. This introductory section is followed by the most-cited publications (see the first column), in which the twenty most-cited leadership and organizational change publications published between 1978 and 2014 were ranked and discussed. In *The Leadership Quarterly* and the *Journal of Change Management* section (see the second column), all issues of each journal since these journals were founded were reviewed in order to identify the emergent and ongoing debates relating to leadership and organizational change. In the academic handbooks section (see the third column), recent leadership handbooks and organizational change handbooks were reviewed in order to gauge a meta-level understanding of leadership and organizational change, as reported by respected handbook editors and expert contributors. The university textbooks section (see the fourth column) informed by earlier reviews creatively asked how we are supporting leadership and organizational change teaching. In the chapter's final section, preliminary conclusions from the literature review are discussed in terms of Ford and Ford's (2012) review of the empirical evidence relating to leadership and organizational change.

LEADERSHIP AND ORGANIZATIONAL CHANGE: THE MOST-CITED PUBLICATIONS (1978–2014)

Parry (2011), as cited in Chapter One, suggested that there were far more practitioner and conceptual scholarship books and papers than theoretical and empirical scholarship, with the implication that any citation count would need to explore this imbalance. Even if our preference is for theoretical and empirical scholarship, exclusively engaging with such literature would misrepresent the state of the sub-field under review. Citation counts

	The Most-Cited Publications	*The Leadership Quarterly* and the *Journal of Change Management*	Academic Handbooks	University Textbooks
Why was this review undertaken?	In order to identify the most influential publications as gauged by citations	In order to follow emerging and ongoing debates featured within focused journals since they were founded	To gain meta-level understanding of leadership and organizational change as identified in respected handbooks	To establish the state of knowledge about leadership and organizational as gauged through textbooks
Which publications were reviewed?	10 most-cited 'leading change' publications 10 most-cited 'transformational leadership' publications	*The Leadership Quarterly* (LQ) The *Journal of Change Management* (J of CM)	Four leadership-focused handbooks Three organizational-change focused handbooks	Organizational change textbooks; Senior and Swailes (2010), Grieves (2010) and Hayes (2014)
When does this review focus upon?	1978–2014	LQ 1990–2014 J of CM 2000–2014	2010–2014	2010–2014
How was this review undertaken?	Using Publish or Perish Software (Harzing, 2007)	All issues of LQ referring to transformation/change and all issues of J of CM referring to leadership	Handbooks reviewed in terms of their coverage of leadership and organizational change	Reviewing specific chapters in terms of their treatment of leadership and organizational change
What did the review reveal?	This literature had a strong practitioner emphasis, stronger on prescription than analysis	Emphasis on: Transformational leadership in LQ And on change leader development, competencies and capabilities In J of CM	Insights were not evident and interest appeared very limited within both fields of study	Textbooks confirm limited knowledge about leadership and organizational change

Figure 2.1 Mapping the leadership and organizational change literature review process and content

offered a means of ranking those publications most frequently cited in order to gauge what was influential within the sub-field of leadership and organizational change, regardless of it being based upon empirical/theoretical scholarship or practitioner/conceptual scholarship.

Substantial bodies of knowledge inform the separate fields of leadership studies and organizational change studies; consequently, the focus here is on that literature informing understanding about how these fields were intertwined. Initially looking to leadership studies revealed that '. . .over the past 30 years transformational leadership has been the single most studied and debated idea within the field of leadership studies' (Diaz-Saenz, 2011:299). This strand of thinking grounded in the transformative capabilities of leaders was inspired by Burns's (1978) original differentiation between transformational and transactional leaders, whereas within the studies of organizational change, Kotter's (1995, 1996) practitioner-orientated writing acted as the main catalyst for greater practitioner and academic engagement with leadership and organizational change. It was consequently necessary to engage with both disparate strands of transformational leadership and leadership of change thinking, focusing on all books and journal papers published between the 1st of January 1978 and the 31st of December 2014 that in their titles referred to:

> 'Change leader/s,' 'change leadership,' 'leadership of change' and 'leading change,' and 'transformational leader/s,' 'transformational leadership,' 'leadership of transformation' and 'leading transformation.'

Only publications in English were reviewed and, given the large bodies of leadership literature and organizational change literature, it was necessary to identify the most influential literature, although 'influential' does not necessarily equate to it being academically the most rigorous. EndNote and the Web of Knowledge were used for the initial citation pilot work; however, this software did not address the applied nature of this sub-field, particularly in terms of the prevalence of organizational change books, rather than papers and the prevalence of practitioner-orientated publications.

The Publish or Perish software (Harzing, 2007) linked to Google scholar citations proved more applicable to the applied nature of this sub-field, enabling the generation of the top 1,000 citations-based league tables for both 'transformational leadership' and the 'leadership of change' strands, including (if heavily cited) both scholarly and practitioner contributions. A ranking of the ten most-cited leadership of change publications and the ten most-cited transformational leadership publications identified on the 2nd of April 2015 are included as Appendices One and Two. There were far more transformational leadership publications than leadership of change publications, and the transformational leadership publications overall received far more citations. In Figure 2.2, the five overall most-cited publications and their citation counts at the time of the review are highlighted.

No.	Citations	Transformation/ Change	Book/ Paper	Title	Author/ Year
1.	6638	Change	Book	Leading change	(Kotter, 1996)
2.	4340	Change	Paper	Leading change: Why transformation efforts fail	(Kotter, 1995)
3.	3539	Transformation	Book	Transformational leadership	(Bass and Riggio, 2006)
4.	3240	Transformation	Paper	Transformational leader behaviors and their effects on followers' trust in leader, satisfaction, and organizational citizenship behaviors	(Podsakoff et al, 1990)
5.	2846	Transformation	Paper	From transactional to transformational leadership: Learning to share the vision	Bass (1990)

Figure 2.2   The top five most-cited publications as of 2nd of April 2015

Please see Appendices One and Two for further rankings of the most-cited publications.

Harvard Professor Emeritus John Kotter's *Leading Change* (1996) was the overall most-cited publication (see Figure 2.2), with the late Bernard Bass having the greatest number of cited publications either authored or co-authored by him and with him and the other transformational leadership publications reflected his influence. A prevalence of books over papers was evident, highlighting the applied nature of these debates, although there were far fewer transformational leadership books than leadership of change books. These books largely spoke to practitioners rather than academic audiences and by association, there was a lack of empirical work if gauged by the publications in refereed journals. Troublingly for the evolution of this sub-field, Figure 2.2 suggests that academics were citing a practitioner-orientated book (Kotter, 1996) and a practitioner-orientated paper (Kotter, 1995) far more than any empirical work, which is highly compatible with Parry's (2011) conclusion. The following two sub-sections discuss Bernard Bass's conceptualisation of transformational leadership and John Kotter's conceptualisation of leading change with numbers (1 = most cited, etc.) after the year of publication referring to positions in the rankings (see Appendices One and Two). The discussion in each section is organized chronologically in order to reflect the evolution of these debates.

Bernard Bass and Transformational Leadership *The Transformational Leader* (Tichy and Devanna, 1986a) (4) (see also paper with the same title, Tichy and Devanna, 1986b) offered an optimistic account of how leaders were transforming American corporations. The book began with an epilogue and ended with a prologue with three acts in between: Act one—recognising the need for revitalisation, act two—creating a new vision and act three—institutionalising change. Whereas Tichy and Devanna employed the contemporary rhetoric of their times, their three acts closely mirrored earlier three-step approaches (Lewin, 1947). These authors used the transformational leadership label, although their writings were closer to organizational change than the transformational leadership that Bass subsequently encouraged. Bass's earliest publication in the citations ranking appeared in 1990, in *From Transactional to Transformational Leadership: Learning to Share the Vision* (Bass, 1990:19) (3) The promise of transformational leadership is caught in the strapline for the paper 'transformational leaders inspire, energize, and intellectually stimulate their employees. Bass argued that through training, managers can learn the techniques and obtain the qualities they need to become transformational leaders.' Bass (1990) differentiated the characteristics of a transformational leader: Charisma, inspiration, intellectual stimulation and individualised consideration from the characteristics of a transactional leader, contingent reward, management by exception (active), management by exception (passive) and laissez faire.

The ranking for the manual for the Multifactor Leadership Questionnaires (MLQ) (Bass and Avolio, 1990) (10) needs to be treated with caution, as the manual appeared in many editions and more recently has been disseminated through websites. The origins of the MLQ can be traced back to Bass, when it appeared in its long form with seventy-three items (Bycio et al, 1995), with subsequent research and development informing revisions of the MLQ. The MLQ in measuring concepts of transformational and transactional leadership has been shortened to forty-five questions that are either self-rated based upon perception or rater rated (see Tejeda et al, 2001 for an overview of the MLQ).

Podsakoff et al (1990) (2) empirically examined the impact of transformational leader behaviours upon organizational citizenship and the potential mediating role of subordinate trust and satisfaction, drawing their data from a diversified petrochemical company. They found that transformational leadership influences organizational citizenship behaviours, suggesting that 'these findings validate the basic notion that transformational behaviors influence followers to perform, above and beyond the call of duty' (Podsakoff et al, 1990:137). Howell and Avolio (1993) (8) used measures of leadership, locus of control and support for innovation to predict the performance of 78 managers. Lowe et al (1996) (5) undertook a meta-analysis of the transformational leadership literature using the MLQ. They found that the MLQ transformational leadership scales were reliable, significantly predicting work unit effectiveness across those studies they examined.

Bass (1997) (7) appeared to have been keen to advance understanding and test the boundaries of transformational leadership, as evidenced by *Does the Transactional-Transformational Leadership Paradigm Transcend Organizational and National Boundaries?* Bass's paper answered his own question in finding that the same conception of phenomena and relationships could be observed in a wide range of organizations and cultures. In *Two Decades of Research and Development in Transformational Leadership*, the research into transformational leadership was evaluated and the rhetorical research question, 'Why is transformational leadership more effective than transactional leadership in business, military, industrial, hospital and educational settings?' was posed and answered (Bass, 1999) (9).

Bass and Steidlmeier (1999) (6) responded to criticisms that transformational leadership was unethical, identifying three ethical pillars: The leader's moral character, the ethical legitimacy of the values within the leader's vision and the morality of the social, ethical choices and actions that the leaders and followers pursue. They differentiated transformational leadership from what they referred to as 'pseudo-transformational leadership.'

> Self-aggrandizing, fantasizing, pseudo-transformational leaders can be branded as immoral. But authentic transformational leaders, as moral agents expand the domain of effective freedom, the horizon of conscience and the scope of altruistic intention
>
> (Bass and Steidlmeier, 1999:211)

Transformational Leadership (Bass and Riggio, 2006) (1) built on the first edition (Bass, 1998), with the book benefitting from a foreword by James Macgregor Burns and Georgia Sorenson. Transformational leaders went beyond exchanges or agreements, achieving superior results through employing one or more of four components: Idealised influence, inspirational motivation, intellectual stimulation and individualised consideration. As well as these four components, the Full Range of Leadership model included components of transactional leadership along with laissez-faire behaviour. Leader-Member Exchange (LMX) focused on the perceived quality of the dyadic relationship between a subordinate and his/her immediate supervisor. LMX unfolded in several stages in which trust, loyalty and respect developed. In the first stage, LMX was transactional; only if the last stage was reached did it become transformational (Bass and Riggio, 2006).

John Kotter and Leading Change In terms of the most-cited publications identified, there were none prior to the mid-nineties. O'Toole's (1995) (3) lesser-known account of *Leading Change: Overcoming the Ideology of Comfort and the Tyranny of Custom* was to be overshadowed by Kotter (1996), but O'Toole was far closer to Burns (1978) in sharing a moral vision and an interest in American political history as a guide to leading change. O'Toole explicitly did not share Kotter's contingent view of leading change, '. . . that to implement change, effective leaders do whatever the circumstances require' (O'Toole, 1995:7).

Kotter's two practitioner-orientated publications are by far the two most-cited publications and are consequently heavily featured here. Earlier academic and societal beliefs that organizational change and organizational cultures could be successfully managed were being questioned. Against this backdrop, Kotter's (1995/1996) identification of leadership errors and his subsequent eight steps presented the right message at the right time (see Figure 2.3).

The influential practitioner magazine *Harvard Business Review* published *Leading Change: Why Transformation Efforts Fail* (Kotter, 1995) (2), which was based upon Kotter's experiences as a consultant. Kotter identified eight errors that explained why transformation efforts failed, although he never explained how he evaluated transformation failure. In

Eight errors that cause transformation failures (Kotter, 1995)	Eight steps to transform your organization (Kotter, 1996)
Error 1: Not establishing a great enough sense of urgency	1. Establishing a sense of urgency
Error 2: Not creating a powerful enough guiding coalition	2. Forming a powerful guiding coalition
Error 3: Lacking a vision	3. Creating a vision
Error 4: Under communicating the vision by a factor of ten	4. Communicating the vision
Error 5: Not removing obstacles to the new vision	5. Empowering others to act on the vision
Error 6: Not systematically planning for, and creating short-term wins	6. Planning for and creating short-term wins
Error 7: Declaring victory too soon	7. Consolidating improvements and producing still more change
Error 8: Not anchoring changes in the corporation's culture	8. Institutionalizing new approaches

Figure 2.3   Eight leadership transformation errors and eight leadership transformation stages

writing *Leading Change*, Kotter (1996) (1) majored upon eight proactive best-practice stages that would result in successful transformation.

By comparison to Kotter's publications, the other leadership of change publications received a fraction of the citations (see Appendix Two). Empirically grounded accounts of the leadership of change proved to be few and far between, with Paglis and Green (2002) (10) a notable exception. They developed and tested a leadership model in a real estate company and an industrial chemicals firm. They focused on the manager's motivation for attempting the leadership of change informed by Bandura's (1986) social cognitive theory. Gill (2002) (9) in his think piece posed a recurrent question within this review: Change management or change leadership? He favoured a combination of management and leadership as articulated within his own model of leadership, which was informed by his literature reviewing and developed further in his textbook (Gill, 2011).

Herold et al (2008:348) (6) offered another empirically grounded account of the leadership of transformation and change. One of the strengths of their paper was their interest in the similarities and differences between the concepts of change leadership and transformational leadership. They regarded change leadership as referring to the here-and-now, focusing on the specific change at hand and how the leader handled it from a tactical point of view (House and Adita, 1997). Transformational leadership referred to a longer-term relationship between a leader and followers, which was built up over many interactions with a more organizational or strategic orientation. Their research, which was informed by the data obtained from 343 employees in 30 organizations, drew upon a cross section of organizations in the southeastern US. Their far-reaching paper drew the following conclusions:

> Transformational leadership was found to be more strongly related to followers' change commitment than change-specific leadership practices, especially when the change had significant personal impact. For leaders were not viewed as transformational, good change-management practices were found to be associated with higher levels of change commitment.
>
> (Herold et al, 2008:346)

In *Leading Change toward Sustainability* (Doppelt, 2009) (5), now in its second edition, the focus was on transforming organizations into better social and environmental citizens. *Change Leadership: A Practical Guide to Transforming Our Schools* (Wagner et al, 2010) (7), based upon the work of the Change Leadership Group at the Harvard Graduate School of Education, sought to develop educators as agents of change. Anderson and Ackerman-Anderson's (2010) (4) book *Beyond Change Management*, aimed at practitioners, was organized around four major sections, with section titles signposting the content: A call for conscious change leaders, people dynamics, process dynamics and answering the call to conscious change leadership. Finally, Quinn's (2011)(10) *Building the Bridge as You Walk on It: A Guide for Leading Change* offered a humanistic conclusion to this section by encouraging everyone to engage in eight leadership practices: Reflective action, authentic engagement, appreciative inquiry, grounded vision, adaptive confidence, detached interdependence, responsible freedom and tough love.

LEADERSHIP AND ORGANIZATIONAL CHANGE: *THE LEADERSHIP QUARTERLY* (1990–2014) AND THE *JOURNAL OF CHANGE MANAGEMENT* (2000–2014) COVERAGE

The focus in the previous section was on the most-cited publications in order to gauge and begin to understand the development of research and scholarship within this sub-field since 1978 and its respective influence (see Appendices One and Two for full rankings). It is acknowledged that the majority of the work that is potentially informing the leadership and organizational change sub-field has not been included, but given that the publications identified were based upon citation rankings, by definition, they have influenced the sub-field. An alternative means of engaging with this sub-field is through the analysis of themes within papers published in two respected, specialised journals. As these papers have gone through an academic review process, they should reflect the editorial policies of the respective journals. Over time, the editors, editorial boards and reviewers of journals have influenced the development of the academic fields and sub-fields of study. Debates and new lines of inquiry are encouraged and discouraged, both knowingly and unknowingly. This influence is rarely perceptible at the level of a single paper or a single issue, but is likely to be more discernible through the analysis of multiple volumes of a specific journal. The analysis reported here focuses on two subject-specific, refereed journals, both open to interdisciplinary contributions in advancing the study of leadership and organizational change, respectively.

The Leadership Quarterly, based in America, was founded in 1990 by Bernard Bass, Bob House and Henry Tosi. The *Journal of Change Management*, based in the UK, was founded by Colin Carnall in 2000. The intention is neutrally to highlight papers that are potentially relevant to advancing understanding about leadership and organizational change. All issues of *The Leadership Quarterly* were reviewed from 1990 until the end of 2014, in order to identify those papers with organizational change and/ or transformation in their titles. By association, these papers would have to relate in some way to the journal's explicit editorial leadership focus, and 87 papers were identified (see Appendix Three for a full listing). In parallel, all issues of the *Journal of Change Management* were reviewed from 2000 until the end of 2014, in order to identify those papers with leader/leadership in their titles. Again, by association, the papers identified would have to relate to the journal's explicit organizational change editorial focus, and 41 papers were identified (see Appendix Four for a full listing). Appendices Three and Four have been annotated in terms of the focus of the papers identified and if they were based upon research. The overall aim of this activity was to establish themes and patterns across the individual papers identified.

The Leadership Quarterly As expected, transformational leadership as initiated by Bernard Bass featured very prominently (see Appendix Three) in a journal that he was involved in founding. What was less expected was the enduring appeal of transformational leadership within this journal from when it was founded until the present day. This prominence (over a quarter of a century) may have been shaped by the editors or may have reflected the independent interests of the contributors, or a combination of the two. If nothing else, transformational leadership was far more than a passing fad/fashion for these scholars. The ongoing focus on transformational leadership gave the journal greater coherence than the pluralism of most leadership and management journals, although this may have been at the expense of competing accounts of leading/leadership of transformation and change.

The papers identified were largely empirical, although provocative editorials and purely conceptual papers were also evident. Quantitative data gathered in order to test hypotheses was the favoured research design, invariably with a focus on advancing knowledge about transformational leadership. Whereas the majority of papers identified favoured a transformational leadership perspective, the editors also published papers offering alternative conceptualisations of leadership and organizational change. The papers identified included papers in the most-cited publications ranking (see Appendix One). The vast majority (69) of the papers identified focused on transformational leadership, approaching transformational leadership from both a positive and positivist perspective. Whilst more than one theme was often dealt with within a single paper, the major themes applied to transformational leadership were as follows: Charisma, levels, contextualisation, ethics, cognitive approaches and parenting/early development. These emerging themes are discussed briefly below.

One of Bass's (1990) original characteristics of transformational leadership charisma was a frequent focus of research. Ehrlich et al (1990) specifically highlighted the charismatic appeal of transformational leadership and subsequently, transformational leadership and charismatic leadership appeared to be dealt with synonymously (Brown and Lord, 1998; Conger, 1999; Conger and Hunt, 1999; Dionne et al, 2012; Hartog, 1999; Hunt, 1999; Rowold and Heinitz, 2007; Yukl, 1999). Another theme related to the origins of transformational leadership and its applicability at different individual, dyad and group levels (Avolio and Bass, 1995; Braun et al, 2013; Menges et al, 2011; Schriesheim et al, 2006; Sosik et al 2004;Wang and Howell, 2012; Yammarino et al, 1998). Closely aligned with a focus on these different levels were studies that focused on leader-follower relations (Dvir and Shamir, 2003; Hu et al, 2012; Nielsen and Daniels, 2012; Podsakoff et al, 1990; Tims et al, 2011; Van Dierendonck et al, 2014).

Another recurrent theme was the desire to test the applicability of transformational leadership in different contexts in order to advance understanding. For example, Berson and Avolio (2004) studied transformational leadership in a telecommunications firm, Nemanich and Keller (2007) and Nemanich and Vera (2009) focused on the context of an acquisition, Osborn and Marion (2009) a strategic alliance and Purvanova and Bono (2009) and Balthazard, Waldman and Warren (2009) virtual teams. Druskat (1994) and Vinkenburg et al (2011) focused on women's experiences of transformational leadership and Zhu et al (2005) and Jung et al (2008) focused on chief executive officers (CEOs) and transformational leadership.

Bass and Steidlmeier (1999:182) explicitly sought to defend transformational leadership against critiques of its morality as ventured by '. . .libertarians, "grass roots" theorists, and organizational development consultants.' Whereas they defended and differentiated authentic transformational leadership from pseudo-transformational leadership, Price (2003:68) was not convinced by such differentiations, fearing that transformational leaders may be encouraged '. . .to believe that they are justified in making exceptions of themselves on the grounds that their leadership behaviour is authentic.' In a similar manner, Carey (1992) critically questioned the moral foundations of transformational leadership, highlighting a shift from Burns's (1978) moral leadership to Bass's perceived emphasis upon change leadership. Simola et al (2010) empirically demonstrated how an ethic of care was more relevant to transformational leadership than an ethic of justice, and Zhu et al (2011) returned to Burns's (1978) original differentiation that transforming leaders were morally uplifting, and empirically attempted to explain how this uplifting process worked.

Academics were drawn to transformational leadership from very different disciplines, with the interest of psychologists in individuals and their development particularly evident. There was ongoing interest in the cognitive aspects of transformational leadership, with Wofford and Goodwin (1994) and Wofford et al (1998) seeking to cognitively understand transactional and transformational leadership. Balthazard et al (2012) even used the latest neurological imaging technology to differentiate transformational from transactional leaders through brain scans. And Parr et al (2013) considered the applicability of transformational leadership for employees with autism spectrum disorder.

A final discernible theme related to parenting and early personal development. Popper et al (2000) creatively explained transformational leadership in terms of attachment theory, emphasising the influence of attachment figures (mainly parents) upon child development, and Popper and Mayseless (2003) subsequently applied a parenting perspective to transformational leadership. Zacharatos et al (2000) applied transformational leadership principles to the development of adolescents. Tucker et al's (2010) interests echoed those of Popper et al (2000) and Popper and Mayseless (2003), finding that, consistent with social learning theory, transformational leaders modelled prosocial behaviours for their followers.

The papers conveyed an almost evangelical belief in transformational leadership: This was more than a theory, this was a way of thinking and behaving and potentially perceived as means to realise Burns's (1978) vision of societies and institutions transformed through moral leadership. The importance of believing in leadership was even demonstrated within Rubin et al's (2009) study of 106 manufacturing managers, highlighting that leader cynicism about organizational change negatively influenced both leader and employee outcomes.

The academic norm of *The Leadership Quarterly* was appreciative inquiries into transformational leadership, rather than critiques. Consequently, it is informative to look at two critical counterpoints published within the journal that generated significant responses from readers in subsequent issues. Beyer's (1999) and Yukl's (1999) papers appeared in part one of a two-part special issue that took stock of the present and future of charismatic and transformational leadership. In the special issue, Conger (1999:147) set the scene for the growth of interest in charismatic and transformational leadership: 'I suspect we also share a general dissatisfaction with earlier models of leadership which have seemed too narrow and simplistic to explain leaders in change agent roles.'

Beyer (1999) was concerned that transformational leadership writer's operationalisation of charisma departed from Weber's original conceptualisation and downplayed integral aspects of charisma, precipitating crisis, the radical vision and systemic change. Beyer referred to herself as an outsider within her paper and Yukl (1999), similarly, was another outsider to this paradigm. Yukl's (1999:286) concern related to a tendency of transformational leadership writers to emphasise positive aspects, yet neglect conceptual weaknesses.

> . . .[T]hey include ambiguous constructs, insufficient description of explanatory processes, a narrow focus on dyadic processes, omission of some relevant behaviors, insufficient specification of limiting conditions (situational variables), and a bias toward heroic conceptions of leadership.

Yukl (1999:295) citing Bryman (1993) raised an issue particularly pertinent to this critical review: '. . .[T]he theories are still weak on explaining how charisma is institutionalized or a major change is actually implemented by the leader.' Conger's (1999) interest in leaders in change agent roles cited earlier reminds us that transformational leadership is not the exclusive explanation of leaders in change agent roles. Whilst in a minority compared to transformational leadership, *The Leadership Quarterly* published insightful papers into leaders in change agent roles, highlighted here in chronological order. Fletcher's (2004) critical essay on post-heroic leadership argued that new models erroneously presented leadership as gender- and power-neutral. Consequently, post-heroic leadership may not live up to its transformative potential. Kan and Parry (2004:486), using grounded theory, investigated nursing leadership in a New Zealand hospital undergoing change.

> A recurring theme in this study was that nurse leaders had the potential to achieve greater influence and change within the healthcare environment. However, an equally recurring theme was that this potential was repressed by cultural and societal factors within and outside nursing.

Tyler and De Cremer (2005) hypothesised that those who more strongly identified with their company would be more influenced by procedural justice information. They tested their hypothesis in a merger situation in which the leaders sought employee acceptance of a change in corporate structure.

> If leaders act fairly then the fairness of their exercise of authority itself becomes a factor motivating employees to buy into changes and accept the new company. In other words, leaders can lead via the procedures they use to implement change.
>
> (Tyler and De Cremer, 2005:543)

It sounds blindingly obvious in its simplicity, but in the context of this review, it is worth emphasising that fairness is not necessarily the organizational norm and is certainly the antithesis of fashionable beliefs in strong leadership. Boje and Rhodes (2006) refreshingly appeared as the postmodern cuckoos within the positivist transformational leadership nest, ironically depicting Ronald MacDonald literally and metaphorically as a leadership clown. They highlighted how Ronald's status as transformational leader was formalised within his quasi-formal executive position as *Chief Happiness Officer* in 2003, persuasively attributing McDonald's transformation into a fashionable, fit and healthy corporation down to Ronald's transformational leadership.

Currie et al (2009) investigated leadership in English secondary schools embedded within a societal context and institutional environment, which the authors believed had previously been neglected. They were able to study two different approaches to leadership within similar contexts: A government-prescribed and results-oriented approach, and a more traditional, value-based approach. They found that the results-oriented approach had not fully replaced value-based leadership. Levay (2010) acknowledged that charismatic leadership for Weber was about social change, subsequently questioning the importance and desirability of charismatic leaders in change processes. Through a historical analysis of two changes in two health departments, she demonstrated how charismatic leadership was actually employed in order to maintain the status quo and to resist change.

Battilana et al's (2010) paper stands out as a paper that explicitly bridges the leadership and organizational change literature through its exploration of relationships between leadership competencies and different activities emphasised in planned organizational change implementation. This relationship was analysed using data from 89 clinical managers in the National Health Service (UK) who implemented change projects between 2003 and 2004. They found that treating planned organizational change as a generic phenomenon may mask idiosyncrasies associated with the different activities involved in the change implementation processes. Hurtzschenreuter et al (2012) adopted a much narrower focus in their review of the literature on the leaders' impact on strategic change in the context of CEO succession events. Their literature reviewing, whilst comprehensive, acknowledged that this literature was still in an immature phase. Stoker et al (2012) also focused on CEOs, this time questioning whether CEO transformational leadership makes a difference for team performance and change effectiveness. Provocatively, for transformational leadership believers, they concluded from their research with 39 top management teams and their CEOs that organizational results could be achieved without a transformational CEO. Nohe et al (2013) examined leaders in times of organizational change, investigating mechanisms through which leaders' change-promoting behaviours are associated with team performance. They found that team leaders were perceived as more charismatic when they engaged in change-promoting behaviours.

In summary, *The Leadership Quarterly*, since it was founded in 1990, has advanced understanding about leadership and organizational change. The majority of papers identified focused on transformational leadership. These theoretical developments had been empirically informed, and there were signs of convergence amongst transformational leadership scholars (see earlier themes). However, as reported within *The Leadership Quarterly*, these theories were weak in explaining how a major change was actually implemented by a leader (Yukl, 1999). The downside of the journal's emphasis upon transformational leadership was potentially overshadowing other research accounts relating leadership to transformation and change. Those papers identified (particularly Tyler and De Cremer, 2005; Currie et al, 2009 and Battilana et al, 2010) appeared very relevant in empirically advancing the sub-field; however, they were very much in the minority. The impression gained was of a jigsaw puzzle with a picture that is recognisable, yet still incomplete.

The Journal of Change Management In reviewing the journal over fourteen years, its early practitioner orientation was very apparent. However, these early contributions soon gave way to critical accounts of organizational change that were almost exclusively written by academics. In parallel to this, there was a move away from single, descriptive, practice-based case studies towards far more empirically grounded papers. There was a far greater emphasis on change leadership/leading change than on transformational leadership, which may partially be explained by the journal editor being located in the UK. Only one paper (Bloch, 2000) made explicit reference to transformational leadership in its title, although there were references to Bernard Bass in the following identified papers: Hawkins and Dulewicz (2009), Higgs (2009), Klaussner (2012), Lyons et al (2009), Michaelis et al (2009), Moorman et al (2012), Parry et al (2002), Young and Dulewicz (2006), and Young and Dulewicz (2006).

There were 41 papers identified with 'lead,' 'leader/s,' 'leading' or 'leadership' in their titles, with four of these editorials. The home page of the journal featured a ranking of the journal's twenty most-cited papers, which included five leadership papers (Gill, 2002; Higgs, 2009; Higgs and Rowland, 2005; Michaelis et al, 2009; Van Dijk and Van Dick, 2009) out of the 41 papers. In 21 of the papers, original research was presented, with the other papers being conceptual, literature-based or practice-based or a combination.

In terms of the themes of the papers, the most common theme (ten papers) related to the competencies, capabilities and development of change leaders (Conger and Toegel, 2002; Good and Sharma, 2010; Higgs and Rowland, 2000, 2001 and 2010; Hyde and Paterson, 2001; Miller, 2001; Vinnicombe and Singh, 2002; Wren and Dulewicz, 2005; Young and Dulewicz, 2006). In recent decades, leadership studies have been informed by new approaches (discussed further in Chapter Four). It was anticipated that these new approaches would be reflected in the leadership themes favoured, although no pattern was evident. Those emergent leadership approaches identified included: Servant leadership (Pepper, 2002), lateral leadership (Kuhl et al, 2005), chaos theory (Karp, 2006 and Karp and Helgo, 2008) and grassroots leadership (Mars 2009; Hartley 2009). Potentially, there is a time lag between the new, generic approaches to leadership studies influencing a sub-field such as leadership and organizational change. The critical leadership studies highlight a darker side of leadership (see Chapter Four), and the expectation was that this would be mirrored in the *Journal of Change Management* papers, but only Higgs's (2009) paper on leadership narcissism really engaged with this darker side of leadership. The 2012 special issue on ethics, justice and leadership (Grover et al, 2012) did give emphasis to the ethics of leading change, Heres and Lasthuizen's (2012) ethical leadership, Innocenti et al's (2012) behavioural integrity, Klaussner's (2012) trust and mistrust and Moorman et al's (2012) leader integrity. At the time of writing, there were indications that the ethics of leading change was becoming a central theme for senior members of the editorial board (see By et al, 2012, 2013).

Van der Voet et al (2014) effectively contributed to the empirical advance of the sub-field of leadership and organizational change through their well-thought-out and executed study of the city works department of the

Dutch city of Rotterdam. Their main research question was, 'What is the role of leadership during planned and emergent processes of organizational change?'

> In an emergent process of change, the leadership of change is distributed over a larger group of individuals and hierarchical levels. . .The leadership of change itself should also be subject to the change in values. By shaping a participatory approach to change and delegating leadership responsibilities, effective change leadership consists of walking the walk instead of merely talking the talk.
>
> (Van der Voet et al, 2014:189)

The caveat with this empirical contribution is that the findings of this study of a Dutch city works department may be a reflection of the local organizational culture or Dutch national culture as much as the influence of leadership. For example, By and Burnes (2011) (discussed further in the next section) argue that planned approaches to change as encouraged by Lewin (1947) were more likely to lead to utilitarian outcomes, and emergent change was more likely to lead to unethical outcomes. These debates normally characterising the advance of fields and sub-fields of study were the exception, rather than the expected norm, but at the very least suggest the beginnings of debates relating leadership to organizational change.

In summary, the *Journal of Change Management*, since it was founded in 2000, has advanced understanding about leadership and organizational change. However, the largest and most enduring theme (ten papers) related to the development, competencies and capabilities of change leaders. Whereas the development agenda is important, it does 'put the cart before the horse.' Background assumptions (Gouldner, 1971) appeared to be at work here that leadership did result in organizational change and that the nature of this relationship is satisfactorily understood (background assumptions are discussed further in Chapter Five).

LEADERSHIP AND ORGANIZATIONAL CHANGE: ACADEMIC HANDBOOKS REVIEWED (2010–2014)

The citation counts and emerging themes featured in the two previous sections offered insights, although they were inevitably fragmented and compartmentalised into leadership and organizational change. They did not feature accumulated leadership and organizational change knowledge, whereas the overarching explanations contained in handbooks and textbooks potentially synthesise what is known (or not known). In seeking such synthesis, recently published leadership studies academic handbooks (Nohria and Khurana, 2010; Bryman et al, 2011, Rumsey, 2012 and Day, 2104) and organizational change studies academic handbooks (Beer and

Nohria, 2000, Burke et al, 2009; Boje et al, 2011; By and Burnes, 2013) were reviewed for their coverage of the sub-field of leadership and organizational change and the potential insights they offered. These handbooks are a fairly recent publishing innovation, synthesising and communicating the cumulative state of knowledge primarily to academic audiences as gauged by the expert editors and contributors in their respective fields. These contributions benefit from the literature reviewing, research and scholarship experiences of the respective contributors. The 35-year time horizon in this section narrows to the handbooks published since 2000, although these are mainly limited to those published in the last five years.

The Handbook of Leadership Theory and Practice (Nohria and Khurana, 2010) is comprised of 26 chapters written by eminent leadership scholars and organized around five sections: The impact of leadership, the theory of leadership, the variability of leadership, the practice of leadership and the development of leaders. This handbook benefitted from different chapters on leadership written from different disciplinary perspectives, including psychological, clinical, organizational behaviour, sociological, economic and historic. Only one chapter explicitly focused on leading change; this is a chapter written by Marshall Ganz, a lecturer in public policy at Harvard Kennedy School. The chapter focused on leading change within social movements and politics rather than the organizational change focus of this critical review. However, the handbook did offer informative insights into leadership and organizational change, informed by the Harvard centennial colloquium underpinning the book. In their chapter, which reviewed the last half-century of leadership research through an organization behaviour lens, Glynn and Dejordy (2010:125) took stock of the leadership theories of change, perceiving newer leadership models as treating leadership as a change process and the leader as the primary catalyst for change.

> Overall, the theoretical trajectory of leadership seems propelled by increasing attribution of agency to leaders, moving from "who they are" to "what they do" to "when they do what."
>
> (Glynn and Dejordy, 2010:126)

Lorsch (2010), in his chapter 'A Contingency Theory of Leadership,' spoke directly to Kotter's influence upon this field. In reflecting back upon the leadership studies of the sixties informed by contingency theory, Lorsch acknowledged their limitations, believing that they were heading in the right direction, citing Kotter as an illustration of the move away from contingent accounts of leadership towards a general theory. However, he argued that the now-popular distinction made between leaders and managers encouraged by Zaleznik (1977) and Kotter (1982) was a false dichotomy.

> According to this view, leaders are individuals who are introducing change. Managers are sustaining the status quo by motivating

organization members to work effectively. The further inference is made that it is impossible, or at least difficult, for the same person to be an effective leader and an effective manager.

(Lorsch, 2010:413)

Whilst acknowledging its popularity, Lorsch believed that this was a false dichotomy because most effective leaders also turned out to be very good managers and the idea that to be a leader requires bringing about change meant many people who were leaders would no longer be leaders. However, he suggested that the distinction proved popular because '. . .it glorifies the notion of leadership, and those who accept this definition enjoy thinking of themselves as high-status leaders rather than mundane managers' (Lorsch, 2010:414).

The second leadership handbook was *The SAGE Handbook of Leadership* (Bryman et al, 2011). It is comprised of five parts: Overview perspectives, macro sociological perspectives, political and philosophical perspectives, psychological perspectives and emerging perspectives. Individual editors took responsibility for the development of each part, with the editors voting on what themes/chapters to include. This resulted in a democratic handbook containing 38 contributions from 64 authors (subject experts in their respective fields). There were chapters on the 'Leader-Member Exchange' and 'Transformational Leadership,' with the latter discussed below. Hansen and Bathurst's (2011) chapter, obliquely entitled 'Aesthetics and Leadership,' initially appeared outside the scope of this critical review, but within its emancipatory conceptualisation, it did address transformation. In terms of understanding leadership and organizational change interrelationships, this area did not merit a separate chapter. Parry's (2011:57) chapter on leadership and organization theory included a sub-section on leadership and organizational change, where he critically took stock of the state of scholarship in this area.

Leadership and organizational change are inextricably intertwined. However, 'organizational change' has become an interest for organizational consultants more so than for empirical researchers. There are many more books and articles on practitioner or conceptual scholarship than on theoretical or empirical scholarship. Much of the practitioner work is case study-based, and anecdotal and not rigorous in its conduct.

This quotation is simultaneously reassuring and troubling: It is reassuring (for this reviewer) in that a respected professor of leadership also acknowledges the absence of the anticipated large body of theoretical/empirical work. However, it is troubling for academics and wider society given that leadership and organizational change are undoubtedly intertwined and very prevalent, yet we know little empirically about their interrelationships. Parry did briefly consider more empirical/theoretical work within his review, identifying Kavanagh and Ashkanasy's (2006) paper as of particular interest. The authors undertook cross-institutional data collection across three universities merging with other colleges of advanced education; this longitudinal research was undertaken over six years. Literature reviewing enabled the development of five propositions that were subsequently tested, with the following conclusions drawn from the paper:

> As such individuals and their perception of the manner in which change is being managed will often determine not only how a leader will be regarded, but who will be regarded as a leader. Leaders need to be competent and trained in the process of transforming organizations and reflect on follower motives when considering how to lead organizational change as prompted by a merger.
>
> (Kavanagh and Ashkanasy, 2006:S100)

Another chapter in the SAGE handbook focused on transformational leadership, with Diaz-Saenz (2011:299) claiming that 'for the past 30 years transformational leadership has been the single most studied and debated idea within the field of leadership studies.' Citing Conger (1999), Diaz-Saenz (2011) attributed its popularity and development to the desire of American businesses to respond to international competition, particularly in the eighties. As well as the references featured earlier in this chapter, Diaz-Saenz highlighted the influence of the transformational leadership inventory developed by Podsakoff et al (1990) and subsequently overshadowed by the MLQ. Diaz-Saenz acknowledged that in early writings on transformational leadership, there was a tendency to use charisma as a synonym for transformational leadership. Diaz-Saenz acknowledged that empirical research supported the view that transformational leadership favourably influenced the follower's performance, but an equal weakness was that idealised notions of transformational leadership gave too much credit to leaders and their limited vision of the scientific community researching transformational leadership. Diaz-Saenz cited Beyer's (1999) criticism of transformational leadership's bias towards psychology at the expense of sociology. When compared to the leadership of change, the study of transformational leadership appeared very convergent, although for Diaz-Saenz (2011:308), 'transformational leadership has progressed over the years. Nevertheless, it seems that efforts are fragmented into diverse isolated groups of researchers, who sometimes seem to ignore each other.'

The third handbook, *The Oxford Handbook of Leadership* (Rumsey, 2012), included the chapter 'From Transactional and Transformational to Authentic Leadership,' but there were no chapters focused on organizational change. Finally, within *The Oxford Handbook of Leadership and Organizations* (Day, 2014), there were chapters on 'Charismatic and Transformational Leadership,' 'Leader-Member Exchange Theory (LMX)' and

'Leading for Proactivity,' but no chapters on organizational change or organizational transformation.

In shifting the focus to organizational change handbooks, did Burke et al (2009), Boje, Burnes and Hassard (2011) and By and Burnes (2013) offer overarching explanations of leadership and organizational change interrelationships? In *Organization Change: A Comprehensive Reader* (Burke et al, 2009), three of the 52 contributions made reference to leaders/leadership in their titles (Burke, 2009; Rioch, 1971; Witherspoon and Cannon, 2004;). Witherspoon and Cannon (2004) focused on executive coaching of leaders in times of transition, which was outside the scope of this review.

Similarly, Rioch's (1971) chapter, with its title a quotation from Isaiah, initially appeared tangential (please note the reference is to the original journal paper, as the supporting Jossey Bass website is no longer operational). However, the chapter's prescience chimes with many leadership debates featured in this critical review. Rioch (1971) suggests that in troubled times, we don't know which way to turn, and we seek a common goal or to belong to a stable community. We look for a good leader with the answer, but we encounter bad leaders responsible for all our ills and ailments. Instead of choices between either top-led change or participative, follower-driven change, Rioch (1971) highlights another perspective. In the absence of participative/community-based change, the leader becomes the surrogate for the agency of the community. Rioch explains the follower's perceived need for leaders through examples drawn from religion, parenting education, drama and Tavistock group conferences. Although her main interest was not with organizational change, her reasoning explains the potential interrelationships between leadership and organizational change. There is a tendency in humans to be aggravated when isolated or faced with unfamiliar situations, and they find the exercise of their own power of mind difficult in these situations (Rioch, 1971). This appears to be an intriguing and plausible psychodynamic explanation of why leadership is increasingly offered up during times of organizational change, which would merit empirical investigation. Finally, Burke's (2009) contribution (see Figure 2.4) is taken from the second edition of his own organizational change textbook.

Prelaunch Phase—Leader self-examination, gathering information from the external environment, establishing a need for change, providing clarity of vision and direction

The Launch Phase—Communicating the need for change, initiating key activities, dealing with resistance

Post-launch Phase—Multiple leverage, taking the heat, consistency, perseverance, repeating the message

Sustaining the Change—Dealing with unanticipated consequences, momentum, choosing successors, launching yet again new initiatives

---

Figure 2.4 Leading organizational change (Burke, 2009)

What is interesting and innovative about this contribution (Figure 2.4) is its emphasis upon four organizational change phases: Prelaunch, launch, post-launch and a sustaining phase, with each phase having implications for the leader's change role and function (see Ford and Ford, 2012, for further discussion about the stages of change leadership). Burke acknowledged that it had been written in a prescriptive fashion, although it drew upon theoretical ideas. By and Burnes (2011), in their contribution to *The Routledge Companion to Organizational Change* (Boje et al, 2011), focused on leadership and change, with their subtitle 'Whatever happened to ethics' signposting their subsequent edited reader *Organizational Change, Leadership and Ethics: Leading Organizations towards Sustainability* (By and Burnes, 2013). Both publications are reviewed given their relevance to this critical review.

By and Burnes (2011) built upon themes first introduced in Burnes (2009) and Burnes and Jackson (2011), commencing with an acknowledgement of major developments with regards to approaches to leadership and change. They then developed this discussion into the case for ethical change leadership. Their concern was that the advance of emergent change had consequences for the development of planned change. Emergent change was critically associated with the egoistic consequentialism personified by Gordon Gecko in the film *Wall Street*, whereas they favoured a planned approach to change that '. . .adopts the utilitarian objective of seeking to achieve the greatest good for the greatest number' (By and Burnes, 2011:302). They drew three conclusions from their chapter: That leadership and change were inextricably linked, that the planned approach to change was more likely to lead to utilitarian outcomes than the emergent approach and that emergent change was more likely to lead to unethical outcomes.

A recurrent theme within this critical review has been that definitions and ambiguities relating to both leadership and to organizational change hamper the development and advancement of convincing theories. The addition of ethics initially only appears to further muddy these waters, but in *Organizational Change, Leadership and Ethics: Leading Organizations Towards Sustainability*, By and Burnes (2013), rather than viewing ethics as an add-on, regarded ethics as integral to achieving sustainable organizational change. This book, which was an edited reader, took a different form to the handbooks: whereas all of the contributors shared a similar vision, the writing styles and favoured perspectives varied considerably. The following contributions appeared particularly pertinent to the interrelationships between leadership and organizational change. Patzer and Voegtlin (2013) highlighted the influence that positivist and post-positivist paradigms had had upon explanations of leadership, ethics and organizational change. Classical leadership theory, adopting a positivist research paradigm, favoured highly quantitative methods and gave impetus to the transformational leadership typical of the research in this paradigm. By contrast, post-positivist paradigms were far more philosophical, with servant leadership and responsible leadership typical of the post-positivist paradigm. Diefenbach (2013) drew attention to how change failure was often attributed to technical aspects of change programmes or employee resistance/lack of support or employee organizational misbehaviour; whereas poor change leadership was largely neglected. He highlighted how leader incompetence and immorality had not featured prominently within organization studies.

Sutherland and Smith (2013) emphasised a dualities-aware approach as beneficial, both in terms of theorising change leadership and change leadership practice (discussed further in Chapter Three). The final chapter, entitled 'Looking Back to Move Forward' (Burnes, 2013) took the form of a reminder that the founding father of planned change, Kurt Lewin, originally offered a participative and democratic model of changing, poignantly informed by his life experiences as a German refugee in the 1940s and his desire to help the disadvantaged. Emergent change in comparison to planned change was believed to lack such a moral compass.

LEADERSHIP AND ORGANIZATIONAL CHANGE: UNIVERSITY TEXTBOOKS REVIEWED (2010–2014)

Interest in leadership of organizational change theories and practices suggests that such interest would be reflected in university textbooks informing the education of undergraduates and postgraduates as the potential leaders of tomorrow. University textbooks do not normally feature in literature reviews, but in seeking to provide their student readers with accessible insights into accumulated knowledge offer a creative means to gauge the state of leadership and organizational change knowledge. The breadth of textbooks is often disparaged when compared to the depth of refereed journal papers, but their strength is synthesising what is known, and in potentially drawing upon a range of disparate sources. However, the initial review of organizational change textbooks (Balogun and Hope Hailey, 2008; Palmer et al 2009) revealed only brief discussions of leadership, with no chapters devoted to leading/leadership of change. The latest editions from Burnes (2014) and Carnall and By (2014) showed signs of increasing emphasis on leadership when compared to earlier editions. These authorial choices may echo Parry's (2011) conclusion about the imbalance between practitioner and empirical evidence or may reflect authors focusing upon managing/management rather than leading/leadership. The following review focuses specifically on the chapters on leadership and organizational change in Grieves's (2010), Senior and Swailes's (2010) and Hayes's (2014) organizational change textbooks.

The academic discipline backgrounds of Senior and Swailes (2010) were occupational psychology and human resource management, respectively. In the fourth edition of *Organizational Change*, one of their nine chapters was devoted to leadership and change. They commenced with a discussion of the differences between leadership and management, followed by a detailed chronological coverage of the different generic leadership theories, including critical approaches (pages 225 to 261). Only pages 261 to 273 focused on leading change, before the chapter concluded. The authors discussed leading changes using Dunphy and Stace's (1988, 1993) differentiation between fine tuning, incremental adjustment, modular transformation and corporate transformation and between collaborative, communicative, directive and coercive leadership. Leading change was discussed as a response to resistance to change with authors such as Ford and Ford (2009) cited, rather than the normal, unsophisticated Kotter and Schlesinger (1979) analysis. There was subsequent coverage of cynicism and scepticism, readiness for change, leader-member exchange, organizational citizenship, force field analysis and responses to resistance, but the anticipated review of specific leadership and organizational change theories did not emerge. The implication of this chapter was that your favoured explanation of leading change would be determined by your favoured generic leadership approach and that this preference would determine your practice.

Grieves's (2010) chapter on leading change initially appeared to follow management and organization studies textbook orthodoxy, celebrating the historic evolution of leadership studies. However, within this overview of the sub-field, perceptive and innovative insights emerged. Debates around differentiating (and not differentiating) management and leadership were introduced (see Chapter Four for further discussion). A norm when differentiating between leadership and management is to go back to Selznick (1957). However, Grieves (2010) highlighted the connection between Selznick and the design school of strategy, citing Mintzberg et al's (1998) provocative strategy typology. Mintzberg et al (1998) noted the Harvard Business School's promotion of such approaches to strategy and that such approaches did not emphasise ethics and values. Grieves (2010:263) wrote that this perspective '. . .fashioned the cult of the strategic leader as the architect of the organization.' Also, Grieves (2010:270) drew attention to Quinn's (1978) notion of logical incrementalism, arguing that '. . .perhaps the most important contribution of strategic management was the critique of change as a neat linear sequence.' Grieves (2010) subsequently discussed transformational leadership, emphasising that originally, Downton (1973) and Burns (1978) placed greater emphasis upon moral imperatives than later business expositions did. Finally, Grieves engaged with results-based leadership, suggesting eight actions that leaders needed to undertake when managing change. Grieves succeeded in writing about leading change without referencing Kotter, although Kotter's mindset haunted Grieves's final eight prescriptions, slightly tainting what was a really thought-provoking chapter.

Hayes (2014) acknowledged that leadership had been given greater attention within the fourth edition of his textbook. One of the seven parts of the book was entitled 'Leading and Managing the People Issues.' Two chapters were of particular interest within his textbook: Chapter Two—'Leading

1. Recognising the need for change and starting the change process
2. Diagnosing what needs to be changed and formulating a vision of a preferred future state
3. Planning how to intervene in order to achieve the desired change
4. Implementing plans and reviewing progress
5. Sustaining the change
6. Leading and managing the people issues
7. Learning

Figure 2.5   Leading change: a process perspective (Hayes, 2014)

Change: A Process Perspective,' and Chapter Nine—'The Role of Leadership in Change Management.' In Chapter Two, Hayes presented a process model of change, with the management of change conceptualised as purposeful, constructed and often contested and as requiring seven core activities to be attended to:

In the context of the textbook entitled *The Theory and Practice of Change Management*, Hayes explained his model, conceptualising the management of change in a chapter entitled 'Leading Change: A Process Perspective,' making frequent references to those leading change. The differentiation between leading and managing within this chapter is blurred, which may have been intentional or unintentional (see Chapter Four for further discussion about the false dichotomy between leading and managing). What is explicit from reading this chapter was the emphasis Hayes placed upon Kurt Lewin's (1947) contribution. Hayes (2014) appears far closer to Burnes (2004) than Kotter (1996) in appreciating Lewin as the original source and making the case for the continued relevance today of Lewin's work. Again, a question surfaces about leading change or managing change: Are these active verbs a modern semantic construction? Hayes's (2014) chapter, 'entitled The Role of Leadership in Change Management,' cited Tichy and Devanna's (1986a) and Kotter's (1996) differentiation between management as maintaining the existing organization and leadership as concerned with change. This was tempered with Bolden's (2004) critique of the differentiation; however, subsequently, the differentiation appears to have been used. Key leadership tasks were discussed in terms of sense making, visioning, sense giving, aligning, enabling, supporting and maintaining momentum and sustaining the change. The chapter then moved into leadership style, introducing transformational leadership under a sub-heading of charismatic leadership, before exploring distributed leadership as a counterbalance to the notions of heroic leadership.

The unusual choice to review textbook coverage was informed by the earlier analyses reported in this chapter. As anticipated, the textbook authors were unable to focus on convincing theories of leadership and organizational change, because such theories do not exist. This reflects significant short-comings of the sub-field, rather than shortcomings of textbook authors (see Hughes, 2010 for another example of such shortcomings).

DISCUSSION AND PRELIMINARY CONCLUSIONS

Ford and Ford's (2012) review of empirical evidence, *The Leadership of Organization Change: A View from Recent Empirical Evidence*, is particularly pertinent to this chapter and this book. As well as offering an important and valuable contribution to the sub-field of leadership and organizational change, they provided a body of evidence with which to compare and contrast the preliminary conclusions of this chapter. Before discussing Ford and Ford's (2012) contribution, it is informative to summarise the preliminary conclusions that may be drawn from the literature review featured in this chapter.

- The two most-cited leading change/transformational leadership publications (Kotter, 1995, 1996) published between 1978 and 2014 were primarily practitioner-orientated, rather than empirical studies. Wheras citations rankings revealed transformational leadership as empirically advancing, this form of leadership was primarily about the transformation of followers, rather than organizations. Yukl (1999) warned that transformational leadership theories were weak on explaining how major change was implemented by the leader. More recently, Bass and Riggio (2006) conceded that there was relatively little research examining how transformational leadership affects organizational change.
- Both *The Leadership Quarterly* and the *Journal of Change Management* published papers that informed understanding about leadership and organizational change. However, the anticipated debate that focused on understanding interrelationships between leadership and organizational change was not evident. In the case of *The Leadership Quarterly*, the papers tended to concentrate on advancing transformational leadership, and in the case of the *Journal of Change Management*, the papers focused on the development, capabilities and competences of change leaders, without exploring the background assumption that leadership does result in organizational change.
- In the leadership handbooks (Bryman et al, 2011; Day, 2014; Nohria and Khurana, 2010; Rumsey, 2012) and organizational change handbooks (Beer and Nohria, 2000, Boje et al, 2011; Burke et al, 2009; By and Burnes, 2013), the anticipated coverage of leadership and organizational change was missing. This may have been a reflection of the lack of empirical work to report upon, or subject experts focusing on

their own fields of leadership studies and organizational change studies rather than the messy intersection between the two fields.

• The organizational change textbook authors may have made similar authorial choices to the handbook contributors. Narrowing the focus to actual chapters (Grieves, 2010; Senior and Swailes, 2010 and Hayes, 2014) highlighted an emphasis on generic leadership studies, rather than studies of leadership and organizational change interrelationships underpinned by empirical evidence, reflecting the deficiencies within the sub-field.

In their review, Ford and Ford (2012) focused exclusively on literature published in peer-reviewed journals between 1990 and 2010, intentionally not reviewing practitioner magazines such as the *Harvard Business Review*. Whilst their choice reflected academic best practice and their stated focus upon empirical evidence, practitioner writing, such as John Kotter's (1995, 1996), is excluded. In Chapter Five, it will be suggested that the writings of both Bass and Kotter have framed academic as well as practitioner thinking about the leadership of organizational change.

Ford and Ford (2012) initially undertook a keyword search of papers published in the *Journal of Change Management*, the *Journal of Organizational Change Management* and the *Journal of Applied Behavioral Science*; however, their search revealed only '. . .a small handful of articles. . .' The authors then expanded their review to include all academic peer-reviewed papers, identifying 27 papers between 1990 and 2010; they subsequently excluded certain papers, which resulted in a final tally of 14 papers (see Figure 2.6).

The fourteen papers Ford and Ford (2012) identified are listed alphabetically in Figure 2.6. In reviewing this literature, they made an interesting differentiation (fourth column) between *focused leadership*, where one person was attributed as leader, and *distributed leadership*, referring to leadership involving multiple people. This resonates with earlier discussions and subsequent discussions, in that leadership and organizational change is often conceived of in terms of strong and individualistic leaders, whereas in the context of organizational change, distributed leadership is likely to be relevant. Ford and Ford (2012) assessed the contributions made by the papers featured in Figure 2.6, but drew similar conclusions about the fragmented and incomplete state of knowledge, similar to the findings reported in this chapter. They commenced their discussion section as follows:

> There is simply too little empirical research that specifically addresses the leadership of change to warrant a prescription for what works. . .we find, the available research equivocal and incomplete regarding both what constitutes effective leadership and the impact of change leaders approaches, behaviors, and activities on change outcomes of any type.
>
> (Ford and Ford, 2012:22)

Author/s	Year	Title	Form of Leadership
Battilana, Gilmartin, Sengul, Pache and Alexander	2010	Leadership competencies for implementing planned organizational change	Focused
Denis, Lamothe and Langley	2001	The dynamics of collective leadership and strategic change in pluralistic organizations	Distributed
Dennis, Langley and Cazale	1996	Leadership and strategic change under ambiguity	Distributed
Eriksen	2008	Leading adaptive organizational change: Self-reflexivity and self-transformation	Focused
Gilley, McMillan, and Gilley	2009	Organizational change and characteristics of leadership effectiveness	Focused
Gioia and Chittipeddi	1991	Sensemaking and sensegiving in strategic change initiation	Distributed
Gioia, Thomas, Clark and Chittipeddi	1994	Symbolism and strategic change in academia: The dynamics of sensemaking and influence	Distributed
Herold, Fedor, Caldwell and Liu	2008	The effects of transformational and change leadership on employee commitment to change: A multilevel study	Focused
Higgs and Rowland	2005	All changes great and small: Exploring approaches to change and its leadership	Focused
Higgs and Rowland	2009	Change leadership: Case study of a global energy company	Focused
Joffe and Glynn	2002	Facilitating change and empowering employees	Distributed
Kavanagh and Ashkanasy	2006	The impact of leadership and change management strategy on organizational culture and individual acceptance of change during a merger	Distributed
Lyons, Swindler and Offner	2009	The Impact of Leadership on Change Readiness in the US Military	Distributed
Wren and Dulewicz	2005	Leading competencies, activities and successful change in the Royal Air Force	Focused

Figure 2.6 Leadership of organizational change papers (Ford and Ford, 2012)

Ford and Ford (2012) acknowledged that they were 'particularly surprised' to find only Herold et al (2008) investigating the relationship between transformational leadership and organizational change. Ford and Ford (2012:31) identified four weaknesses within the literature that they had reviewed:

1) An over-emphasis on the role of the individual leader in a position of authority.
2) The use of subjective assessments of change implementation and leadership without addressing the original intended outcomes for the leadership of a successful change.
3) The single-point data collection of many studies that does not include the temporality of change and its implications for the processes and interactions of leadership.
4) A vocabulary that adds confusion and vagueness to both the research and its conclusions.

All of these weaknesses were encountered when independently undertaking the literature reviewing informing this chapter. These weaknesses do not just impede literature reviewing, they are likely to be impediments to anyone undertaking leadership and organizational change research and scholarship. As Jeffrey Ford and Laurie Ford are highly respected in the field organizational change, the final sentence of their review of the empirical evidence offered a sad epitaph to the state of leadership of organizational change knowledge they encountered.

> With regard to Burke's assumption that leaders have a significant influence on organization change, we're willing to agree but unfortunately can't say what that influence is, what leader actions and interactions are responsible for it, or whether the influence is only on the subjective perceptions of people affected by the change or also impacts the objective outcomes of change.
>
> (Ford and Ford, 2012:33)

In conclusion, the interrelationships between leadership and organizational change have been acknowledged (Conger, 1999; By and Burnes, 2011, Parry, 2011). However, the findings of this chapter and the writings of Parry (2011) and Ford and Ford (2012) suggest that we still lack the anticipated empirical understanding into the nature, practices and consequences of such interrelationships. The greatest progress to date appears to have been made in empirically advancing transformational leadership, which attempted to realise Burns's (1978) vision of transforming societies and institutions through leadership. However, the form of transformational leadership (Bass and Riggio, 2006) that has evolved is primarily concerned with transforming followers through leadership is distinct from transforming organizations (see Bass and Riggio, 2006, Yukl, 1999, and Ford and Ford, 2012 for further discussion of this limitation). A more narrow focus on the leadership of organizational change empirical progress appears to have been far more limited and fragmented, typified by the most-cited publications, which were Kotter's (1995, 1996) practitioner-orientated writings. The conclusion drawn from the literature review reported in this chapter is that the sub-field of leadership and organizational change is potentially informed by the fields of organizational change studies and leadership studies. However, to date, scholars in both fields have neither taken on responsibility for advancing the sub-field nor appear interested in advancing this sub-field, which in mitigation may dilute their primary interest in either organizational change studies or leadership studies. Consequently, the next two chapters look separately to each of these fields in order to better understand how these fields are advancing and how they might subsequently contribute to advancing understanding about the sub-field of leadership and organizational change.

REFERENCES

This reference list includes full references for citations in Appendix One and Appendix Two.

Anderson, D., and L. Ackerman-Anderson. 2001 and 2010. *Beyond Change Management: How to Achieve Breakthrough Results Through Conscious Change Leadership*. Chichester: John Wiley and Sons.

Avolio, B.J., and B.M. Bass. 1995. "Individual Consideration Viewed at Multiple Levels of Analysis: A Multi-Level Framework for Examining the Diffusion of Transformational Leadership". *The Leadership Quarterly* 6 (2): 199–218.

Avolio, B.J., J.J. Sosik, S.S. Kahai and B. Baker. 2014. "E-Leadership: Re-Examining Transformations in Leadership Source and Transmission". *The Leadership Quarterly* 25 (1): 105–131.

Balogun, J. and V. Hope Hailey. 2008. *Exploring Strategic Change*, 3rd ed. Harlow: FT Prentice Hall.

Balthazard, P.A., D.A. Waldman and J.E. Warren. 2009. "Predictors of the Emergence of Transformational Leadership in Virtual Decision Teams." *The Leadership Quarterly* 20 (5): 651–663.

Balthazard, P.A., D.A. Waldman, R.W. Thatcher and S.T. Hannah. 2012. "Differentiating Transformational and Non-Transformational Leaders on the Basis of Neurological Imaging". *The Leadership Quarterly* 23 (2): 244–258.

Bandura, A. 1986. *Social Foundations of Thought and Action: A Social Cognitive Theory*. Englewood Cliffs, NJ: Prentice-Hall.

Bass, B.M. 1985. *Leadership and Performance Beyond Expectations*. New York: Free Press.

Bass, B.M. 1990a. "Editorial: Transformational Leaders Are Not Necessarily Participative". *The Leadership Quarterly* 1 (4): 219–272.

Bass, B.M. 1990b. From Transactional to Transformational Leadership: Learning to Share the Vision. *Organizational Dynamics* 18 (3): 19–31.

Bass, B.M. 1995. "Theory of Transformational Leadership Redux". *The Leadership Quarterly* 6 (4): 463–478.

Bass, B.M. 1997. "Does the Transactional–Transformational Leadership Paradigm Transcend Organizational and National Boundaries?" *American Psychologist* 52 (2): 130–139.

Bass, B.M. 1998. *Transformational Leadership: Industrial, Military and Educational Impact*. Mahwah, NJ: Lawrence Erlbaum & Associates.

Bass, B.M. 1999. Two Decades of Research and Development in Transformational Leadership. *European Journal of Work and Organizational Psychology* 8 (1): 9–32.

Bass, B.M., and B.J. Avolio. 1990. *Transformational Leadership Development: Manual for the Multifactor Leadership Questionnaire*. Palo Alto, CA: Consulting Psychologists Press.

Bass, B.M., and R.E. Riggio. 2006. *Transformational Leadership*, 2nd ed. Mahwah, NJ: Lawrence Erlbaum Associates Inc/Psychology Press.

Bass, B.M., and P. Steidlmeier. 1999. "Ethics, Character and Authentic Transformational Leadership Behaviour". *The Leadership Quarterly* 10 (2): 181–217.

Battilana, J., M. Gilmartin, M. Sengul, A.C. Pache and J.A. Alexander. 2010. "Leadership Competencies for Implementing Planned Organizational Change". *The Leadership Quarterly* 21 (3): 422–438.

Beer, M., and N. Nohria, eds. 2000. *Breaking the Code of Change*. Boston: Harvard Business School Press.

Benefiel, M. 2005. "The Second Half of the Journey: Spiritual Leadership for Organizational Transformation". *The Leadership Quarterly* 16 (5): 723–747.

Berson, Y., and B.J. Avolio. 2004. "Transformational Leadership and the Dissemination of Organizational Goals: A Case Study of a Telecommunication Firm". *The Leadership Quarterly* 15 (5): 625–646.

Beyer, J.M. 1999. "Taming and Promoting Charisma to Change Organizations". *The Leadership Quarterly* 10 (2): 307–330.

Bloch, S. 2000. "Positive Deviants and Their Power on Transformational Leadership". *Journal of Change Management* 1 (3): 273–279.

Boje, D.M., B. Burnes and J. Hassard, eds. 2011. *The Routledge Companion to Organizational Change*. London: Routledge.

Boje, D.M., and C. Rhodes. 2006. "The Leadership of Ronald McDonald: Double Narration and Stylistic Lines of Transformation". *The Leadership Quarterly* 17 (1): 94–103.

Bolden, R. 2004. *What Is Leadership?* Research Report, Leadership South West: University of Exeter.

Bommer, W.H., R.S. Rubin and T.T. Baldwin. 2004. "Setting the Stage for Effective Leadership: Antecedents of Transformational Leadership Behavior". *The Leadership Quarterly* 15 (2): 195–210.

Braun, S., C. Peus, S. Weisweiler and D. Frey. 2013. "Transformational Leadership, Job Satisfaction, and Team Performance: A Multilevel Mediation Model of Trust". *The Leadership Quarterly* 24 (1): 270–283.

Brown, D.J., and L.M. Keeping. 2005. "Elaborating the Construct of Transformational Leadership: The Role of Affect." *The Leadership Quarterly* 16 (2): 245–272.

Brown, D.J., and R.G. Lord. 1998. "The Utility of Experimental Research in the Study of Transformational/Charismatic Leadership". *The Leadership Quarterly* 9 (1): 531–539.

Bryman, A. 1993. "Charismatic Leadership in Organizations: Some Neglected Issues". *The Leadership Quarterly* 4 (3–4): 289–304.

Bryman, A., D. Collinson, K. Grint, B. Jackson and M. Uhl-Bien, eds. 2011. *The SAGE Handbook of Leadership*. London: Sage Publications Ltd.

Burke, W.W. 2009. "Leading Organization Change". In *Organization Change: A Comprehensive Reader*, eds. W.W. Burke, D.G. Lake and J.W. Paine, 737–761. San Francisco: Jossey Bass.

Burnes, B. 2004. "Kurt Lewin and the Planned Approach to Change: A Re-appraisal", *Journal of Management Studies* 41 (6): 977–1002.

Burnes, B. 2009. "Reflections: Ethics and Organizational Change – Time for a Return to Lewinian Values". *Journal of Change Management* 9(4): 359–381.

Burnes, B. 2013. "Looking Back to Move Forward". In *Organizational Change, Leadership and Ethics: Leading Organizations Towards Sustainability*, eds. R.T. By and B. Burnes, 243–258. London: Routledge.

Burnes, B. 2014. *Managing Change*, 6th ed. Harlow: Pearson.

Burnes, B. and Jackson, P. 2011. "Success and Failure in Organizational Change: An Exploration of the Role of Values." *The Journal of Change Management* 11(2): 133–162.

Burns, J.M. 1978. *Leadership*. New York: Harper Row Publishers.

By, R.T., and B. Burnes, eds. 2013. *Organizational Change, Leadership and Ethics: Leading Organizations Towards Sustainability*. London: Routledge.

By, R.T., and B. Burnes. 2011. "Leadership and Change: Whatever Happened to Ethics?" *The Routledge Companion to Organizational Change*, eds. D.M. Boje, B. Burnes, and J. Hassard, 295–309. London: Routledge.

By, R.T., B. Burnes and C. Oswick. 2012. "Change Management: Leadership, Values and Ethics". *Journal of Change Management* 12 (1): 1–5.

By, R.T., B. Burnes and C. Oswick. 2013. "Creating a Leading Journal and Maintaining Academic Freedom". *Journal of Change Management* 13 (1): 1–8.

Bycio, P., R.D. Hackett and J.S. Allen. 1995. "Further Assessments of Bass's (1985) Conceptualization of Transactional and Transformational Leadership". *Journal of Applied Psychology* 80 (4): 468–478.

Carey, M.R. 1992. "Transformational Leadership and Fundamental Option for Self—Transcendence". *The Leadership Quarterly* 3 (3): 217–236.

Carnall, C. 2000. "Editorial". *Journal of Change Management* 1(1): 4.

Carnall, C.A., and R.T. By. 2014. *Managing Change in Organizations*, 6th ed. Harlow: Pearson.

Cavazotte, F., V. Moreno and M. Hickmann. 2012. "Effects of Leader Intelligence, Personality and Emotional Intelligence on Transformational Leadership and Managerial Performance." *The Leadership Quarterly* 23 (3): 443–455.

Conger, J.A. 1999. "Charismatic and Transformational Leadership in Organizations: An Insider's Perspective of These Developing Streams of Research." *The Leadership Quarterly* 10 (2): 145–179.

Conger, J.A., and J.G. Hunt. 1999. "Charismatic and Transformational Leadership: Taking Stock of the Present and the Future (Part 1)". *The Leadership Quarterly* 10 (2): 121–127.

Conger, J.A., and G. Toegel. 2002. "Action Learning and Multi-Rater Feedback as Leadership Development Interventions: Popular But Poorly Deployed". *Journal of Change Management* 3 (4): 332–348.

Currie, G., A. Lockett and O. Suhomlinova. 2009. "Leadership and Institutional Change in the Public Sector: The Case of Secondary Schools in England". *The Leadership Quarterly* 20 (5): 664–679.

Day, D, ed. 2014. *The Oxford Handbook of Leadership and Organizations (Oxford Library of Psychology)*. New York: Oxford University Press.

Denis, J.L., L. Lamothe and A. Langley. 2001. "The Dynamics of Collective Leadership and Strategic Change in Pluralistic Organizations". *Academy of Management Journal* 44 (4): 809–837.

Denis, J.L., A. Langley and L. Cazale. 1996. "Leadership and Strategic Change Under Ambiguity". *Organization Studies* 17 (4): 673–699.

Diaz-Saenz, H.R. 2011. "Transformational Leadership". In *The SAGE Handbook of Leadership*, eds. A. Bryman., D. Collinson, K. Grint, B. Jackson and M. Uhl-Bien, 299–310. London: Sage Publications Ltd.

Diefenbach, T. 2013. "Incompetent or Immoral Leadership? Why Many Managers and Change Leaders Get It Wrong". In *Organizational Change, Leadership and Ethics: Leading Organizations Towards Sustainability*, eds. By. R.T and B. Burnes, 149–170. London: Routledge.

Dionne, S.D., J.U. Chun, C. Hao, A. Serban, F.J. Yammarino and W.D. Spangler. 2012. "Article Quality and Publication Impact via Levels of Analysis Incorporation: An Illustration with Transformational/Charismatic Leadership". *The Leadership Quarterly* 23 (6): 1012–1042.

Doppelt, B. 2009. *Leading Change Toward Sustainability*, 2nd ed. Sheffield, UK: Greenleaf Publishing.

Downton, J.V. 1973. *Rebel Leadership: Commitment and Charisma in the Revolutionary Process*. New York: Free Press.

Druskat, V.U. 1994. "Gender and Leadership Style: Transformational and Transactional Leadership in the Roman Catholic Church". *The Leadership Quarterly* 5 (2): 99–119.

Dunphy, D., and D. Stace. 1988. "Transformational and Coercive Strategies for Planned Organizational Change: Beyond the OD Model". *Organization Studies* 9 (3): 317–334.

Dunphy, D., and D. Stace. 1993. "The Strategic Management of Corporate Change". *Human Relations* 46 (8): 905–920.

Dvir, T., and B. Shamir. 2003. "Follower Developmental Characteristics as Predicting Transformational Leadership: A Longitudinal Field Study". *The Leadership Quarterly* 14 (3): 327–344.

Ehrlich, S.B., J.R. Meindl and B. Viellieu. 1990. "The Charismatic Appeal of a Transformational Leader: An Empirical Case Study of a Small, High-Technology Contractor". *The Leadership Quarterly* 1 (4): 229–247.

Epitropaki, O., and R. Martin. 2005. "The Moderating Role of Individual Differences in the Relation Between Transformational/transactional Leadership Perceptions and Organizational Identification". *The Leadership Quarterly* 16 (4): 569–589.

Epitropaki, O., and R. Martin. 2013. "Transformational—Transactional Leadership and Upward Influence: The Role of Relative Leader Member Exchanges (RLMX) and Perceived Organizational Support (POS)." *The Leadership Quarterly* 24 (2): 299–315.

Eriksen, M. 2008. "Leading Adaptive Organizational Change: Self Reflexivity and Self-Transformation". *Journal of Organizational Change Management* 21 (5): 622–640.

Ewen, C., A. Wihler, G. Blickle, K. Oerder and B.P. III Ellen. 2013. "Further Specification of the Leader Political Skill-Leadership Effectiveness Relationships: Transformational and Transactional Leader Behavior as Mediators." *The Leadership Quarterly* 24 (4): 516–533.

Ferdig, M.A. 2007. "Sustainability Leadership: Co-Creating a Sustainable Future". *Journal of Change Management* 7 (1): 25–35.

Fletcher, J.K. 2004. "The Paradox of Postheroic Leadership: An Essay in Gender, Power, and Transformational Change". *The Leadership Quarterly* 15 (5): 647–661.

Ford, J.D., and L.W. Ford. 2009. "Decoding Resistance to Change". *Harvard Business Review* 87 (4): 99–103.

Ford, J.D. and L.W. Ford. 2012. "The Leadership of Organization Change: A View from Recent Empirical Evidence". In *Research in Organizational Change and Development (Research in Organizational Change and Development, Volume 20)*, eds. In Abraham B. (Rami) Shani, William A. Pasmore, Richard W. Woodman (eds.) 1–36. Emerald Group Publishing Limited.

Gill, R. 2002. "Change Management—or Change Leadership?" *Journal of Change Management* 3 (4): 307–318.

Gill, R. 2011. *Theory and Practice of Leadership*. London: Sage Publications Ltd.

Gilley, A., H.S. McMillan and J.W. Gilley. 2009. "Organizational Change and Characteristics of Leadership Effectiveness". *Journal of Leadership and Organizational Studies* 16 (1): 38–47.

Gioia, D.A., and K. Chittipeddi. 1991. "Sensemaking and Sensegiving in Strategic Change Initiation". *Strategic Management Journal* 12 (6): 433–448.

Gioia, D.A., J.B. Thomas., S.M. Clark and K. Chittipeddi. 1994. "Symbolism and Strategic Change in Academia: The Dynamics of Sensemaking and Influence". *Organization Science* 5 (3): 363–383.

Glynn, M.A., and R. DeJordy. 2010. "Leadership Through an Organization Behaviour Lens: A Look at the Last Half-Century of Research". In *Handbook of Leadership Theory and Practice: A Harvard Business School Centennial Colloquium*, eds. N. Nohria and R. Khurana, 119–157. Harvard (Boston): Harvard Business Press.

Good, D.J., and G. Sharma. 2010. "A Little More Rigidity: Firming the Construct of Leader Flexibility." *Journal of Change Management* 10 (2): 155–174.

Gouldner, A.W. 1971. *The Coming Crisis of Western Sociology*. London: Heinemann.

Grieves, J. 2010. *Organizational Change: Themes and Issues*. Oxford: Oxford University Press.

Grint, K. 2000. *The Arts of Leadership*. Oxford: Oxford University Press.

Grint, K. 2008. "Forward to the past or back to the future? Leadership, 1965-2006". In *Mapping the Management Journey: Practice, Theory and Context*, eds. S, Dopson., M, Earl, and P. Snow, 104–18. Oxford: Oxford University Press.

Grover, S.L. 2014. "Moral Identity as a Lens for Interpreting Honesty of Indirect Leaders". *Journal of Change Management* 14 (1): 48–65.

Grover, S.L., T. Nadisic and D.L. Patient. 2012. "Bringing Together Different Perspectives on Ethical Leadership". *Journal of Change Management* 12 (4): 377–381.

Hansen, H., and R. Bathurst. 2011. "Aesthetics and Leadership". In *The SAGE Handbook of Leadership*, eds. A. Bryman, D. Collinson, K. Grint, B. Jackson and M. Uhl-Bien, 255–266. London: Sage Publications Ltd.

Hartley, M. 2009. "Leading Grassroots Change in the Academy: Strategic and Ideological Adaptation in the Civic Engagement Movement." *Journal of Change Management* 9 (3): 323–338.

Hartog, D.N., R.J. House, P.J. Hanges, S.A. Ruiz-Quintanilla and P.W. Dorfman. 1999. "Culture Specific and Cross—Culturally Generalizable Implicit Leadership Theories: Are Attributes of Charismatic/transformational Leadership Universally Endorsed?" *The Leadership Quarterly* 10 (2): 219–256.

Harzing, A.W. 2007. *Publish or Perish*. Available from http://www.harzing.com/pop.htm.

Hawkins, J., and V. Dulewicz. 2009. "Relationships Between Leadership Style, the Degree of Change Experienced, Performance and Follower Commitment in Policing". *Journal of Change Management* 9 (3): 251–270.

Hayes, J. 2014. *The Theory and Practice of Change Management*. 4th Edition, Houndmills: Palgrave Macmillan.

Heres, L., and K. Lasthuizen. 2012. "What's the Difference? Ethical Leadership in Public, Hybrid and Private Sector Organizations". *Journal of Change Management* 12 (4): 441–466.

Herold, D.M., D.B. Fedor, S. Caldwell and Y. Liu. 2008. "The Effects of Transformational and Change Leadership on Employee Commitment to Change: A Multilevel Study". *Journal of Applied Psychology* 93 (2): 346–357.

Higgs, M. and D. Rowland.2001. "Developing Change Leaders: Assessing the Impact of a Development Programme". *Journal of Change Management* 2 (1): 47–64.

Higgs, M. 2009. "The Good, the Bad and the Ugly: Leadership and Narcissism". *Journal of Change Management* 9 (2): 165–178.

Higgs, M. and D. Rowland 2010. "Emperors with Clothes on: The Role of Self-Awareness in Developing Effective Change Leadership". *Journal of Change Management* 10 (4): 369–385.

Higgs, M., and D. Rowland. 2000. "Building Change Leadership Capability: 'The Quest for Change Competence.'" *Journal of Change Management* 1 (2): 116–130.

Higgs, M., and D. Rowland. 2005. "All Changes Great and Small: Exploring Approaches to Change and Its Leadership". *Journal of Change Management* 5 (2): 121–151.

Higgs, M., and D. Rowland. 2009. "Change Leadership: Case Study of a Global Energy Company". *Strategic Change* 18 (1/2): 45–58.

Hooijberg, R., and J. Choi. 2000. "From Selling Peanusts and Beer in Yankee Stadium to Creating a Theory of Transformational Leadership: An Interview with Bernie Bass". *The Leadership Quarterly* 11 (2): 291–306.

House, R.J., and R.N. Adita. 1997. "The Social Scientific Study of Leadership: Quo Vadis?" *Journal of Management* 23: 409–473.

Howell, J.M., and B.J. Avolio. 1993. "Transformational Leadership, Transactional Leadership, Locus of Control and Support for Innovation: Key Predictors of Consolidated-Business-Unit Performance". *Journal of Applied Psychology* 78 (6): 891–902.

Hu, J., Z. Wang, R.C. Liden and J. Sun. 2012. "The Influence of Leader Core Self-Evaluation on Follower Reports of Transformational Leadership". *The Leadership Quarterly* 23 (5): 860–868.

Hughes, M. 2010. *Managing Change: A Critical Perspective.* London: CIPD Publishing.

Hunt, J.G. 1999. "Transformational/Charismatic Leadership's Transformation of the Field: An Historical Essay". *The Leadership Quarterly* 10 (2): 129–144.

Hur, Y.H., P.T. Van den Berg and C.P.M. Wilderom. 2011. "Transformational Leadership as a Mediator Between Emotional Intelligence and Team Outcomes". *The Leadership Quarterly* 22 (4): 591–603.

Hutzschenreuter, T., I. Kleindienst and C. Greger. 2012. "How New Leaders Affect Strategic Change Following a Succession Event: A Critical Review of the Literature". *The Leadership Quarterly* 23 (5): 729–755.

Hyde, A., and J. Paterson. 2001. "Leadership Development as a Vehicle for Change during Merger". *Journal of Change Management* 2 (3): 266–271.

Innocenti, L., A.M. Peluso and M. Pilati. 2012. "The Interplay Between HR Practices and Perceived Behavioural Integrity in Determining Positive Employee Outcomes". *Journal of Change Management* 12 (4): 399–415.

James, M., and K. Ward. 2001. "Leading a Multinational Team of Change Agents at Glaxo Wellcome (now Glaxo Smithkline)". *Journal of Change Management* 2 (2): 148–159.

Joffe, M., and Glynn, S. 2002. "Facilitating Change and Empowering Employees". *Journal of Change Management* 2 (4): 369–379.

Jung, D.I., A. Wu and C. Chow. 2008. "Towards Understanding the Direct and Indirect Effects of CEOs' Transformational Leadership of Firm Innovation". *The Leadership Quarterly* 19 (5): 582–594.

Jung, D.I., C. Chow and A. Wu. 2003. "The Role of Transformational Leadership in Enhancing Organizational Innovation: Hypotheses and Some Preliminary Findings". *The Leadership Quarterly* 14 (4–5): 525–544.

Kan, M.M., and K.W. Parry. 2004. "Identifying Paradox: A Grounded Theory of Leadership in Overcoming Resistance to Change." *The Leadership Quarterly* 15 (5): 467–491.

Karp, T. 2006. "Transforming Organizations for Organic Growth: The DNA of Change Leadership". *Journal of Change Management* 6 (1): 3–20.

Karp, T., and T.I.T. Helgo. 2008. "From Change Management to Change Leadership: Embracing Chaotic Change in Public Service Organizations". *Journal of Change Management* 8 (1): 85–96.

Kavanagh, M.H., and N.M. Ashkanasy. 2006. "The Impact of Leadership and Change Management Strategy on Organizational Culture and Individual Acceptance of Change during a Merger". *British Journal of Management* 17, Special Issue: S81–S103.

Klaussner, S. 2012. "Trust and Leadership: Toward an Interactive Perspective". *Journal of Change Management* 12 (4): 417–439.

Koivisto, S., J. Lipponen and M.J. Platow. 2013. "Organizational and Supervisory Justice Effects on Experienced Threat During Change: The Moderating Role of Leader in Group Representativeness". *The Leadership Quarterly* 24 (4): 595–607.

Kotter, J.P. 1982. *The General Managers*. New York: The Free Press.

Kotter, J.P. 1995. "Leading Change: Why Transformation Efforts Fail". *Harvard Business Review* 73 (2): 44–56.

Kotter, J.P. 1996. *Leading Change*. Boston MA: Harvard Business School Press.

Kotter, J.P. and Schlesinger, L.A. 1979. "Choosing Strategies for Change". *Harvard Business Review* 57 (2): 106–114.

Kuhl, S., T. Schnelle and F. Tillman. 2005. "Lateral Leadership: An Organizational Approach to Change". *Journal of Change Management* 5 (2): 177–189.

Lakshman, C. 2005. "Top Executive Knowledge Leadership: Managing Knowledge to Lead Change at General Electric". *Journal of Change Management* 5 (4): 429–446.

Levay, C. 2010. "Charismatic Leadership in Resistance to Change". *The Leadership Quarterly* 21 (1): 127–143.

Lewin, K. 1947. "Frontiers in Group Dynamics". In *Field Theory in Social Science*, ed. D. Cartwright, 188–237. London: Social Science Paperbacks.

Liu, W., R. Zhu and Y. Yang. 2010. "I Warn You Because I like You: Voice Behaviour, Employee Identifications, and Transformational Leadership". *The Leadership Quarterly* 21 (1): 189–202.

Loewe, K.B., K.G. Kroeck and N. Sivasubramaniam. 1996. "Effective Correlates of Transformational and Transactional Leadership: A Meta-Analytic Review of the MLQ Literature". *The Leadership Quarterly* 7 (3): 385–415.

Lorsch, J. 2010. "A Contingency Theory of Leadership". In *Handbook of Leadership Theory and Practice: A Harvard Business School Centennial Colloquium*, eds. N. Nohria and R. Khurana, 411–429. Harvard (Boston): Harvard Business Press.

Lyons, J.B., S.D. Swindler and A. Offner. 2009. "The Impact of Leadership on Change Readiness in the US Military". *Journal of Change Management* 9 (4): 459–475.

Mars, M.M. 2009. "Student Entrepreneurs as Agents of Organizational Change and Social Transformation: A Grassroots Leadership Perspective". *Journal of Change Management* 9 (3): 339–357.

Maslin-Wicks, K. 2007. "Forsaking Transformational Leadership: Roscoe Conkling, the Great Sentator from New York". *The Leadership Quarterly* 18 (5): 463–476.

Menges, J.I., F. Walter, B. Vogel and H. Bruch. 2011. "Transformational Leadership Climate: Performance Linkages, Mechanisms, and Boundary Conditions at the Organizational Level". *The Leadership Quarterly* 22 (5): 893–909.

Michaelis, B., R. Stegmaier and K. Sonntag. 2009. "Affective Commitment to Change and Innovation Implementation Behavior: The Role of Charismatic Leadership and Employees' Trust in Top Management." *Journal of Change Management* 9 (4): 399–417.

Miller, D. 2001. "Successful Change Leaders: What Makes Them? What Do They Do That Is Different?" *Journal of Change Management* 2 (4): 359–368.

Mintzberg, H., B. Ahlstrand and J. Lampel. 1998. *Strategy Safari: The Complete Guide Through the Wilds of Strategic Management*, 1st edition. London: FT Prentice Hall.

Moorman, R.H., T.C. Darnold and M. Priesemuth. 2012. "Toward the Measurement of Perceived Leaders Integrity: Introducing a Multidimensional Approach". *Journal of Change Management* 12 (4): 383–398.

Ndofor, H.A., R.L. Priem, J.A. Rathbun and A.K. Dhir. 2009. "What Does the New Boss Think?: How New Leaders' Cognitive Communities and Recent 'Top-Job' Success Affect Organizational Change and Performance". *The Leadership Quarterly* 20 (5): 799–813.

Nemanich, L.A., and R.T. Keller. 2007. "Transformational Leadership in an Acquisition: A Field Study of Employees". *The Leadership Quarterly* 18 (1): 45–68.

Nemanich, L.A., and D. Vera. 2009. "Transformational Leadership and Ambidexterity in the Context of an Acquisition". *The Leadership Quarterly* 20 (1): 19–33.

Nielsen, K., and B. Cleal. 2011. "Under Which Conditions Do Middle Managers Exhibit Transformational Leadership Behaviors?—An Experience Sampling Method Study on the Predictors of Transformational Leadership Behaviors". *The Leadership Quarterly* 22 (2): 344–352.

Nielsen, K., and K. Daniels. 2012. "Does Shared and Differentiated Transformational Leadership Predict Followers' Working Conditions and Well-Being?" *The Leadership Quarterly* 23 (3): 383–397.

Nohe, C., B. Michaelis, J.I. Menges, Z. Zhang and K. Sonntag. 2013. "Charisma and Organizational Change: A Mutilevel Study of Perceived Charisma, Commitment to Change, and Team Performance". *The Leadership Quarterly* 24 (2): 378–389.

Nohria, N., and R. Khurana. 2010. *Handbook of Leadership Theory and Practice: A Harvard Business School Centennial Colloquium*. Harvard (Boston): Harvard Business Press.

Osborn, R.N., and R. Marion. 2009. "Contextual Leadership, Transformational Leadership and the Performance of International Innovation Seeking Alliances". *The Leadership Quarterly* 20 (2): 191–206.

Ospina, S., and E. Foldy. 2010. "Building Bridges from the Margins: The Work of Leadership in Social Change Organizations". *The Leadership Quarterly* 21 (2): 292–307.

O'Toole, J. 1995. *Leading Change: Overcoming the Ideology of Comfort and the Tyranny of Custom*. San Francisco: Jossey Bass—An Imprint of Wiley.

Paglis, L.L., and Green, S.G. 2002. "Leadership Self Efficacy and Managers' Motivation for Leading Change". *Journal of Organizational Behavior* 23 (2): 215–235.

Palmer, I., R. Dunford and G. Akin. 2009. *Managing Organizational Change: A Multiple Perspectives Approach*, 2nd ed. Boston: McGraw-Hill International Editions.

Parr, A.D., S.T. Hunter and G.S. Ligon. 2013. "Questioning Universal Applicability of Transformational Leadership: Examining Employees with Autism Spectrum Disorder". *The Leadership Quarterly* 24 (4): 608–622.

Parry, K.W. 2011. "Leadership and Organization Theory". In *The SAGE Handbook of Leadership*, eds. A. Bryman, D. Collinson, K. Grint, B. Jackson and M. Uhl-Bien, 53–70. London: Sage Publications Ltd.

Parry, K.W., and S. Proctor-Thompson. 2002. "Leadership, Culture and Performance: The Case of the New Zealand Public Sector". *Journal of Change Management* 3 (4): 376–399.

Patzer, M., and C. Voegtlin. 2013. "Leadership Ethics and Organizational Change: Sketching the Field". In *Organizational Change, Leadership and Ethics: Leading Organizations Towards Sustainability*, eds. R.T. By and B. Burnes, 9–34. London: Routledge.

Pepper, A. 2002. "Leading Professionals: A Science, a Philosophy and a Way of Working". *Journal of Change Management* 3 (4): 349–360.

Pillai, R., E.A. Williams, K.B. Lowe and D.I. Jung. 2003. "Personality, Transformational Leadership, Trust and the 2000 U.S. Presidential Vote". *The Leadership Quarterly* 14 (2): 161–192.

Podsakoff, P.M., S.B. MacKenzie and R.H. Moorman. 1990. "Transformational Leader Behaviors and Their Effects on Followers' Trust in Leader, Satisfaction, and Organizational Citizenship Behaviors". *The Leadership Quarterly* 1 (2): 107–142.

Podsakoff, P.M., S.B. MacKenzie, H. Moorman and R. Fetter. 1990. "Transformational Leader Behaviors and Their Effects on Followers' Trust in Leader, Satisfaction, and Organizational Citizenship Behaviors". *The Leadership Quarterly* 1 (2): 107–142.

Popper, M., and O. Mayseless. 2003. "Back to Basics: Applying a Parenting Perspective to Transformational Leadership". *The Leadership Quarterly* 14 (1): 41–65.

Popper, M., O. Mayseless and O. Castelnovo. 2000. "Transformational Leadership and Attachment." *The Leadership Quarterly* 11 (2): 267–289.

Price, T.L. 2003. "The Ethics of Authentic Transformational Leadership". *The Leadership Quarterly* 14 (1): 67–81.

Purvanova, R.K., and J.E. Bono. 2009. "Transformational Leadership in Context: Face-to-Face and Virtual Teams". *The Leadership Quarterly* 20 (5): 343–357.

Quinn, J.B. 1978. *Strategies for Change: Logical Incrementalism*. Homewood, IL: R.D. Irwin, Inc.

Quinn, R.E. 2011. *Building the Bridge as You Walk on It: A Guide for Leading Change*. San Francisco, CA: Wiley.

Rafferty, A.E., and M.A. Griffin. 2004. "Dimensions of Transformational Leadership: Conceptual and Empirical Extensions". *The Leadership Quarterly* 15 (3): 329–354.

Reeves, D.B. 2009. *Leading Change in Your School: How to Conquer Myths, Build Commitment and Get Results*. Alexandria, VA: Association for Supervision and Curriculum Development.

Reichard, R.J., R.E. Riggio, D.W. Guerin, P.H. Oliver, A.W. Gottfried and A. Eskeles. 2011. "A Longitudinal Analysis of Relationships Between Adolescent Personality and Intelligence with Adult Leader Emergence and Transformational Leadership". *The Leadership Quarterly* 22 (3): 471–481.

Rioch, M.J. 1971. " 'All We like Sheep' (Isaiah 53:6): Followers and Leaders". *Psychiatry: Interpersonal and Biological Processes* 34 (3): 258–273.

Rowold, J., and K. Heinitz. 2007. "Transformational and Charismatic Leadership: Assessing the Convergent, Divergent and Criterion Validity of the MLQ and the CKS". *The Leadership Quarterly* 18 (2): 121–133.

Rubin, R.S., E.C. Dierdorff, W.H. Bommer and T.T. Baldwin. 2009. "Do Leaders Reap What They Sow? Leader and Employee Outcomes of Leader Organizational Cynicism about Change". *The Leadership Quarterly* 20 (5): 680–688.

Rumsey, M.G. 2012. *The Oxford Handbook of Leadership (Oxford Library of Psychology)*. New York: Oxford University Press.

Schriesheim, C.A., S.L. Castro, X. Zhou and L.A. DeChurch. 2006. "An Investigation of Path-Goal and Transformational Leadership Theory Predictions at the Individual Level of Analysis". *The Leadership Quarterly* 17 (1): 21–38.

Selznick, P. 1957. *Leadership in Administration: A Sociological Interpretation*. Evanston, IL: Row Peterson.

Senior, B., and S. Swailes. 2010. *Organizational Change*, 4th ed. Harlow: Pearson Education Limited.

Simola, S.K., J. Barling and N. Turner. 2010. "Transformational Leadership and Leader Moral Orientation: Contrasting an Ethic of Justice an Ethic of Care". *The Leadership Quarterly* 21 (1): 179–188.

Smid, G., E. Hout and Y. Burger. 2006. "Leadership in Organizational Change: Rules for Successful Hiring in Interim Management". *Journal of Change Management* 6 (1): 35–51.

Sosik, J.J., V.M. Godshalk and F.J. Yammarino. 2004. "Transformational Leadership, Learning Goal Orientation, and Expectations for Career Success in Mentor-Protege Relationships: A Multiple Levels of Analysis Perspective". *The Leadership Quarterly* 15 (2): 241–261.

Stoker, J.I., H. Grutterink and N.J. Kolk. 2012. "Do Transformational CEOs Always Make the Difference? The Role of TMT Feedback Seeking Behavior". *The Leadership Quarterly* 23 (3): 582–592.

Sutherland, F., and A.C.T. Smith. 2013. "Leadership for the Age of Sustainability: A Dualities Approach to Organizational Change". In *Organizational Change, Leadership and Ethics: Leading Organizations Towards Sustainability*, eds. R.T. By and B. Burnes, 216–239. London: Routledge.

Tejeda, M.J., T.A. Scandura and R. Pillai. 2001. "The MLQ Revisited: Psychometric Properties and Recommendations". *The Leadership Quarterly* 12 (1): 31–52.

Tichy, N.M., and M.A. Devanna. 1986a. *The Transformational Leader: The Key to Global Competitiveness*. New York: John Wiley and Sons.

Tichy, N.M., and M.A. Devanna. 1986b. "The Transformational Leader". *Training and Development Journal* 40 (7): 27–32.

Tims, M., A.B. Bakker and D. Xanthopoulou. 2011. "Do Transformational Leaders Enhance Their Followers' Daily Work Engagement". *The Leadership Quarterly* 22 (1): 121–131.

Tse, H.H., M, X. Huang and W. Lam. 2013. "Why Does Transformational Leadership Matter for Employee Turnover? A Multi-Foci Social Exchange Perspective". *The Leadership Quarterly* 24 (5): 763–776.

Tucker, S., N Turner, J. Barling and M. McEvoy. 2010. "Transformational Leadership and Childrens' Aggression in Team Settings: A Short-Term Longitudinal Study". *The Leadership Quarterly* 21 (3): 389–399.

Tyler, T.R., and D. De Cremer. 2005. "Process-Based Leadership: Fair Procedures and Reactions to Organizational Change". *The Leadership Quarterly* 16 (4): 529–545.

Van Dierendonck, D., D. Stam and P. Boersma. 2014. "Same Difference? Exploring the Differential Mechanisms Linking Servant Leadership and Transformational Leadership to Follower Outcomes". *The Leadership Quarterly* 25 (3): 544–562.

Van Dijk, R., and R.Van Dick. 2009. "Navigating Organizational Change: Change Leaders, Employee Resistance and Work-Based Identities". *Journal of Change Management* 9 (2): 143–163.

Van der Voet, J., S. Groeneveld and B.S. Kuipers. 2014. "Talking the Talk or Walking the Walk? The Leadership of Planned and Emergent Change in Public Organization". *Journal of Change Management* 14 (2):171–191.

Vinkenburg, C.J., M.L. Van Engen, A.H. Eagly and M.C. Johannessen-Schmidt. 2011. "An Exploration of Stereotypical Beliefs about Leadership Styles: Is Transformational Leadership Route to Women's Promotion?" *The Leadership Quarterly* 22 (1): 10–21.

Vinnicombe, S., and V. Singh. 2002. "Women-Only Management Training: An Essential Part of Women's Leadership Development". *Journal of Change Management* 3 (4): 294–306.

Wagner, T., R. Kegan, L.L. Lahey, R.W. Lemons, J. Garnier, D. Helsing, A. Howell and H.T. Rasmussen, eds. 2010. *Change Leadership: A Practical Guide to Transforming Our Schools*. San Francisco, CA: Jossey Bass—An Imprint of Wiley.

Wang, X., and J.M. Howell. 2012. "A Multilevel Study of Transformational Leadership, Identification, and Follower Outcomes". *The Leadership Quarterly* 23 (5): 775–790.

Weymes, E. 2002. "Relationships Not Leadership Sustain Successful Organizations". *Journal of Change Management* 3 (4): 319–331.

Williams, E.A., R. Pillai, B. Deptula and K.B. Lowe. 2012. "The Effects of Crisis, Cynicism about Change, and Value Congruence on Perceptions of Authentic Leadership and Attributed Charisma in the 2008 Presidential Election". *The Leadership Quarterly* 23 (3): 324–341.

Witherspoon, R., and M.D. Cannon. 2004. "Coaching Leaders in Transition: Lessons from the Field in Creative Consulting: Innovative Perspectives on Management Consulting, Information Age Publishing". In *Organization Change: A Comprehensive Reader*, eds. W.W.Burke, D.G. Lake and J.W. Paine, 599–625. San Francisco: Jossey Bass.

Wofford, J.C., and V.L. Goodwin. 1994. "A Cognitive Interpretation of Transactional and Transformational Leadership Theories". *The Leadership Quarterly* 5 (2): 161–186.

Wofford, J.C., V.L. Goodwin and J.L. Whittington. 1998. "A Field Study of a Cognitive Approach to Understanding Transformational and Transactional Leadership". *The Leadership Quarterly* 9 (1): 55–84.

Woodward, S., and C. Hendry. 2004. "Leading and Coping with Change". *Journal of Change Management* 4 (2): 155–183.

Wren, J., and V. Dulewicz. 2005. "Leading Competencies, Activities and Successful Change in the Royal Air Force". *Journal of Change Management* 5 (3): 295–309.

Yammarino, F.J., W.D. Spangler and A.J. Dubinsky. 1998. "Transformational and Contingent Reward Leadership: Individual, Dyad and Group Levels of Analysis". *The Leadership Quarterly* 9 (1): 27–54.

Yammarino, F.J., W.D. Spangler and B.M. Bass. 1993. "Transformational Leadership and Performance: A Longitudinal Investigation". *The Leadership Quarterly* 4 (1): 81–10.

Young, M., and V. Dulewicz. 2006. "Leadership Styles, Change Context and Leader Performance in the Royal Navy". *Journal of Change Management* 6 (4): 383–396.

Yukl, G. 1999. "An Evaluation of Conceptual Weaknesses in Transformational and Charismatic Leadership Theories". *The Leadership Quarterly* 10 (2): 285–305.

Zacharatos, A., J. Barling and E.K. Kelloway. 2000. "Development and Effects of Transformational Leadership in Adolescents". *The Leadership Quarterly* 11 (2): 211–226.

Zaleznik, A. 1977. "Managers and Leaders: Are They Different?" *Harvard Business Review* 15 (5): 67–80.

Zhang, W., H. Wang and C.L. Pearce. 2014. "Consideration for Future Consequences as an Antecedent of Transformational Leadership Behavior: The Moderating Effects of Perceived Dynamic Work Environment." *The Leadership Quarterly* 25 (2): 329–343.

Zhu, W., I.K.H. Chew and W.D. Spangler. 2005. "CEO Transformational Leadership and Organizational Outcomes: The Mediating Role of Human-Capital-Enhancing Human Resource Management". *The Leadership Quarterly* 16 (1): 39–52.

Zhu, W., B.J. Avolio, R.E. Riggio and J.J. Sosik. 2011. "The Effect of Unauthentic Transformational Leadership on Follower and Group Ethics". *The Leadership Quarterly* 22 (5): 801–817.

3 Understanding Organizational Change

INTRODUCTION

> . . .[T]here is much to question and challenge within the field of organizational change.
>
> (Frahm, 2007:952)

The sceptical conclusion of Frahm (2007) about the state of the field of organizational change is echoed within this chapter's unifying narrative. However, within the critiques and challenges featured in this chapter, there are reasons for optimism about the critical development of the field of organizational change. Studies of organizational change differ from physics or economics, which gain their legitimacy from their relative maturity as academic disciplines, particularly in comparison with a field such as organizational change. The downside of these established disciplines is that their rules, laws and theories become very fixed. Paradigm shifts, which interested Kuhn (1962), particularly regarding his own discipline of physics, were rare and significant events. Inevitably, an emerging field such as organizational change is far more malleable and possesses considerable critical potential for reshaping, rethinking and reimagining. Whereas critiques imply the failure/death of organizational change and its management (see Hughes, 2011, forthcoming for further discussion), these critiques may also be read as healthy indicators of critical questioning of an evolving field such as organizational change studies.

There remains a danger that critiquing the field of organizational change may remove academics from debates that have a profound influence upon societies, institutions, organizations and individuals. In the previous chapter, Parry (2011) and Ford and Ford's (2012) critical conclusions about the state of leadership and organizational change knowledge may be regarded as a wake-up call, but also an explanation for an absence of expected critical academic engagement. Influential and respected critical scholars (Grey, 2003; Kahn, 1974; Sturdy and Grey, 2003) successfully critiqued the field of organizational change and, by association, those working and thinking about working in the field. The danger is that the empirical scholar's avoidance of the field of organizational change becomes a self-fulfilling prophecy: The field is perceived as lacking empirical rigour, so academics avoid the field, leading to the field being perceived as lacking empirical rigour, etc. One of the unintended and perverse consequences of critiques is that practitioner accounts of leading change, such as Kotter's (1996), now command over 6,000 citations (see Figure 2.2). This chapter argues for a critical understanding of organizational change in order to inform our understanding of leadership and organizational change, with the intention that critique should advance critical understanding, rather than create an academic void for exclusively practitioner literature to occupy. This chapter is organized around six closely related sections informing the explanation and elaboration of the development of the field of organizational change studies.

Firstly, organizational change as a field of academic study is similar to other progressive fields. There are innovation studies (Fagerberg and Verspagen, 2009) and studies of projects (Soderlund, 2011), as well as leadership studies, with each field of study prone to debates, contradictions and controversies. It is consequently necessary to understand how such fields work and how they differ from academic disciplines, which requires engagement with Kuhn's (1962) paradigms and scientific revolutions.

Secondly, Chapters One and Two emphasised the historical nature of reviewing leadership and organizational change literature over 35 years since 1978, raising issues about the dominant accounts of history and how such histories were written. A short historiography of organizational change demonstrates how dominant accounts of organizational change have been constructed in a certain way, privileging certain explanations and disparaging other explanations. The implication is that fields of study are subject to historiographical processes, with the sub-field of leadership and organization change likely to be subject to similar processes. Thirdly, whilst acknowledging accounts of organizational change are subject to such historiographical processes, it is still informative to go back to the theoretical milestones of the last 35 years, chronologically mapping the development of explanations of organizational change over 35 years. In this way, the development of organizational change as a field of study is made tangible.

In the fourth section, the focus narrows to one of the explanations of organizational change featured in the previous section, *Philosophies of Organizational Change* (Smith and Graetz, 2011). Smith and Graetz's (2011) pluralistic typology features rational, biological, institutional, resource, psychological, systems, cultural, critical and dualities philosophies. All philosophies are believed to inform understanding organizational change, but a dualities-aware approach is encouraged, as it informs both theory and practice. In Chapter Five, this approach is applied to leadership and organizational change.

The focus further narrows in the fifth section to seven organizational change empirical/theoretical advances that respond to the deficiencies in leading change orthodoxy and more proactively imagine what might be. The seven featured empirical/theoretical advances relate to resistance, ethics, power and politics, process thinking, learning, agency and discourse, context and evaluation, and they are gathered together using the mnemonic REPLACE.

The final section revisits the chapter introduction, now informed by discussions in previous sections. The contested nature of organizational change is acknowledged and the positions taken by critical scholars are revisited. There is never going to be a consensus understanding of organizational change and there never should be, for the reasons discussed in this chapter. However, critical understanding is small and marginal in comparison to rationalist/organizational change orthodoxy, which offers a means to rethink, reshape and reimagine organizational change understanding.

ORGANIZATIONAL FIELD STUDIES

> It seems natural enough to think of knowledge and its properties and relationships in terms of landscapes, and to saturate epistemological discussion with spatial metaphors: fields and frontiers, pioneering, exploration, false trails, charts and landmarks.
>
> (Becher and Trowler, 2001:58)

While Becher and Trowler (2001) worked within education studies, they were interested in all of the knowledge landscapes evident within universities. The field of organizational change, imagined geographically for a moment, raises questions about frontiers and boundaries: How has organizational change been explained over time, who have been the pioneers and what have been their landmark studies? Universities tend to focus and organize in terms of academic disciplines rather than fields of study. However, there is a problem with notions of a 'hierarchy of sciences' (Cole, 1983) depicting natural sciences as a model of scientific progress, which social science should seek to emulate (see Hassard et al, 2008 for further discussion). Kuhn's (1962) famously mapped scientific revolutions concerned primarily academic communities at the disciplinary level, rather than their specialisms/fields, believing that paradigms provided scientists not only with a map, but also provided directions essential for map-making. Unfortunately, the unified science aspirations of convergent natural sciences that Kuhn (1962) encouraged were mirrored in expectations about newly emerging studies of organizations and management. Whitley (1984, 2000), in his studies of management, highlighted a privileging of science, tracing the origins of the goal of an integrated, coherent and relevant 'science of management' back to the halcyon days of the 1950s.

In Becher and Trowler's (2001) studies, spatial metaphors were used to contrast urban and rural ways of academic life. In urban specialisms, academics worked closely on a narrow range of related problems, whereas within rural specialisms, academics were far more dispersed, working on a broad range of problems. They cited physics as a highly convergent discipline, with respondents commenting upon an overriding sense of collective kinship, mutual interests, shared intellectual style, consensus around profound simplicities and a quasi-religious belief in the unity of nature. In contrast, sociology, mechanical engineering, modern languages, geography and pharmacy were cited as being divergent disciplines in terms of how research was conducted. Using such language, the 'rural' field of organizational change lacks the convergence of physics and judged against such criteria, would be regarded as inferior. By contrast, transformational leadership (featured in Chapter Two), in being more 'urban' and converging around a common quest to advance transformational leadership, would be regarded as superior.

However, more generally, Whitley (1984) found that management studies did not integrate around common theoretical goals and research skills, but instead developed into multiple sub-fields with differing goals, problems and research approaches. The convergence similar to natural sciences envisaged within management and organization studies was never realised, and instead we witness divergence as many fields and sub-fields developed and continue to develop (see McKinley et al, 1999 who reached similar conclusions in their account of the development of schools of thought in organization theory). The review of leadership and organizational change developments since 1978 requires an appreciation of the dynamic nature of organization studies during this era, particularly the influence of paradigms, the so-called paradigm wars and developments up until the present day.

Whilst *Sociological Paradigms and Organisational Analysis* (Burrell and Morgan, 1979) received many bouquets and brickbats (see Deetz, 1996, Grant and Perren, 2002 and Shepherd and Challenger, 2013 for overviews) since its publication over thirty years ago, the book made a significant contribution to understanding the territorial nature of organization studies. They (1979) explained competing philosophical assumptions in terms of four polarised debates: Ontological, epistemological, human nature and methodological. Philosophical assumptions were acknowledged as underpinning the four paradigms of functionalism, interpretivism, radical humanism and radical structuralism. Deetz (1996) acknowledged that alternative scholars had embraced the four-paradigm grid that Burrell and Morgan promoted as an alternative to the more mainstream functionalist accounts of organization. The rethinking of Burrell and Morgan (1979) by Deetz (1996) offered an important milestone in terms of developments in the debate about the territorial nature of organization studies in general and organizational change in particular. Deetz argued persuasively that we needed to move away from Burrell and Morgan's reification. Deetz was interested in how the linguistic turn in modern philosophy informed organization studies. Research orientation differences could be contrasted in terms of 'local/emergent' and 'elite/a priori' and in terms of 'dissensus' and 'consensus' (see Chapter Five for application to leadership and organizational change). Deetz was influential in encouraging movement away from paradigms towards discourses, and this linguistic turn has been significant for organizational change scholars (see Phillips and Oswick, 2011 for further discussion).

More recently, Shepherd and Challenger (2013) in revisiting management and organization studies paradigms acknowledged Weick's (1999) call for the dissolution of the paradigm wars and Deetz's (1996) and Hassard and Kelemen's (2002) encouragement to move away from paradigms towards discourses. However, Shepherd and Challenger (2013) acknowledged that paradigm(s) in business and management research continue to be popular. In reviewing editorial statements in *Organization Studies*, Hinings (2010) offered an overview of the state of the field of organization studies. Hinings identified three interrelated themes: A desire and respect for diverse theoretical perspectives and methodological approaches, a concern with more than the organization per se, and sustaining an interdisciplinary range. Today, divergence appears to have become a respected norm, with such divergence appearing equally applicable to the field of organizational change. It will feature in the subsequent chapters.

A SHORT HISTORIOGRAPHY OF ORGANIZATIONAL CHANGE

According to Huczynski (2006), there have been only six truly popular management idea families over the past one hundred years: Bureaucracy, scientific management, administrative management, human relations, neo-human relations and guru theory. Each management idea family has informed understanding about organizational change (see Hughes, 2010 for further discussion); these ideas reflect particular accounts of history. Cooke (1999:81) argued persuasively that 'change management's very construction has been a political process which has written the left out, and shaped an understanding of the field as technocratic and ideologically neutral.' The implication is that there is never a singular or exclusive history of a field or an academic discipline; instead, multiple histories exist and compete for our attention. Dominant accounts of a field's history are shaped by the powerful and the influential. In the next chapter, similar historiographical processes are at work with regards to the perceived leadership studies orthodoxy, with what is focused upon being highly selective.

Historiography is relevant here, because it is not just about historically understanding organizational change, but also understanding the strong influence of the past on how organizational change is perceived and theorised today. Burke (2014), as a respected organizational change scholar, within his textbook included a chapter entitled 'A Brief History of Organizational Change,' which informatively mapped important forerunners to the modern study of organizational change. For Burke, these were scientific management, the Hawthorne studies, industrial psychology, survey feed-back, sensitivity training, sociotechnical systems, organization development (OD), the managerial grid and OD, coercion and confrontation and management consulting. However, the danger with such linear histories covering approximately one hundred years is that they reflect an apparent accretion of knowledge with reassurance achieved through the implied progress. The reassurance that solidifies orthodoxy is at the expense of advancing understanding and at the expense of alternative explanations of organizational change. The following discussion focuses historiographically upon scientific management, Hawthorne studies, planned change and Kurt Lewin and OD. The intention is to highlight how certain accounts of organizational change have been favoured and encourage caution when imagining a linear, neutral and rational development of the field of organizational change. This will be a recurrent theme throughout this critical review, that certain readings have been favoured at the expense of others in understanding leadership and organizational change.

F.W.Taylor's (1911) scientific management may be understood in terms of the following scientific principles: Divorce of conception from execution, fragmentation and standardisation, financial incentives, scientific selection of staff and cooperation (Gabriel, 2008). Over a century later, these principles are still evident within organizations and evident within prescriptions about how organizations should change (see, for example, business process reengineering, Grint and Case, 1998). Taylor's (1911) concept of scientific management was given added legitimacy through his research undertaken at the Midvale Steel Company and Bethlehem Steel Company. However, Wrege and Hodgetts's (2000) analysis of the original documents, upon which Taylor's famous pig-iron observations of 1899 were based, found that his observations were erroneous. Taylor and his associates made many mistakes, the most important of which was the simplification of their results. However, the underlying message of scientific management was an encouragement to de-skill work and increase management control. The message appealed to managers, ensuring its longevity, how it is presented to students today and its application today.

In terms of Huczynski's (2006) popular management idea families, the Hawthorne studies followed on from scientific management, emphasising worker motivation as social, rather than economic, and offering a counterpoint to scientific management (Gabriel, 2008). The Hawthorne studies gained considerable legitimacy from being research-based and again influenced organizational change, particularly in terms of OD and the relationships between human resource management and organizational change. However, Hassard (2012) has encouraged a critical rethinking of the famous Hawthorne Studies (1924–32) undertaken at Western Electric. Human relations, which was attributed to Elton Mayo's arrival in 1928, was actually found to predate Mayo's arrival. Instead, the favoured human relations approach was found to be underpinned by Western Electric's hard-edged paternalism and tough-minded anti-unionism, with the organizational climate becoming increasingly challenging during the 1930s. This contrasts with Burke's (2014) depiction of the Hawthorne studies as a significant precursor to understanding organizational change signposting more humanistic treatment of workers.

Cooke (1999), in his analysis of the historiography of the management of change, illustrated how the writings of Kurt Lewin, John Collier and Edgar Schein were depicted in a certain way in order to reflect managerialist historiography; however, such depictions diverged from these authors' original intentions. Kurt Lewin (1890–1947) is acknowledged as the intellectual father of planned change (Schein, 1988). However, it became fashionable to misrepresent Kurt Lewin and then critique the misrepresentation (see Burnes, 2004 for further discussion and re-evaluation). Cooke (1999), Burnes (2004) and Burnes and Cooke (2013) revisited Lewin's original writings, challenging common misrepresentations and acknowledging Lewin's considerable contribution to understanding organizational change.

Cooke (1999:83) explained how historiographical processes work: '[H]istory, our knowing of the past, is constructed by identifying some of these events as significant, and, by implication, others as not, and by giving these events particular meaning.' Burnes (2004:979), through careful reading of Lewin's original work and setting Lewin's work within its own political and social context, countered the criticisms, writing that 'for most of his life Lewin's main preoccupation was the resolution of social conflict and, in particular, the problems of minority or disadvantaged groups.' Burnes and Cooke's (2013) long history of OD differs from the short histories of OD, which suggest that OD originated in the late 1950s. For Burnes and Cooke, OD can be traced back to Lewin's work in the late 1930s. They questioned accounts of OD being revised and revitalised in response to its perceived decline in the 1980s, instead arguing that it is not fundamentally different from the past.

In this discussion, the way that certain theoretical explanations are favoured and privileged has been highlighted. In seeking to understand organizational change, historiographical processes are equally applicable to wider depictions of the environments in which organizational change takes place. Burrell (1992) challenged notions of linearity and chronarchy, instead favouring notions of spiral time (depicted pictorially as a coiled serpent). Similarly, Cummings (2002:180) challenged assumptions about the linearity of organizational change, arguing for 'a vision of time not as a straight line but as a spiral, with past, present and future intermingled.' In this way, business process reengineering is scientific management revisited, rather than a radical new change methodology, as originally rhetorically depicted (see Grint and Case, 1998). In a similar manner, historiography questions popular rhetoric that we are living through turbulent times depicting uniquely turbulent environments (Eccles and Nohria, 1992; Sorge and Van Witteloostuijn, 2004; Thompson and O'Connell Davidson, 1995). The historiographic nature of the accounts of leadership and organizational change informs the discussions in Chapter Five and the explanations in Chapter Six.

EXPLAINING ORGANIZATIONAL CHANGE: THE LAST 35 YEARS

The caveat to the short historiography of organizational change featured in the previous section is that all understanding of management and organization theory is historiographically shaped (Cooke, 1999). Critical histories of organizational change are as susceptible to historiographical processes as managerialist histories of organizational change.

> In the field of organizational change, theories are necessarily infused with ideology. Our theories are value driven, often self-serving, grounded in social movements and driven by social forces.
>
> (Dunphy, 1996:542)

Studying organizational change really does depend upon who you ask. Organizational change scholars have their own preferred explanations, and may be conscious or unconscious of their preferences (positive and negative). In the next section, Smith and Graetz's (2011) *Philosophies of Organizational Change* offers a framework for highlighting such preferences and preferred explanations. Explanations of leadership and organizational change are shaped and framed by paradigms, perspectives and philosophies. However, whilst such mental models point authors in certain directions, they may not be aware of their influence (Palmer et al, 2009). The quest is further complicated by organizational change theories and practices drawing upon different social science disciplines and traditions (Van de Ven and Poole, 1995; Burnes, 2014). In this section, the pluralist understanding of organizational change as encouraged by Eisenhardt (2000) is favoured. The 35-year window has been used to focus on leadership and organizational change and through this window, developments informing the study of organizational change are equally apparent. Chronological study milestones offer a means to document developments in studying organizational change and a resource to critically evaluate leadership and organizational change (Chapter Five). Whilst concerns about linear accounts of history and chronarchy are acknowledged (Burrell, 1992; Cummings, 2002), the implication here is not that each development is an improvement upon the previous one, although greater theoretical sophistication becomes evident over time, but that these milestones offer different lenses for viewing explanations of leadership and organizational change.

In the previous section, the landscape of organization studies was surveyed, and stretching the geographical metaphor, this section explores the geology beneath the landscape, beginning to make explicit assumptions underpinning the studies of organizational change. Underpinning assumptions feature in the critiques of the shortcomings of what is known about leadership and organizational change, and they potentially offer ways forward (see Chapters Five and Six for further discussion of the assumptions underpinning the sub-field). Pettigrew et al (2001), in their overview of the challenges of studying organizational change, cited Kahn's (1974) provocative characterisation of organizational change literature, which was cited in Chapter One. In a manner similar to Kahn (1974), organizational change scholars take critical stock of the state of knowledge in order to establish overarching explanations of organizational change. These overviews appear motivated by a mixture of frustration with the state of knowledge and attempts to legitimise ongoing work and proactively map ways forward for the field. In the following section, seven reviews are featured that reflect the explanations offered over the last thirty-five years. They specifically underpin organizational change as well as inform the explanations of leadership and organizational change (see Figure 3.1).

Author/s	Year	Characteristics
Burrell and Morgan	1979	Radical humanist, Radical structuralist, Interpretive, Functionalist
Dunphy and Stace	1988	Participative evolution, Charismatic transformation, Forced evolution, Dictatorial transformation
Van de Ven and Poole	1995	Evolution, Dialectic, Life cycle, Teleology
Pettigrew, Woodman and Cameron	2001	Multiple contexts/levels of analysis, Time, history, process and action, Change processes and organizational performance outcomes, International comparisons on organizational change, Receptivity and customization, Engagement between scholars and practitioners
Van de Ven and Poole	2005	Variance studies (organizational entities) Variance studies (dynamic modelling) Process studies (organizational entities) Process studies (narrating emergent actions)
Smith and Graetz	2011	Philosophies: Rational, biological, institutional, resource, psychological, systems, cultural, critical and dualities
Langley, Smallman, Tsoukas and Van de Ven	2013	Process questions: the centrality of time Process ontology: change and becoming Process data: longitudinal, rich and varied Process comparisons: cross-case replication Process decomposition: longitudinal replication Process representations: rethinking boxes and arrows Process generalisation: abstracting from the particular The prevalence of paradox and dialectics Emergence and evolution through multilevel interaction The processual dynamics of stability

Figure 3.1   35 years of explaining organizational change

These frameworks (see Figure 3.1) are neither the most fashionable nor the most recent. They have been chosen because they correspond with shifts in thinking over the 35-year chronology of this critical review and because they highlight the pluralist diversity of the philosophical and methodological explanations. When Eisenhardt (2000) encouraged pluralism in ideas with regards to change as a driver of change, pluralism was very much in vogue. Pluralism with regards to understanding organizational change connects theories, models and concepts in ways that a single favoured perspective cannot.

> . . .[C]oordinating the pluralistic insights from the four approaches provides a richer understanding of organizational change than any one approach provides by itself.
>
> (Van de Ven and Poole, 2005:1377)

> . . . I see the field as evolving through a process of sedimentation where earlier theories continue to coexist with more recent approaches. Basic epistemological, theoretical, and methodological differences remain that maintain the conceptual diversity of the field.
>
> (Demers, 2007:xiv)

Whereas for some, the consistency of a single perspective is favoured over conceptual diversity, in the context of furthering understanding about leadership and organizational change, conceptual diversity is likely to be more informative than a single perspective. Research identities appear to be far more explicit these days: Post-structuralists, post-modernists and Critical Theorists deeply immerse themselves within particular philosophies and social theories that enable them to write and talk with a greater unity of purpose and with fewer contradictions. In reviewing the field of organizational change over thirty-five years, over the last decade there were signs that the leading scholars were aligning themselves with process/practice theory (see below for further discussion). Equally, in the previous section, there were signs of a historical turn with regards to understanding organizational change (Cooke, 1999). The following discussion features the frameworks (Figure 3.1) for studying organizational change in chronological order.

Social Paradigms and Organizational Analysis (Burrell and Morgan, 1979) was published at a similar time to when Burns (1978) took critical stock of the state of leadership studies. It is the only featured publication that is not organizational-change specific, although Wilson (1992), Collins (1998) and Randall (2004) have all effectively applied Burrell and Morgan's framework to explain strategic change, organizational change and managing change, respectively (see Hughes, 2010 for further discussion). Burrell and Morgan (1979) distinguished between the sociology of regulation and radical change. They differentiated theorists primarily concerned with explanations of society that emphasised underlying unity and cohesiveness (the sociology of regulation) from those interested in the deep-seated structural conflict, modes of domination and structural contradiction that characterise modern society (the sociology of radical change). Burrell and Morgan's second axis differentiated theorists in terms of their research interest into either individual's subjective experiences or the hard, objective realities of scientific research. Four paradigms of functionalism, interpretivism, radical humanism and radical structuralism, each underpinned by philosophical assumptions, were highlighted. However, to this day, functionalism remains the most prevalent explanation of organizational change and, by association, is likely to feature prominently in orthodox explanations of leadership and organizational change. Burrell and Morgan (1979) received many bouquets and brickbats since its publication over thirty years ago (see Grant and Perren, 2002 for an overview).

Moving into the eighties, Dunphy and Stace's (1988) differentiation between participative evolution, charismatic transformation, forced evolution and dictatorial transformation, which was cited previously, inevitably appears dated. However, it has considerable relevance to the ongoing leadership debates about followership, distributed leadership and transformational leadership. In essence, Dunphy and Stace contrasted incremental and transformational accounts of organizational change. They suggested that transformative change had been more appropriate than incrementalism, but since the mid- to late 1970s, environments characterised by stability and growth had given way to more competitive and turbulent environments. This perceived shift in environments with implications for leadership was very evident within Kotter's (1996) *Leading Change* and Bass and Riggio's (2006) *Transformational Leadership* (although earlier caveats about the social construction of turbulent environments remain relevant).

In the nineties, Van de Ven and Poole (1995) offered a highly respected typology that enabled theories explaining organizational change processes to be classified and differentiated. It is included here because it surfaces underlying assumptions in terms of how change is explained as a life cycle, as teleology, a dialectic or as evolution. Their work benefitted from extensive interdisciplinary literature reviewing of theories explaining processes of change in the social, biological and physical sciences. Four ideal-type theories were used as a means of distinguishing the characteristics of these theories:

> These four types represent fundamentally different event sequences and generative mechanisms—we will call them motors—to explain how and why changes unfold.
>
> (Van de Ven and Poole, 1995:511)

Van de Ven and Poole's (1995) analysis offered change scholars an influential typology of different explanations for why organizations change, with the featured theories not being hierarchically superior, but providing alternative images of similar organizational processes. Life-cycle theories viewed change as imminent with an underlying form, logic, program or code regulating the process of change, moving the entity toward a subsequent end that is prefigured in the present state. Teleological explanations of organizational change are particularly evident in goal setting, planning, functionalist, social constructionist and symbolic interactionist theories, reflecting the doctrine that a purpose or goal guides the movement of an entity. According to dialectical theory, change occurs when opposing values, forces or events gain enough power to challenge the status quo (Van de Ven and Poole, 1995), whereas evolutionary explanations of change emphasise the recurrent and cumulative progression of the variation and selection of organizational entities, suggesting that those organizations best able to adapt are the most likely to survive.

Pettigrew et al (2001) highlighted six interconnected analytical issues relating to where organizational change literature remained underdeveloped (see Figure 3.1). They offered a framework to critique the literature in terms of weaknesses as acknowledged by leading scholars. After identifying underdeveloped organizational change areas, Pettigrew et al (2001) proactively demonstrated within their special issue how the ten papers they accepted addressed these areas. Their cautionary conclusions are mirrored within this chapter.

> . . .[T]here is the need to straddle the social and organizational sciences; to conceive of researchers and users as coproducers; to transcend current beliefs of scholars and users while also engaging with those beliefs, and to supplement disciplinary knowledge on change rather than attempt to supplant that knowledge. As ever in science as a human activity, the most fundamental challenges are to our own scholarly routines.
>
> (Pettigrew et al, 2001:710)

This quotation offers many perceptive insights into explaining organizational change in general and leadership and organizational change in particular. Firstly, leadership and organizational change explanations will need to straddle social and organizational sciences and build upon earlier disciplinary work, suggesting that dissensus and divergence is likely to characterise explanations, rather than artificial consensus. Secondly, there is an implication that academics will have their favoured explanations for leadership and organizational change and that these explanations may not be amenable to change with a goal to challenge academic routines.

As a follow up to their 1995 paper, Van de Ven and Poole (2005) differentiated accounts of organizational change in terms of whether scholars regarded organizations as consisting of things (variances) or processes and again, their typology informs different critiques of organizational change.

The common thread running through these works is the difference between scientific explanations, cast in terms of independent variables causing changes in a dependent variable, and explanations that tell a narrative or story about how a sequence of events unfolds to produce a given outcome.

(Van de Ven and Poole, 2005:1381)

This quotation suggests that explanations of leadership and organizational change may be explained in terms of variances, potentially drawing upon quantitative data and testing hypotheses, or explained in terms of processes, potentially drawing upon qualitative, longitudinal data. Van de Ven and Poole (2005) emphasise time as the 'ether' of change, noting that we tend to judge occurrences of change against a background of time. However, they warned that because time has been taken for granted, it has largely been neglected within organizational scholarship. Smith and Graetz's (2011) *Philosophies of Organizational Change* was a development of the ideas in their paper (Graetz and Smith, 2010). The philosophies of organizational change they focused on were rational, biological, institutional, resource, psychological, systems, cultural, critical and dualities, favouring a dualities philosophy (their typology is the main focus of the next section).

Langley et al's (2013) contribution builds upon some of the earlier studies cited here and is included because it highlights the influence of process studies on understanding organizational change. The editors received more than 100 potential contributions to their special issue of the *Academy of Management Journal*, which was themed around process studies of change in organization and management. Their paper took the form of an editorial that identified themes from the 13 contributions selected, organized around the major headings of the nature of process research, process research methods and substantive advances to process theories.

In terms of the nature of process research, Langley et al (2013) emphasised the centrality of time and differentiated process research from variance questions that emphasised co-variation between dependent and independent variables (compatible with Van de Ven and Poole, 2005). They acknowledged that different ontologies were evident within the process and temporality studies featured in their special issue. All submissions in terms of process research methods featured longitudinal data, although some relied upon quantitative analysis and some upon qualitative analysis. In some papers, submissions process comparisons were made through cross-case comparisons. Langley et al (2013) emphasised that the sample size for a process study was not the number of cases, but instead the number of temporal observations. In the featured process studies, there was a tendency to draw upon visual maps and diagrams in representing processes and their iterative dynamics. The editors found inferences from the particular to the general in research designs. The special issue also highlighted substantive advances to process theories. The editors (2013:9) found more sophisticated process conceptualisations than within the earlier work that had been reviewed; in particular, they found that '. . . the central role of tension, contradiction, paradox, and dialectics in driving patterns of change emerges strongly throughout these studies.' Contributions revealed emergence and evolution taking place through multi-level interaction. Finally, the editors highlighted the dynamics of processual stability, in particular, the overwhelming emphasis that management research places on the importance of outcomes. They argued that from a process perspective, the outcomes measured at particular points of time were way stations within an ongoing flow of activities. Process studies of change have a long history, but what this paper highlights is process studies gaining wider acceptance amongst the academic community within a leading journal.

> Process questions take a researcher into a conceptual terrain of events, episodes, activity, temporal ordering, fluidity, and change. We see that process conceptualizations offer ways to understand emergence and change as well as stability, and they incorporate understandings of causality as constituted through chains of events rather than abstract correlations.
>
> (Langley et al, 2013:10)

This section has demonstrated different explanations of organizational change being offered over the last 35 years, with more recent studies either contradicting or complimenting earlier studies. If you delve back into process studies, you find Whitehead's (1929) influential writings on process metaphysics. In this way, the last bookend of this review (Langley et al, 2013) does not suggest an end to the quest, but rather the existence of multiple, pluralistic insights into understanding organizational change, some with roots going way back, others more recent. In the next section, the focus shifts to *Philosophies of Organizational Change* (Smith and Graetz, 2011) and how dualities-aware philosophies enable pluralistic organizational change insights to be drawn upon and integrated in order to understand organizational change.

PHILOSOPHIES AND DUALITIES OF ORGANIZATIONAL CHANGE

> The world appears differently to everyone: there is no universal way to see organizations.
>
> (Smith and Graetz, 2011:15)

Philosophies of Organizational Change (Smith and Graetz, 2011) refines and elaborates upon earlier typologies (Graetz and Smith, 2008, 2010) and also is the precursor to Sutherland and Smith's (2013) account of a dualities-aware approach towards leadership and organizational change. They effectively capture the essence of their book in the following quotation: '[P]hilosophies describe a way of looking at organizational change: a paradigm incorporating structured assumptions and premises and beliefs presupposing the way change works in organizations' (Smith and Graetz, 2011:5). *Philosophies of Organizational Change* is believed to be particularly pertinent to leadership and organizational change for the following reasons. The authors focus on the assumptions, premises and beliefs that presuppose how change works in organizations and how it speaks to both academic and practitioner explanations of leadership and organizational change. In particular, their typology explains what underpins the popular/prevalent explanations of leadership and organizational change. Their typology is pluralistic, featuring rational, biological, institutional, resource, psychological, systems, cultural, critical and dualities philosophies. It is able to engage with the competing explanations likely to be offered for leadership and organizational change. The authors' preferred dualities-aware philosophical position again is very appropriate to leadership and organizational change's major dualities: Leadership/management and change/continuity.

They warn that '. . . all prominent change philosophies, despite strengths and weaknesses, hold unassailable assumptions and enforce rigid limitations' (Smith and Graetz, 2011:15). Whilst they were not writing specifically about leadership and organizational change, the implication is that there will never be a satisfactory explanation using a single philosophy. Each philosophy of organizational change potentially informs the explanations of leadership and organizational change highlighted in Chapter Two. However, rational, psychological, critical and dualities philosophies appear particularly relevant and as meriting further discussion. Before that, the other five are briefly introduced by way of introducing the typology as a whole, as the final dualities philosophy requires an understanding of all of the philosophies.

Biological philosophies depict the nature of organizational change in ecological, organic and evolutionary terms, with leaders focusing on environmental positioning, envisaging their organizations as progressing through life cycles. The strength of this philosophy is the utility of life-cycle explanations that emphasise fitness and survival, whereas the weakness is an over-emphasis on environmental factors. In a similar manner, institutional philosophies depict the nature of organizational change as determined by institutional (industry) pressure, resulting in leaders placing emphasis upon industrial standards and benchmarks. Their strength is that they reveal the importance of environmental and institutional pressures to conform, whereas their weakness is not encouraging a search for advantages against competitors/other providers.

Resource-based philosophies depict the nature of organizational change as determined by access to resources; consequently, leaders focus on acquiring and discharging resources and core competencies. The strength of this philosophy is an emphasis on acquiring resources in order to initiate and sustain change, and its weakness is an assumption that change cannot occur without internal resources. System-based philosophies emphasise the interconnections of all aspects of organizations, resulting in leaders who initiate change by considering all of the constituents and components of an organization. The strength of this philosophy is its avoidance of an assumption that change is contained within one organizational area, and its weakness is the practicalities of keeping track of many different relationships between organizational variables. Culture-based philosophies depict the nature of organizational change as determined by entrenched values, encouraging leaders to attend to 'deep' rites, rituals and values. The strength of this philosophy is that it shows the importance of collective beliefs and norms, and its weakness is the difficulty of directly addressing intangible organizational cultures.

The rational, psychological, critical and dualities philosophies are now discussed in greater detail, as the rational and psychological philosophies potentially inform practitioner-orientated explanations, and the critical and dualities philosophies potentially offer academic explanations of leadership and organizational change. The rational philosophy depicts the nature of organizational change as planned and directed, in which leaders focus on strategy and planning. Smith and Graetz (2011) described the rational philosophy as the most common philosophy governing organizational change. It is informative, to revisit Burrell and Morgan's (1979:48) depiction of a functionalist paradigm cited earlier, which corresponds to Smith and Graetz rational philosophy of organizational change.

> The functionalist paradigm has provided the dominant framework for academic sociology in the twentieth century and accounts for by far the largest proportion of theory and research in the field of organization studies.

Smith and Graetz (2011) acknowledge that the rational philosophy also equates to Van de Ven and Poole's (1995) teleological theories, in that the final destination represents the guiding logic, the planned change. Any attempt to understand leadership and organizational change is informed by this enduring orthodoxy of functionalist/rationalist/teleological explanations of organizational change. This mindset is particularly pertinent to leadership and organizational change, which Smith and Graetz (2011:43) capture in discussing change management gurus:

> ... that successful change lies firmly in the hands of leaders, all of whom can benefit by introducing the steps advocated. Conversely, unsuccessful change must be due to managerial or leadership inadequacy.

Subsequently writing about the rational philosophy, they suggest that there is a belief that 'change can be controlled because everything in an organization should be subservient to the will, vision and action of leaders' (Smith and Graetz, 2011:45). This insight is informative and reoccurs in the next leadership studies chapter. In essence, the leadership of organizational change may be critically understood as the submission to and the imposition of the leader's will.

Smith and Graetz (2011) in their discussion of the rational philosophy identify three disadvantages associated with organizational leaders leading a change process. Firstly, in the event of a structural obstacle or argument between senior staff, there is no one to make objective appeals to. Secondly, if the chief executive officer (CEO) becomes involved in day-to-day change processes, then his or her normal operational work will likely suffer. Thirdly, a CEO in the driver's seat of change conveys the impression, true or false, that the change is the autocratic will of the leader, with the dangerous implication that the organization is an autocratic dictatorship. A more general weakness of the rational philosophy relates directly to assumptions about the nature of organizational change as certain and controllable: '. . .[N]o matter how logical, future action can rarely be clearly defined and calculated in advance' (Smith and Graetz, 2011:45). Conversely, the perceived strengths of the rational philosophy explain its enduring practitioner appeal, presuming that the sequential and planned pursuit of optimal solutions results in successful change, 'rational models follow a set pattern that resonates intuitively, but they also enjoy an unparalleled, and sometimes blindly optimistic popularity' (Smith and Graetz, 2011:45).

The psychological philosophy depicts the nature of organizational change as embedded within the minds of those affected. It is discussed here with regards to organizational change, but also has been very influential in terms of leadership studies, particularly with regards to transformational leadership (Fairhurst, 2008). The psychological philosophy encourages leaders to manage employee transitions and psychological adjustments to change based on the belief that 'the impact of change is complex, powerful and potentially severe' (Smith and Graetz, 2011:105). The practical implications of the psychological philosophy are a need to share knowledge and decision-making, and to acknowledge all contributions within the processes of organizational change. The psychological philosophy depicts resistance to change as a psychological response to organizational change that is likely to diminish as employees take ownership of change through bottom-up approaches to change. Smith and Graetz (2011:113) identify OD as a particular psychological philosophy addressing human responses to organizational change: '. . . OD commits to the premise that change must emanate from a critical mass of engaged employees. Better performance comes with interested, valued and empowered employees.' The strengths of the psychological philosophy are its emphasis upon individuals within processes of organizational change, acknowledging that individuals are central to change and that individuals may have had positive and/or negative experiences of organizational change and that these human transitions require managing. The weakness of the psychological philosophy is that by focusing on individuals, the more systemic aspects of organizational change, such as structure, are ignored. The rational and psychological philosophies are particularly useful when explaining practitioner understandings of how organizational change works. They have equally appealed to many academics.

Critical and dualities philosophies have not been so prevalent, but in offering alternative explanations, they challenge the orthodoxy and potentially advance understanding. Critical approaches are not a new phenomenon, with Burrell and Morgan (1979) highlighting 'radical humanism' and 'radical structuralism' as part of their sociology of radical change, acting as a critical counterpoint to the sociology of regulation (functionalism and interpretivism). Equally, Van de Ven and Poole (1995) highlighted that according to the dialectical theory, change occurs when opposing values, forces or events gain enough power to challenge the status quo. More recently, process theory (Langley et al, 2013) critically challenged the dominant assumptions underpinning how organizational change is understood.

Critical philosophy in its depictions of the nature of organizational change places a different emphasis to the other philosophies upon conflict, power and the rejection of universal rules. Critical philosophies are not motivated by a desire to inform management and leadership practices; instead, their logic emphasises attention to power and genuine empowerment and emancipatory practices. Smith and Graetz (2011) subtitled their critical philosophy chapter, 'Changing Reality,' and depicted critical philosophy mainly as postmodernism.

> The postmodern approach to change is less concerned with overarching, grand theories describing social behaviour and more interested in the indeterminacy, ambiguity and contradiction of organizational life . . . However, for most postmodern thinkers, organizational change will never work if it conforms to the uptight demands of rationalist leaders seeking to impose corporate objectives and performance measures.
>
> (Smith and Graetz, 2011:166)

Smith and Graetz (2011) acknowledge Marx and Hegel, but radical structuralist explanations of organizational change do not feature prominently. In terms of power, they favour Foucault's (1980, 1982) view of power, with its novel way of looking at how and why change occurs. In essence, organizational change occurs through discourses within organizations: '[I]n fact, most discourse theorists suggest that reality itself is a social construction laid down by the discourses in operation' (Smith and Graetz, 2011:169). Social construction and discourses are discussed in more detail in the next chapter, given their applicability to leadership studies. The strengths of critical philosophy are the highlighting of the centrality of power, ideology clashes and contradictions that are inherent within organizational change. The potential weakness of critical philosophy is that all organizational change is being explained by power at the expense of other explanations.

The dualities philosophy subtitled 'changing tensions' depicts the nature of organizational change as complex and dynamic, emphasising that managers and leaders face a challenge of managing tensions, such as continuity and change. In the first few pages of their concluding chapter, Smith and Graetz explain the dualities philosophy of organizational change by revisiting all of the preceding philosophies, and acknowledge that each contributes in different ways to understanding organizational change. They conclude that no single philosophy can encapsulate organizational change; consequently, a more dynamic and inclusive philosophy is warranted. They acknowledge the dilemma that '. . . change leaders struggle to instigate change from the top while the operational bottom demands continuity' (Smith and Graetz, 2011:183), concluding that change management cannot just be about change: Paradoxically, it does also need to incorporate continuity.

In Figure 3.2, the managing and leading and continuity and change dualisms that surface throughout this critical review are emphasised through a 2 x 2 matrix. Thinking in terms of 'either/or' dualisms is not favoured and potentially does more harm than good, although they have proved influential in terms of leadership and organizational change and need to be addressed within any informed understanding of leadership and organizational change. The current orthodoxy may be paraphrased as managing change superseded by leading change, with an implication that leading is superior to managing and that change is superior to stability/continuity (the cultural aspects informing this shift are discussed in Chapter Four). Subsequently, managing is now associated with organizational stability/ continuity and differentiated from leading, which is now associated with organizational change (this problematic orthodoxy is elaborated upon and challenged in subsequent chapters).

It is informative to understand how dualisms work before returning to the dualities-aware approach favoured by Smith and Graetz (2011). Knights (1997) acknowledged that organization studies suffered from a polarisation of theoretical positions, although Knights did not favour dualisms, rejecting them for three reasons. Firstly, dualistic thinking privileges knowledge most compatible with the natural sciences over the social sciences, which is

Managing	Leading
Organizational Stability/ Continuity	Organizational Change

Figure 3.2 Managing and leading, continuity and change dualisms

compatible with Cole's (1983) concerns about a 'hierarchy of the sciences.' Secondly, dualisms always privilege one side over the other. So in Figure 3.2, leading organizational change is privileged over managing organizational stability. Thirdly, and related to the second criticism, binary oppositions encourage thinking about what is present and what is absent or marginal. The next chapter will look in more detail at depictions of leader-manager differentiations.

Lewis (2000:767) in her exploration of paradox, identified the tensions within organization studies: '[I]f we use a paradox framework, organizing appears to inherently juxtapose contradictions.' Lewis notes ironically that as organizations become more complex, diverse and dynamic, traditional 'either/or' thinking begins to oversimplify management. In terms of Figure 3.2, organizations respond to perceptions of a more turbulent operating environment through leading change, rather than managing continuity regardless of the institutional importance of managing continuities: Health and safety, personnel policies, auditing etc. The change and continuity dualism is particularly pertinent to this critical review.

> Change and continuity come together when old and new forms of organizing operate in a two-way, bidirectional partnership, mediated through the planning, organizing, co-ordinating and controlling functions. These well-established functions form the metaphorical engine room of the organization.
>
> (Graetz and Smith, 2008:266)

In both Chapters Two and Four, there are discussions about change leadership apparently superseding change management, a belief that can and will be questioned. However, Smith and Graetz's (2011) encouragement to be dualities-aware about change and continuity highlights that they are not in competition, but that they complement each other. Graetz and Smith (2008) acknowledged that there were extensive separate literatures relating to forms of organizing and to dualities, but limited overlapping literature. Their literature review enabled them to identify five duality characteristics: Simultaneity, relational, minimal thresholds, dynamism and improvisation, which they believed operated in collaboration. Sutherland (previously known as Graetz) and Smith (2013) revisited earlier writings (Graetz and Smith, 2008; Smith and Graetz, 2011) with particular reference to leadership and organizational change, which is very pertinent to this critical review.

> We argue that change and continuity do not exist as opposite sides of the leadership see-saw, but co-exist as dualities that sit side by side without compromising one another.
>
> (Sutherland and Smith, 2013:216)

They describe leadership decision-making as traditionally character-ised by 'either/or' choices or an uneasy compromise between the assumed opposites of change and continuity. Instead, they favour a dualities-aware approach towards leadership.

> Effective change leadership means appreciating how dualistic forces can shape and enable change. By adopting a dualities aware perspective, leaders can come to terms with the intuitive desire to resolve contradic-tion by instead managing the complementarities within contradictory forces.
>
> (Sutherland and Smith, 2013:220)

They argue that the leadership and organizational change duality involves *simultaneous*, but potentially competing and contradictory, change interven-tions, which are *relational* in that they are symbiotic and require *minimal thresholds* in order to function. The leadership duality is characterised by the *dynamism* of continuity and change with each of the four duality char-acteristics evolving through the fifth duality characteristic—the *improvisa-tion* of the leader. These five leadership duality characteristics (signposted through italics) require further elaboration, as they are very different from orthodox leadership typologies.

Sutherland and Smith (2013) depict *simultaneity* as the foundational duality characteristic from which other duality characteristics escalate. Leadership *simultaneity* encourages 'both/and' kind of thinking, highlight-ing novel perspectives and new opportunities, rather than the traditional 'either/or' leadership thinking. As well as duality-aware leaders address-ing *simultaneity*, dualities are *relational* in their interdependence, empha-sising the interdependence and complementary forces that exist between apparently opposing dualities. They offer examples of manifestations of these dualities, such as attempting to increase efficiency at the same time as creativity, and providing strong leadership at the same time as support-ing empowerment. There still remains a characteristic of *minimal threshold* with regards to dualities, and the challenge for a leader is to determine this *minimal threshold* between extremes on an organizing continuum. As this characteristic is less obvious than others, an illustration may help.

> . . .[M]inimal contentment and minimal affluence encourage commit-ment, yet also mediate against complacency and inertia. A degree of ambiguity, contradiction and incoherence provides the catalyst for organizational learning, diversity and renewal.
>
> (Smith and Graetz, 2011:191)

It's odd to find ambiguity, contradiction and incoherence presented posi-tively; yet for a dualities-aware leader, they may have beneficial purposes within organizations. The caveat remains that dualities are interdependent, so *minimal thresholds* depend upon tensions between the *simultaneity* and *relational* duality characteristics.

> Dynamism, in conjunction with the simultaneity and relational characteristics, fuels exploitation and exploration, thereby guarding against inertia and complacency, the show stopping accoutrements of success.
> (Sutherland and Smith, 2013:228)

Sutherland and Smith introduce *dynamism* as their fourth leadership duality characteristic, offering an example of dynamic interaction between duality poles such as integration and differentiation. Their final duality characteristic is *improvisation*: '[I]mprovisation can therefore be seen as the ongoing, iterative action which works in sync with the characteristics of simultaneity, relational, minimal thresholds and dynamism to manage continuity and change' (Sutherland and Smith, 2013:229). In making their case for the role of dualities in organizing, Graetz and Smith (2008) pose the following questions:

- What sorts of tensions exist in organizations?
- Why might existing tensions reinforce cycles leading to polarization and inertia?
- How might actors manage dualities as a catalyst for change and understanding?

These questions inform alternative explanations of organizing and begin to question the traditional notions of resistance to change, offering practitioners as well as academics a very different framework to meaningfully engage with and engage others in organizational change processes.

RETHINKING LEADERSHIP AND ORGANIZATIONAL CHANGE

The preliminary conclusions of Chapter Two and the findings of Parry (2011) Ford and Ford (2012) with regards to the state of understanding about leadership and organizational change give impetus and urgency to the academic rethinking of leadership and organizational change. Kotter's (1996) practitioner-orientated *Leading Change*, by far the most-cited publication within this sub-field (see Figure 2.2), provides a catalyst for such rethinking. Rethinking does need to encourage the theoretical and empirical work that subsequently informs practice, rather than the current preference for practitioner-orientated accounts to be used as surrogates for evidence. In this spirit, this section builds upon earlier discussions in this chapter through acknowledging and celebrating the organizational change research, theory and research-informed practice advances of recent years (see Figure 3.3).

Why transformation explanations fail	Rethinking leadership and organizational change
Employees depicted as change resistors	Resistance
Ethics, power and politics underplayed	Ethics, power and politics
Overemphasis upon a sequence of linear steps	Process thinking
Disparaging history limits learning and an appreciation of incremental change	Learning
Leader and leader communications overemphasised	Agency and discourse
Under emphasis of unique cultural contexts	Context
Rhetorical treatment of organizational success/ failure	Evaluation

Figure 3.3 Failings of transformation explanations: rethinking leadership and organizational change

In Figure 3.3, the first column responds to Kotter's (1995, 1996) transformation explanations cited in the previous chapter (see Figure 2.3) through identifying weaknesses. The second column more proactively highlights the academic advances since 1996. The focus is on Kotter as the most-cited author within the sub-field of leadership and organizational change, but more generally illustrates the anecdotal, case-study-based, practitioner-orientated work lacking rigour in its conduct (Parry, 2011) that currently characterises this sub-field. The perceived failures of Kotter's transformation explanations are elaborated upon within the critical evaluation (Chapter Five). In this chapter, the focus is upon organizational change as featured in the second column, introducing the REPLACE framework.

Empirical/theoretical advances are gathered together using the mnemonic REPLACE: Resistance, Ethics, Power and politics, process thinking, Learning, Agency and discourse, Context and Evaluation. The mnemonic is shorthand for a need to literally replace the specific deficiencies of *Leading Change* (Kotter, 1995, 1996) and, more generally, the deficiencies of anecdotal/practitioner-orientated work (highlighted in Chapter Two). The REPLACE mnemonic privileges theoretical/empirical accounts of leadership and organizational change over practitioner-orientated accounts in the belief that they are the best means to advance understanding about leadership and organizational change. A single explanation is unlikely to suffice, given the complexities and ambiguities of both the fields of leadership studies (see Chapter Four) and organizational change studies as featured in this chapter; REPLACE encourages thinking in terms of seven interconnected advances. This discussion deliberately concentrates on publications since 2000, privileging references within respected, refereed journals and critical monographs (for an extended discussion of REPLACE and a critique of Kotter's *Leading Change*, please see Hughes, forthcoming.

Resistance to change—*Leading Change* (Kotter, 1996) worked with an assumption that resistance to change was the problem and strong leadership was the solution. However, critical scholars have increasingly questioned the utility of overcoming resistance to change and crude categorisations of people being either for or against a leader's particular change (Piderit, 2000). Ford et al (2008) took critical stock of what was now known about resistance to change, updating developments since Ford et al (2002) and warning that the presence of change agents may even be part of the problem, rather than the solution (see also Oreg, 2003 and Hughes, 2010). Rethinking resistance as a subtle and diverse response to ongoing organizational change processes would involve employees within organizational change processes, rather than marginalising them as resistant bystanders.

Ethics, power, politics and organizational change—*Leading Change* (Kotter, 1996) at best minimises ethical concerns, whereas by contrast, critical scholars foreground ethical approaches towards leading change (see for example Wall, 2007). Rhodes et al (2010) warned that strong collective narratives in organizations may limit the scope of ethical deliberation and action, and By and Burnes (2011) reminded us that those promoting particular approaches to leadership and change must explicitly acknowledge the ethics of the approaches championed (see also By and Burnes, 2013). *Leading Change*'s (Kotter, 1996) social construction of leaders as the powerful ones in times of change may explain its enduring popularity, but the book fails to really deal theoretically with power and politics. Use of management power in times of organizational change as logical and inevitable was recognised as far back as the early seventies (see Bradshaw and Boonstra, 2004; Hardy and Clegg, 2004 for discussion). However, as Hardy and Clegg (2004) warn, much of the organizational change literature assists change management failure, due to a lack of pragmatism with regards to power. Similarly, Buchanan and Badham (2008), whilst encouraging greater engagement with power and politics, conceded that academics tend to neglect political behaviour with regards to organizational change (see also Thomas and Hardy, 2011). Rethinking ethics, power and politics introduces important dynamics and choices often absent within the typical explanations of leading change.

Process thinking and organizational change—The similarity between Kotter's (1996) eight steps and Lewin's (1947) unfreeze, change and refreeze is indicative of the sequential temporality common within organizational change explanations (Burnes, 2004; Cummings, 2002; Hendry, 1996). Dawson (2014) acknowledged the prevalence of such temporality, as well as the need to engage with alternative explanations of organizational change, revisiting Tsoukas and Chia's (2002) notion that organizations consist of processes of becoming (see earlier discussion of Van de Ven and Poole, 2005 and Langley et al, 2013). Rethinking in terms of process thinking disrupts the sequentialism and linearity that is currently evident within the leading change explanations.

Learning and organizational change—The danger with Kotter's (1996) leadership preoccupation with looking forwards is its neglect of looking backwards and the temporal dimensions of organizational change (Ybema, 2010), and its neglect of the contribution of learning theory (Starkey et al, 2002). Organizational learning grew up almost 'underground' until the explosion of interest in the late 1980s (Easterby Smith et al, 2000). Ongoing learning is believed to be the best preparation for the future (Lakomski, 2001; Sugarman, 2001). Senge (1990) gave impetus to burgeoning interest in the 'learning organization' (Mintzberg et al, 2009) with a revised and updated edition of *The Fifth Discipline* (Senge, 2006), highlighting its enduring popularity. However, learning discourses depicting learning as always a good thing have been critiqued (Clegg et al, 2005; Contu et al, 2003; Friedman et al, 2005; Jackson, 2001; Ortenblad, 2007). Rethinking organizational learning acknowledges the past as well as the future and the often evolutionary/incremental nature of strategic change, potentially involving employees within processes of organizational change.

Agency, discourse and organizational change—*Leading Change* (Kotter, 1996) depicted leaders/powerful guiding coalitions as the agents of change. However, Caldwell (2003) was sceptical about claims made for change leaders, over-emphasising leaders transforming organizations, the failure to differentiate leaders and managers, underestimating leadership at different organizational levels and conflating leadership with change. Caldwell (2003) developed a fourfold literature-based classification of change agency as located within leadership, management, consultants and teams. In synthesising and re-conceptualising the nature of change agency, Caldwell emphasised that there was neither a universal model of change agency nor a single type of change agent with a fixed set of competencies (see also Caldwell, 2005 and Caldwell, 2007). Ongoing change agency studies have highlighted the problems of dispersed change agency (Doyle, 2001) as well as distributed change agency used successfully (with caveats) to implement a complex organizational change (Buchanan et al, 2007) (see also Battilana and Casciaro, 2012).

Kotter's (1996) depiction of a leader/powerful guiding coalition as the change agent privileges one-way communication at the expense of listening to or engaging with employees. Communication is frequently treated as a tool for promoting change or as an unproblematic component of organizing (McClellan, 2011), with 'organizational silence' (Morrison and Milliken, 2000) erroneously conveying acceptance of a change. Dutton et al (2001) analysed how managers successfully shaped change through issue selling, and Heracleous and Barrett (2001) highlighted the role of discourse in shaping organizational change processes. Similarly, Tsoukas (2005) encouraged engagement with discourse in the context of organizational change through differentiating, behaviourist, cognitivist and discourse-analytical approaches (see Phillips and Oswick, 2011 for a comprehensive overview of organizational discourse developments). Rethinking agency challenges belief in a change leader's exclusive agency, highlighting choices with regards to where change agency is located, dispersal of power and the construction of change discourses.

Contextualising organizational change—In terms of locating strategic change case studies within their own unique contexts, Hope Hailey and Balogun's (2002) context-sensitive account of change within Glaxo Wellcome is an exemplar as well as a critical counterpoint to *Leading Change*'s (Kotter, 1996) acontextual transformation cases. Hope Hailey and Balogun warn against descriptive contingency models offering 'recipes' for making complex business simpler and more manageable, citing Kotter and Schlesinger (1979) as illustrative of such formulaic recipes. Instead, they encourage a rigorous analysis of context, considering the different implementation options, being aware of personal preferences and how this limits the options considered and the development of change judgement.

> Strategic change is ultimately a product of a legitimization process shaped by gross changes in the outer context of the firm and by political and cultural considerations inside the firm, though often expressed in rational/analytical terms.
>
> (Pettigrew, 2012:1308)

Rethinking acontextual accounts of leading change in favour of acknowledging unique contexts and cultures encourages movement away from formulaic recipes and refocuses on the diverse choices reflexive change leaders have to make.

Evaluating organizational change—Leading change is depicted as either failing, with improved leadership the solution (Kotter, 1995), or leading change will be successful if the leaders follow eight successful transformation steps (Kotter,1996). However, very few empirical studies link change capacity and action to organizational performance. The evaluation of the success of change initiatives is practically very difficult, as success may be related to notions of quantity, quality and pace of change, which all give different outcomes (Pettigrew et al, 2001). Vaara's (2002) study of the discursive constructions of post-merger integration highlighted success stories as being overly optimistic and failure narratives as overly pessimistic about management's ability to control change processes. Amis et al (2004) questioned the common assumptions evident within the literature about the pace, sequence and linearity of organizational change, challenging the belief that rapid change throughout organizations was sufficient to bring about radical change. Buchanan et al (2005) highlighted the emerging academic interest in the sustainability of organizational change initiatives, identifying eleven factors affecting sustainability: Substantial, individual, managerial, financial, leadership, organizational, cultural, political, processual, contextual and temporal (see Hughes, 2011, for further discussion about evaluating organizational change). Rethinking academic evaluations of organizational change evaluation offers an antidote to the simplistic generalisations that transformations fail or succeed exclusively as a consequence of leadership.

The REPLACE mnemonic encourages debate around seven related advances grounded in empirical and theoretical work that are believed to be particularly pertinent to informing understanding about leadership and organizational change interrelationships. The academic advances discussed separately here are likely to be closer to Chia's (1999) rhizome analogy of organizational change, rather than the traditional conceptualisations of a tree of knowledge.

ORGANIZATIONAL CHANGE: CRITICAL AND CONTESTED

> Most scholars agree that organizational change is a topic that is central and important to organization studies. However, they disagree on the meaning of organization change and how to study it.
>
> (Van de Ven and Poole, 2005:1377)

The dilemma Van de Ven and Poole (2005) highlight is at the heart of this chapter and this critical review. Academic understanding of organizational change can always be articulated, but a chosen/favoured explanation will never be the only explanation. Any informed understanding of leadership and organizational change requires an understanding of organizational change in general and an acknowledgement of the dissensus characterising particular explanations of organizational change.

Applied and practical engagement with organizational change, change management and managing/leading change necessitates answering 'how' questions, potentially at the expense of the'what' and 'why' questions. In this chapter, with the exception of the last section, which looked at how critical research and scholarship (REPLACE) could potentially inform practice, the focus has been upon the 'why' and 'what' questions of organizational change. The pluralism of competing explanations has been introduced, although with a bias towards more critical/scholarly explanations. Organizational change critiques often appear to be reactions to practitioner influence on the field and an over-emphasis upon prescription at the expense of analysis. The danger, as Chapter Two highlighted, is that practitioner-orientated accounts become the norm.

In an academic context, critical engagement is integral, as the field of organizational change has neither the history nor the legitimacy of an academic discipline such as physics. It is only by critically questioning existing knowledge that understanding advances. One must engage in critical thinking and in questioning the taken-for-granted myths and assumptions that characterise this field. Kuhn (1962) characterised physics as an academic discipline converging around a few major research questions driving physics research and how physics was understood. The expectation was that management sciences would mirror the natural sciences, with the early history of management science reflecting belief in the 'hierarchy of science' (Cole, 1983) aspirations. However, social science, in engaging with societies, institutions, organizations and individuals, engages with ambiguities and uncertainties far removed from the rules and laws of natural science. The so-called 'paradigm wars' featured in this chapter imply that a victor would lead to convergence around a unifying management and organization studies paradigm. This never happened and it never could happen: Dissensus and paradigm incommensurability define organizational studies fields, rather than impeding these fields.

Multiple accounts rather than universal understanding of organizational change have been presented in this chapter, which complicates an understanding of leadership and organizational change. The situation is further complicated by leadership studies (Chapter Four) displaying similar dissensus and paradigm incommensurability. The implication is that the lack of progress made in theorising leadership and organizational change may partially be explained in terms of both organizational change studies and leadership studies being subject to ongoing critical contests, which is reflected in the pluralistic, rather than universalistic, explanations.

Practitioner orthodoxy depicts organizational change as rational and linear, with the application of recipes, steps, tools and techniques apparently making change happen and with such orthodoxy mirrored with regards to the mainstream orthodoxy of leadership studies (see Chapter Four). So when Parry (2011) and Ford and Ford (2012) encountered a lack of theoretical/empirical accounts of leadership and organizational change, this may be a consequence of practitioner convergence around unified, rational, linear and consensus understandings of leadership and organizational change, whereas academic understandings of both leadership and organizational change are favoured here, reflecting a lack of consensus and convergence that may be less persuasive.

The dissensus and divergence favoured here complicates explanations of leadership and organizational change, yet is preferable to the socially constructed artificial consensus of practitioner orthodoxy. The concern when eavesdropping on organizational change debates is that critiques do not limit themselves to 'how,' 'what' or 'why' questions, but instead encompass the whole utility of the field of organizational change. The dissensus of competing paradigms engaging with change may raise a gamut of emotional organizational change responses '. . . ranging from nostalgia to hope, from anxiety to resignation, from anticipation to despondency' (Antonacopoulou and Gabriel 2001:446). It is understandable that organizational change provoked strong emotions; for Grey (2003:11) it had become a troublesome fetish, and he wrote that '. . . the whole business of change management should be given up on' (see also, Sturdy and Grey, 2003). And as well as emotional responses, we sometimes forget our own competing, embedded assumptions about how organizational change should be managed, such as directing, navigating, caretaking, coaching, interpreting and nurturing (Palmer and Dunford, 2008).

Whereas management and organizational studies appear to have moved beyond the 'paradigm wars,' a field such as organizational change still appears at times to be impeded by the critical factionalism that characterised the eighties and nineties. On one level, critique is a logical consequence of paradigm incommensurability and the pluralistic nature of organizational change, the view informing this chapter. On another level, a concern remains that the success of clever, socially constructed critiques of the field of organizational change informed by emotional responses and working with particular embedded assumptions towards organizational change may diminish rather than further understanding. It may well be that academic discipline explanations such as sociology, economics or political science may be the way forward, but this would be at the expense of the field of organizational change as an interdisciplinary 'melting pot.' The other concern is that the void created by giving up on or moving beyond organizational change is inevitably filled by practitioner-orientated accounts. In Chapter Two, 6,000+ academic citations of Kotter's (1996) practitioner-orientated *Leading Change* were highlighted. It is impossible to assert why academics turned away from academic accounts towards such practitioner-orientated books. But what can be asserted is that without a healthy field of organizational change characterised by critical thinking, academics will have to default to the only remaining literature, which is practitioner-orientated, thus fuelling the critiques of the sub-field of leadership and organizational change featured in Chapter Two.

REFERENCES

Amis, J., T. Slack and C.R. Hinings. 2004. "The Pace, Sequence, and Linearity of Radical Change". *Academy of Management Journal* 47 (1):15–39.

Antonacopoulou, E.P., and Y. Gabriel. 2001. "Emotion, Learning and Organizational Change: Towards an Integration of Psychoanalytic and other Perspectives". *Journal of Organizational Change Management* 14 (5): 435–451.

Bass, B.M., and R.E. Riggio. 2006. *Transformational Leadership*. Mahwah, NJ: Lawrence Erlbaum Associates Inc/Psychology Press.

Battilana, J., and T. Casciaro. 2012. "Change Agents, Networks, and Institutions: A Contingency Theory of Organizational Change". *Academy of Management Journal* 55(2): 381–398.

Becher, B., and P.R. Trowler. 2001. *Academic Tribes and Territories: Intellectual Enquiry and the Cultures of Disciplines*. Buckingham: Open University Press/SRHE.

Bradshaw, P., and J. Boonstra. 2004. "Power Dynamics in Organizational Change: A Multi-Perspective Approach". In *Dynamics of Organizational Change and Learning*, ed. J.J. Boonstra, 279–299. Chichester: John Wiley & Sons.

Buchanan, D.A., and R. Badham. 2008. *Power, Politics and Organizational Change: Winning the Turf Game*, 2nd ed. London: Sage Publications Ltd.

Buchanan, D.A., R. Addicot, L. Fitzgerald, E. Ferlie and J.I. Baeza. 2007. "Nobody in Charge: Distributed Change Agency in Healthcare". *Human Relations* 60 (7): 1065–1090.

Buchanan, D.A., L. Fitzgerald, D. Ketley, R. Gollop, J.L. Jones, S.S. Lamont, A. Neath and E. Whitby. 2005. "No Going Back: A Review of the Literature on

Sustaining Organizational Change". *International Journal of Management Reviews* 7 (3): 189–205.

Burke, W.W. 2014. *Organization Change: Theory and Practice*, 4th ed. Thousand Oaks: Sage Publications Ltd.

Burnes, B. 2004. "Kurt Lewin and the Planned Approach to Change: A Re-appraisal". *Journal of Management Studies* 41 (6): 977–1002.

Burnes, B. 2014. *Managing Change*, 6th ed. Harlow: FT Prentice Hall.

Burnes, B., and B. Cooke. 2013. "Kurt Lewin's Field Theory: A Review and Re-evaluation". *International Journal of Management Reviews* 15 (4): 408–425.

Burns, J.M. 1978. *Leadership*. New York: Harper Row Publishers.

Burrell, G. 1992. "Back to the Future: Time and Organization". In *Rethinking Organization: New Directions in Organization Theory and Analysis*, eds. M. Reed and M. Hughes, 165–83. London: Sage Publications Ltd.

Burrell, G., and G. Morgan. 1979. *Sociological Paradigms and Organizational Analysis*. London: Heinemann.

By, R.T., and Burnes, B. 2011. "Leadership and Change: Whatever Happened to Ethics?" In *The Routledge Companion to Organizational Change*, eds. D.M. Boje, B. Burnes and J. Hassard, 295–309. London: Routledge.

By, R.T., and Burnes, B. eds. 2013. *Organizational Change, Leadership and Ethics: Leading Organizations Towards Sustainability*. London: Routledge.

Caldwell, R. 2003. "Models of Change Agency: A Fourfold Classification". *British Journal of Management* 14 (2) 131–142.

Caldwell, R. 2005. "Things Fall Apart? Discourses on Agency and Change in Organizations". *Human Relations* 58 (1): 83–114.

Caldwell, R. 2007. "Agency and Change: Re-evaluating Foucault's Legacy". *Organization* 14 (6): 769–791.

Chia, R. 1999. "A 'Rhizomic' Model of Organizational Change and Transformation: Perspectives from the Metaphysics of Change". *British Journal of Management* 10 (3) 209–227.

Clegg, S.R., M. Kornberger and C. Rhodes. 2005. "Learning/Becoming/Organizing". *Organization* 12 (2): 147–167.

Cole, S. 1983. "The Hierarchy of the Sciences?" *American Journal of Sociology* 89 (1): 111–139.

Collins, D. 1998. *Organizational Change: Sociological Perspectives*. London: Routledge.

Cooke, B. 1999. "Writing the Left Out of Management Theory: The Historiography of the Management of Change". *Organization* 6 (1): 81–105.

Contu, A., C. Grey and A. Ortenblad. 2003. "Against Learning". *Human Relations* 56 (8):931–952.

Cummings, S. 2002. *Recreating Strategy*. London: Sage Publications Ltd.

Dawson, P. 2014. "Reflections: On Time, Temporality and Change in Organizations". *Journal of Change Management* 14 (3): 285–308.

Deetz, S. 1996. "Crossroads—Describing Differences in Approaches to Organization Science: Rethinking Burrell and Morgan and their Legacy". *Organization Science* 7 (2): 191–207.

Demers, C. 2007. *Organizational Change Theories: A Synthesis*. Los Angeles: Sage Publications.

Doyle, M. 2001. "Dispersing Change Agency in High Velocity Change Organisations: Issues and Implications". *Leadership and Organization Development Journal* 22 (7): 321–329.

Dunphy, D. 1996. "Organizational Change in Corporate Settings". *Human Relations* 49 (5): 541–552.

Dunphy, D., and D. Stace. 1988. "Transformational and Coercive Strategies for Planned Organizational Change: Beyond the O.D. Model". *Organization Studies* 9 (3): 317–334.

Dutton, J.E., S.J. Ashford, R.M. O'Neil and K.A. Lawrence. 2001. "Moves that Matter: Issue Selling and Organizational Change". *Academy of Management Journal* 44 (4):716–736.

Easterby Smith, M., M. Crossan and D. Nicolini. 2000. "Organizational Learning: Debates Past, Present and Future". *Journal of Management Studies* 37 (6): 783–796.

Eccles, R.G., and N. Nohria. 1992. *Beyond the Hype: Rediscovering the Essence of Management*. Boston: Harvard Business School Press.

Eisenhardt, K.M. 2000. "Paradox, Spirals and Ambivalence: The New Language of Change and Pluralism". *Academy of Management Review* 25 (4): 703–705.

Fagerberg, J., and B. Verspagen. 2009. "Innovation Studies-The Emerging Structure of a New Scientific Field". *Research Policy* 38: 218–233.

Fairhurst, G.T. 2008. "Discursive Leadership: A Communication Alternative to Leadership Psychology". *Management Communication Quarterly* 21(4): 510–521.

Frahm, J. 2007. "Organizational Change: Approaching the Frontier, Some Faster than Others (combined review of five books)". *Organization* 14 (6): 945–955.

Friedman, V., R. Lipshitz and M. Popper. 2005. "The Mystification of Organizational Learning". *Journal of Management Inquiry* 14 (1): 19–30.

Foucault, M. 1982. "The Subject and Power". In *Michel Foucault, Beyond Structuralism and Hermeneutics*, eds. H.L. Dreyfus, P. Rabinow and M. Foucault, 208–226. Chicago: University of Chicago Press.

Foucault, M., and C. Gordon. 1980. *Power/Knowledge Selected Interviews and Other Writings 1972–1977*. New York: Pantheon.

Ford, J.D. and L.W. Ford. 2012. "The Leadership of Organization Change: A View from Recent Empirical Evidence". In *Research in Organizational Change and Development (Research in Organizational Change and Development, Volume 20)*, eds. In Abraham B. (Rami) Shani, William A. Pasmore, Richard W. Woodman (eds.) 1–36. Emerald Group Publishing Limited.

Ford, J.D., L.W. Ford and A. D'Amelio. 2008. "Resistance to Change: The Rest of the Story". *Academy of Management Review* 33 (2): 362–377.

Ford, J.D., L.W. Ford and R.T. Mcnamara. 2002. "Resistance and the Background Conversations of Change". *Journal of Organizational Change Management* 15 (2): 105–121.

Gabriel, Y. 2008. *Organizing Words*. Oxford: Oxford University Press.

Graetz, F., and A.C.T. Smith. 2008. "The Role of Dualities in Arbitrating Continuity and Change in Forms of Organizing". *International Journal of Management Reviews* 10 (3): 266–280.

Graetz, F., and A.C.T. Smith. 2010. "Managing Organizational Change: A Philosophies of Change Approach". *Journal of Change Management* 10 (2):135–154.

Grant, P., and Perren, L. 2002. "Small Business and Entrepreneurial Research: Meta-Theories, Paradigms and Prejudices". *International Small Business Journal* 20 (2): 185–211.

Grey, C. 2003. "The Fetish of Change". *TAMARA Journal of Critical Postmodern Organization Science* 2 (2): 1–18.

Grint, K., and Case, P. 1998. "The Violent Rhetoric of Re-engineering: Management Consultancy on the Offensive". *Journal of Management Studies* 35 (5): 557–77.

Hardy, C., and Clegg, S. 2004. "Power and Change: A Critical Reflection". In *Dynamics of Organizational Change and Learning*, ed. J.J. Boonstra, 343–370. Chichester: John Wiley and Sons.

Hassard, J.S. 2012. "Rethinking the Hawthorne Studies: The Western Electric Research in Its Social, Political and Historical Context". *Human Relations* 65 (11): 1431–1461.

Hassard, J.S., and M. Kelemen. 2002. "Production and Consumption in Organizational Knowledge: The Case of the 'Paradigms Debate'". *Organization* 9 (2): 331–355.

Hassard, J.S., M. Kelemen and J. Wolfram Cox. 2008. *Disorganization Theory: Explorations in Alternative Organizational Analysis.* London: Routledge.

Heracleous, L., and M. Barrett. 2001. Organizational Change as Discourse: Communicative Actions and Deep Structures in the Context of Information Technology Implementation. *Academy of Management Journal* 44 (4): 755–778.

Hendry, C. 1996. "Understanding and Creating Whole Organizational Change Through Learning Theory". *Human Relations* 48 (5): 621–41.

Hinings, C.R. 2010. "Thirty Years of Organization Studies: Enduring Themes on a Changing Institutional Field." *Organization Studies* 31 (6): 659–675.

Hope Hailey, V., and J. Balogun. 2002. "Devising Context Sensitive Approaches to Change: The Example of Glaxo Wellcome". *Long Range Planning* 35 (2): 153–178.

Huczynski, A. 2006. *Management Gurus*, rev. ed. London: Routledge.

Hughes, M. 2010. *Managing Change: A Critical Perspective.* London: CIPD Publishing.

Hughes, M. 2011. "Do 70 percent of all Organizational Change Initiatives Really Fail?" *Journal of Change Management* 11 (4): 451–464.

Hughes, M. forthcoming. "Leading Changes: Why Transformation Explanations Fail." *Leadership*.

Hughes, M. forthcoming. "Who Killed Change Management?" *Culture and Organization*.

Jackson, B. 2001. *Management Gurus and Management Fashions.* London: Routledge.

Kahn, R.L. 1974. "Organizational Development: Some Problems and Proposals". *Journal of Applied Behavioural Science* 10 (4): 485–502.

Knights, D. 1997. "Organization Theory in the Age of Deconstruction: Dualism, Gender and Postmodernism Revisited". *Organization Studies* 18 (1): 1–19.

Kotter, J.P. 1995. "Leading Change: Why Transformation Efforts Fail". *Harvard Business Review* 73 (2): 44–56.

Kotter, J.P. 1996 and 2012. *Leading Change.* Boston MA: Harvard Business School Press.

Kotter, J.P., and L.A. Schlesinger. 1979. "Choosing Strategies for Change". *Harvard Business Review* 57 (2): 106–114.

Kuhn, T.S. 1962. *The Structure of Scientific Revolutions.* Chicago: The University of Chicago Press.

Lakomski, G. 2001. "Organizational Change, Leadership and Learning: Culture as Cognitive Process". *The International Journal of Educational Management* 15 (2): 68–77.

Langley, A., C. Smallman, H. Tsoukas and A.H. Van de Ven. 2013. "Process Studies of Change in Organization and Management: Unveiling Temporality, Activity and Flow". *Academy of Management Journal* 56 (1): 1–13.

Lewin, K. 1947. "Frontiers in Group Dynamics". In *Field Theory in Social Science*, ed. D. Cartwright, 188–237. London: Social Science Paperbacks.

Lewis, M.W. 2000. "Exploring Paradox: Toward a More Comprehensive Guide". *Academy of Management Review* 25 (4): 760–776.

McCellan, J.G. 2011. "Reconsidering Communication and the Discursive Politics of Organizational Change". *Journal of Change Management* 11 (4): 465–480.

Mckinley,W., M.A. Mone and G. Moon. 1999. "Determinants and Development of Schools in Organization Theory". *Academy of Management Review* 24 (4): 634–648.

Mintzberg, H., B. Ahlstrand and J. Lampel. 2009. *Strategy Safari: The Complete Guide Through the Wilds of Strategic Management*, 2nd ed. London: FT Prentice Hall.

Morrison, E.F., and F.J. Milliken. 2000. "Organizational Silence: A Barrier to Change and Development in a Pluralistic World". *Academy of Management Review* 25 (4): 706–725.

Oreg, S. 2003. "Resistance to Change: Developing an Individual Differences Measure". *Journal of Applied Psychology* 88 (4): 680–693.

Ortenblad, A. 2007. "Senge's Many Faces: Problem or Opportunity?" *The Learning Organization* 14 (2): 108–122.

Palmer, I., and R. Dunford. 2008. "Organizational Change and the Importance of Embedded Assumptions". *British Journal of Management* 19, Special Issue: S20–S32.

Palmer, I., R. Dunford and G. Akin. 2009. *Managing Organizational Change: A Multiple Perspectives Approach*, 2nd ed. Boston: McGraw-Hill International Editions.

Parry, K.W. 2011. "Leadership and Organization Theory". In *The SAGE Handbook of Leadership*, eds. A. Bryman, D. Collinson, K. Grint, B. Jackson and M. Uhl-Bien, 53–70. London: Sage Publications Ltd.

Pettigrew, A.M. 2012. "Context and Action in the Transformation of the Firm: A Reprise". *Journal of Management Studies* 49 (7): 1304–1328.

Pettigrew, A.M., R.W. Woodman and K.S. Cameron. 2001. "Studying Organizational Change and Development: Challenges for Future Research". *Academy of Management Journal* 44 (4): 697–713.

Phillips, N., and C. Oswick. 2011. "Organizational Discourse: Domains, Debates, and Directions". *The Academy of Management Annals* 6 (1): 435–481.

Piderit, S.K. 2000. "Rethinking Resistance and Recognizing Ambivalence: A Multidimensional View of Attitudes Towards an Organizational Change". *Academy of Management Review* 25 (4): 783–794.

Randall, J. 2004. *Managing Change/Changing Managers*. London: Routledge.

Rhodes, C., A. Pullen and S.R. Clegg. 2010. "'If I Should Fall from Grace. . .': Stories of Change and Organizational Ethics". *Journal of Business Ethics* 91 (4): 535–551.

Schein, E.H. 1988. *Organizational Psychology*, 3rd ed. London: Prentice Hall.

Senge, P. 1990 and 2006. *The Fifth Discipline: The Art and Practice of the Learning Organization*. London: Random House Business Books.

Shepherd, C., and Challenger, R. 2013. "Revisiting Paradigm(s) in Management Research: A Rhetorical Analysis of the Paradigm Wars". *International Journal of Management Reviews* 15 (2): 225–244.

Smith, A.C.T., and Graetz, F.M. 2011. *Philosophies of Organizational Change*. Cheltenham: Edward Elgar Publishing Ltd.

Soderlund, J. 2011. "Theoretical Foundations of Project Management: Suggestions for a Pluralistic Understanding". In *Oxford Handbook on the Management of Projects*, eds. P.W.G. Morris, J. Pinto and J. Soderlund, 15–36. Oxford: Oxford University Press.

Sorge, A., and Van Witteloostuijn, A. 2004. "The (Non) Sense of Organizational Change: An Essai about Universal Management Hypes, Sick Consultancy Metaphors and Healthy Organization Theories". *Organization Studies* 25 (7): 1205–1231.

Starkey, K., S. Tempest and A. Mckinlay. 2002. "Introduction". In *How Organizations Learn: Managing the Search for Knowledge*, eds. K. Starkey, S. Tempest and A. Mckinlay, 1–10. London: Thomson Learning.

Sturdy, A., and C. Grey. 2003. "Beneath and Beyond Organizational Change Management: Exploring Alternatives". *Organization* 10 (4): 651–662.

Sugarman, B. 2001. "A Learning-Based Approach to Organizational Change: Some Results and Guidelines". *Organizational Dynamics* 30 (1): 62–76.

Sutherland, F., and A.C.T. Smith. 2013. "Leadership for the Age of Sustainability: A Dualities Approach to Organizational Change". In *Organizational Change, Leadership and Ethics: Leading Organizations Towards Sustainability*, eds. R.T. By and B. Burnes, 216–239. London: Routledge.

Taylor, F.W. 1911. *The Principles of Scientific Management*. New York: Harper and Row.

Thomas, R., and C. Hardy. 2011. "Reframing Resistance to Organizational Change". *Scandinavian Journal of Management* 27 (3): 322–331.

Thompson, P., and J. O'Connell Davidson. 1995. "The Continuity of Discontinuity: Managerial Rhetoric in Turbulent Times". *Personnel Review* 24 (4): 17–33.

Tsoukas, H. 2005. "Afterword: Why Language Matters in the Analysis of Organizational Change". *Journal of Organizational Change Management* 18 (1): 96–104.

Tsoukas, H., and R. Chia. 2002. "On Organizational Becoming: Rethinking Organizational Change". *Organization Science* 13 (5): 567–582.

Van de Ven, A.H., and M.S. Poole. 1995. "Explaining Development and Change in Organizations". *Academy of Management Review* 20 (3): 510–540.

Van de Ven, A.H., and M.S. Poole. 2005. "Alternative Approaches for Studying Organizational Change". *Organization Studies* 26 (9): 1377–1404.

Vaara, E. 2002. "On the Discursive Construction of Success/Failure in Narratives of Post-Merger Integration". *Organization Studies* 23 (2): 211–248.

Wall, S. 2007. "Organizational Ethics, Change and Stakeholder Involvement: A Survey of Physicians". *HEC Forum* 19 (3): 227–243.

Weick, K.E. 1999. "Theory Construction as Disciplined Reflexivity: Trade-offs in the 90s". *Academy of Management Review* 24 (4): 797–806.

Whitehead, A.N. 1929. *The Aims of Education and Other Essays*. Free Press: New York.

Whitley, R. 1984. "The Fragmented State of Management Studies: Reasons and Consequences." *Journal of Management Studies* 21 (3): 331–348.

Whitley, R. 2000. *The Intellectual and Social Organization of the Sciences*. Oxford: Oxford University Press.

Wilson, D. 1992. *A Strategy for Change*. London: Routledge.

Wrege, C.D., and R.M. Hodgetts. 2000. "Frederick W. Taylor's 1899 Pig Iron Observations Examining Fact, Fiction, and Lessons for the New Millennium". *Academy of Management Journal* 43 (6): 1283–1291.

Ybema, S. 2010. "Talk of Change: Temporal Contrasts and Collective Identities". *Organization Studies* 31 (4): 481–503.

4 Leadership Studies

INTRODUCTION

In this chapter, the focus turns to thinking critically about leadership studies in order to inform understanding about leadership and organizational change in subsequent chapters. However, throughout this chapter, concepts will be applied to leadership and organizational change for illustrative purposes. In particular, critical/alternative accounts of leadership are privileged that challenge the normal, progressive accounts of the linear accretion of leadership knowledge.

> . . .[L]eadership scholars must critically analyse one another's theories and models and engage in dialogic conversations about those conceptual frameworks. Leadership studies would be vastly improved with a large dose of critical thought and methodology.
>
> (Rost, 1993:183)

In this Rostian spirit, the chapter provokes and challenges, and whereas it is conceded that books are more monologic than dialogic, there has been a conscious effort to understand leadership and organizational change from different paradigms and perspectives. The field of leadership studies is characterised by lots of industry, certainly if gauged by the quantity of publications and theories (Grint, 2005a). However, an assumption that the quantity of publications correlates with the quality of leadership knowledge is not supported. Storey (2011:8), in the introduction to his edited leadership reader, wrote, '. . .[T]he accumulation of weighty and extensive reports to date tend, in the main, to regurgitate a now familiar thesis—but it is a thesis which remains incomplete, insufficiently tested and inadequately debated or scrutinized.' And Gill (2011:98) expressed similar frustration within his comprehensive textbook treatment of leadership.

> No theory or model of leadership so far has provided a satisfactory explanation of leadership; indeed there is no consensus on the meaning

of leadership in the first place. Many theories are partisan or partial, reflecting particular philosophical or ideological points of view. Many are based on limited, even biased, research: the answers one gets depend on the questions one asks.

Kotter (1990:3) has described leadership as '. . .an ageless topic. . .,' which he contrasted with management as '. . . largely the product of the last 100 years. . .' This notion of an 'ageless topic' privileges leadership over the newcomer—'management.' Certainly, formal studies of management are typically traced back to the turn of the last century (Fayol, 1916; Taylor, 1911), with interest in leaders going back to the origins of civilisation. However, 'leadership as a word and leadership as a subject of inquiry and study are distinctly 20th century phenomena' (Rost, 1997:6). The rhetoric of an 'ageless topic' implies that this quest is almost complete, that the leadership studies Holy Grail is about to be discovered. As this chapter suggests, this may be an illusion, with leadership studies presented as a historical narrative fuelling such illusions. Grint (2005a:8) eloquently captures this when he writes, '[I]ndeed, the metaphorical straight line that connects the problems of the past to the solutions of the future resonates with the popularity of the quest for the 'answer' to the leadership 'question."' Critical depictions of leadership studies inevitably have implications for leadership practices. Institutions, policy makers and politicians place faith in leadership as both a reactive solution to their problems and proactively as a positive vision of successful futures. Again, the implication is that this faith is not blind faith, but a faith underpinned by many years of accumulated knowledge and reified through chronologically structured textbook treatments (see, for example Gill, 2011). In this chapter, the intention is to critically move beyond the traditional orthodoxy, identifying those aspects of leadership studies that inform leadership and organizational change.

In terms of the chapter structure, the chapter commences with two landmark books, *Leadership* (Burns, 1978) and *Leadership for the Twenty-First Century* (Rost, 1993). Rost emerged from his deep engagement with the leadership literature simultaneously troubled yet convinced that the field of leadership studies needed to evolve. Rost highlighted fault lines within the orthodox accounts of leadership that are still evident today, orientating this chapter and the current state of leadership studies. These fault lines provide a bridge into social constructionism and related concepts of language and discourse, concluding with the concept of frames and how frames frame our thinking about leadership in particular ways. There are echoes of Rost in Grint's more contemporary leadership narratives, with Grint's influential writings illustrating the concepts of social construction and discourse introduced in the previous section and how they might advance understanding about leadership and organizational change. The neglect of followers (collaborators) within leadership studies repeatedly arises, which requires further discussion, given their relevance to leadership and organizational change. These earlier discussions underpin theorising differences between leaders and managers. Predating fashionable postmodern organization studies, Selznick's (1957) *Leadership in Administration: A Sociological Interpretation*, which is often cited as the earliest reference differentiating leadership and management, referred to leadership as elaborating a socially integrating myth. The section revisits influential milestones informing this perceived differentiation, which are integral to the conceptualisation of leadership producing change and management producing stability. The final section tempers the darkness of the critical accounts of leadership with the light of emerging understanding about leadership. In critically revisiting the leadership literature, there are many moments when leadership authors offered a positive, moral and egalitarian vision of leadership studies, one which would have benefitted wider society, rather than very narrow, sectional interests. And these moments lost in translation, either intentionally or unintentionally, are remembered.

TRANSFORMING TWENTY-FIRST CENTURY LEADERSHIP

Leadership (Burns, 1978) was chosen as the leadership study milestone to commence the 35-year critical history of leadership and organizational change featured in this book. A huge volume of leadership studies literature predates 1978, reflecting competing historiographies and a tendency to depict leadership studies knowledge as progressively improving. Similarly, the writing since 1978 may be critiqued, but by narrowing the focus to 35 years, it is possible to take critical stock of leadership and organizational change as a sub-field of the field of leadership studies. Rost was a student of Burns, with *Leadership for the Twenty-First Century* (Rost, 1993) benefiting from a foreword written by Burns. The following discussion reflects back on both literary landmarks and their implications for leadership studies today. *Leadership* (Burns, 1978) was exceptionally well received within the leadership studies community.

> . . .James Macgregor Burns's *Leadership* not only stands up well but, like great wine, ages beautifully. It is a book which every social scientist and citizen-student of power must read.
>
> (Bennis, 1982:205)

It is still frequently cited by critical leadership scholars (Evans et al, 2013) as well as more mainstream leadership scholars (Gill, 2011). *Leadership* (Burns, 1978), as well as being influential within leadership studies, is particularly pertinent to understanding leadership and organizational change. Bennis (1982) captures the essence of Burns's thesis in the following quotation, taken from his favourable book review published in the *American Journal of Sociology*:

Leadership is collective; there is a symbiotic relationship between leaders and followers, and what makes it collective is the subtle interplay between followers' needs and wants and the leaders' capacities to understand, one way or another, these collective aspirations. Leadership is dissensual: that is, without conflict (peacefully managed); we would all be trapped in a false utopian dream. Leadership is "causative," meaning that-and here is where Burns makes one of his most stunning contributions-leadership can invent and create institutions (or ideas or documents or even memories) that can empower followers to satisfy their needs.

(Bennis, 1982:204)

Burns's pioneering approach encouraged greater engagement with followers (collaborators) within meaningful studies of leadership. Leadership as dissensual is intriguing, given the preference for consensus; Burns's emphasis upon dissensus tends to be missing within contemporary treatments of transformational leadership (see for example, Bass and Riggio, 2006). It echoes the creative destruction of innovation theorists (and Burns even cites Joseph Schumpeter) and even has parallels with Kotter's (1996) emphasis on creating a sense of urgency. Burns (1978:454) believed that 'conflict unifies people just as it divides them.' This is an interesting political science insight, disrupting unitarist beliefs often used by human resource departments and strategic planners to characterise today's organizations. '[I]t would probably be better for most organizations, including corporations, unions, and university faculties, for dissensus to be built into their structures' (Burns, 1978:453). This quotation challenges the taken-for-granted consensus orthodoxy of organizational life today. Equally, the idea of leaders inventing/creating institutions, ideas and memories is a recurrent theme within this chapter, pre-dating the postmodern interest in social construction and discourse accounts of leadership. Downton (1973) originally coined the phrase transformational leadership, although it was *Leadership* (Burns, 1978) that gave emphasis to the differentiation between transformational and transactional leadership that is at the heart of Bernard Bass's later conceptualisation of transformational leadership. However, Burns's vision of transforming leadership was very different from Bass's transformational leadership:

Moral leadership emerges from, and always returns to the fundamental wants and needs, aspirations, and values of the followers.

(Burns, 1978:4)

In Bass's transformational leadership, this emphasis upon morality is believed to be missing (see Carey 1992 and Simola et al, 2010). Burns (1978:20) refers to transforming leadership as occurring when '. . .one or more persons engage with others in such a way that leaders and followers raise one another to higher levels of motivation and morality.' Morality is integral to Burns's depiction of transforming leadership; it is the heart and soul of this form of leadership. Burns (1978:415) remarked upon the absence of artistic, intellectual, political or social leadership in the processes of change he encountered, suggesting, '[I]t is as though change took place mechanically, apart from human volition or participation.' Burns was convinced that leadership without followership was not leadership: '[L]eaders and followers are engaged in a common enterprise; they are dependent on each other, their fortunes rise and fall together, they share the results of planned change together' (Burns, 1978:426). In the context of this critical review of the leadership of organizational change, Burns's belief that leaders and followers share together the results of planned change appears revolutionary even today. Typically, today the strong/heroic leader transforms/ turns around the failing hospital or supermarket chain, dealing robustly with employees who resist the leader's will, disparagingly depicted as being resistant to change.

Rost's (1993) passionate polemic *Leadership for the Twenty-First Century* argued for a new school of leadership, and in many ways can be regarded as an extension of Burns's belief in transforming leadership. Rost's (1993) background in educational administration may explain why he has been frequently cited in the general leadership literature but does not feature prominently within the management and organization studies literature. However, Evans et al's (2013) emphasis on Rost in *Critical Leadership* may help to rectify this situation. *Leadership for the Twenty-First* Century, which is dedicated to James MacGregor Burns, includes a foreword by Burns; however, unusual within the context of a foreword, Burns criticises Rost. This criticism is understandable when you read Rost's fundamentalist pleas for a deeper understanding of leadership with his searching critique of almost everything ever written about leadership, including, incidentally, Burns. Two decades later, Rost's vision of leadership still provokes and informs. Echoing Burns, Rost despaired about the state of leadership studies, highlighting the lack of definitions and the lack of interdisciplinary accounts of leadership. However, out of his dark night of the soul, he encouraged the development a new school of leadership. It is a humanistic vision of leadership that still offers hope. More specifically, there are reasons why Rost's account of leadership fits within the leadership and organizational change focus of this critical review.

(1) Rost was interested in movement between what he referred to as an industrial paradigm, critically characterised by leadership as good management, and a post-industrial paradigm, with a new definition of leadership for new times. This is comparable with the perceived shift from change management towards change leadership, with leadership as good management offering an explanation for this shift.

(2) Rost was obsessed with the centrality of definitions in conceptualising leadership, to the extent that two of his eight chapters concentrate

exclusively upon definitions. The positive outcome of Rost's fetish was the generation of his definition, favoured in this critical review, that 'leadership is an influence relationship among leaders and collaborators who intend real changes that reflect their mutual purposes' (Rost, 1997:11).

(3) Rost's emphasis upon real, intended change fits the organizational change aspect of this critical review. In Rost's configuration, organizational change is not just a subsequent consequence of leadership; without real, intended change, leadership is not taking place. Incidentally for Rost, a change may fail or succeed, but both leaders and collaborators must intend change. This intention to change is out of step with today's emphasis upon successful outcomes.

(4) Rost offered a fresh perspective on leadership and management differentiations, again pertinent to the perceived contemporary movement from change management towards change leadership which privileges change leadership over change management.

Rost channelled his annoyance with earlier leadership studies in what he referred to as an industrial paradigm covering the 20th century, and contrasted them with how he wanted the field of leadership studies to develop into the twenty-first century post-industrial paradigm, as he referred to it. In his critical overview of leadership studies, Rost (1993) identified the following characteristics/shortcomings of leadership studies in the industrial paradigm (see Figure 4.1).

Rost believed that these characteristics of industrial leadership paradigm (see Figure 4.1) were no longer applicable to the twenty-first century post-industrial leadership paradigm (these characteristics are discussed in the next section). He believed that we were at a turning point, although in 1993, this appears to have been more of an aspiration than a paradigm shift. Unfortunately, over two decades later, many of the characteristics (see Figure 4.1) still apply to leadership orthodoxy.

Only Rost (1993:37) could write 'definitions are boring to many people' whilst defending his own fascination with definitions. He explained in detail

---

1) A structural-functionalist view of organizations

2) A view of management as the preeminent profession

3) A personalistic focus on the leader

4) A dominant objective of goal achievement

5) A self-interested and individualistic outlook

6) A male model of life

7) A utilitarian and materialistic ethical perspective

8) A rational, technocratic, linear, quantitative, and scientific language and methodology

---

Figure 4.1   Major characteristics of the industrial leadership paradigm (Rost, 1993)

how the different terms 'lead,' 'leader' and 'leading' go back many centuries. However, he found that the term leadership came into popular use at the turn of the last century, with the earliest books on leadership published in the 1930s. He cited Bass's (1981:16) revised edition of *Stogdill's Handbook of Leadership*, defining leadership as '. . .an interaction between members of a group. Leaders are agents of change, persons whose acts affect people more than other people's acts affect them. . .Leadership occurs when one group member modifies the motivation or competencies of others in the group.' It is intriguing that *Stogdill's Handbook of Leadership*, a respected milestone of leadership studies, features leaders explicitly defined as agents of change. Change featured prominently in Rost's (1993:102) leadership definition:

> Leadership is an influence relationship among leaders and followers who intend real changes that reflect their mutual purposes. (Subsequently revised in 1997 to feature collaborators, rather than followers)

These are more than mere words, as Rost sought to express his belief in the post-industrial leadership paradigm, and these four elements merit further discussion. The relationship based upon influence is multi-directional, and the influencing behaviours are non-coercive. The influence relationship is comprised of leaders and followers. Followers are active and there must be more than one follower and typically more than one leader, but the influence patterns are inevitably unequal. Leaders and followers intend real changes, with real changes being substantive and transforming. Leaders and followers do not have to produce change, but must intend change. The mutual purposes of leaders and followers are forged in non-coercive influence relationships. Leaders and followers develop purposes, not goals. Their intended changes are reflected rather than realised through mutual purposes, and these mutual purposes become common purposes. The inclusion in the definition of 'influence relationship,' 'followers' and 'mutual purposes' was ahead of the more recent leadership studies debates encouraging shared, distributed and collaborative leadership. A later section in this chapter is devoted to collaborative leadership, given its potential relevance to leadership and organizational change.

In revisiting Rost's (1993) passionate writings from over two decades earlier, he appears to have anticipated where critical leadership studies was heading. However, Rost, whilst critical of the industrial paradigm of leadership studies, was never a Critical Theorist; his hope was that his vision of a post-industrial leadership paradigm as a new school of leadership studies would become the mainstream orthodoxy. This begs the question, why didn't his writings have greater influence upon leadership studies orthodoxy? In order to answer this question, it is necessary to understand the leadership orthodoxy that so troubled Rost, and why such orthodoxy is still problematic today.

BEYOND LEADERSHIP ORTHODOXY

At the time of writing, Rost (1993) was concerned that leadership studies was trapped in an industrial paradigm. As Calas and Smircich (1991:568) highlighted in their highly cited review of leadership studies, '. . .the more things change, the more they remain the same.' Barker (1997:350) appeared to share Burns's (1978) and Rost's (1993) frustrations.

> The paradigm relies upon the simplistic concept of the leader as a giver of direction and as a manipulator of will, who frames and solves specific management or social problems.

This is particularly pertinent to this 35-year review of leadership and organizational change. Subsequent sections will critically move beyond this perceived leadership orthodoxy, but the leadership orthodoxy that is being implicitly and explicitly critiqued requires introduction, as it is still believed to be at work. Consequently, the following discussion is structured around the characteristics of the theory of the industrial leadership paradigm (see Figure 4.1) that Rost (1993) identified through his extensive leadership literature reviewing. Kotter's (1996) *Leading Change* and Bass and Riggio's (2006) *Transformational Leadership*, identified and introduced in Chapter Two as the most-cited leadership and organizational change publications, are used to illustrate these characteristics, which are believed to characterise the mainstream leadership literature today.

Structural-functionalism, which was originally applied to how societies were structured, was increasingly applied to organizations, and it was this application that Rost believed was characterising industrial-era leadership studies. Burrell and Morgan (1979) (discussed in Chapter Three) in their study of paradigms and organizational analysis at this time highlighted the functionalist orthodoxy of organization studies, citing Salaman and Thompson (1973:1):

> . . .tends to adopt theories and models of organizational functioning, and to focus on areas of empirical investigation, that are highly oriented towards managerial conceptions of organizations, managerial priorities and problems, and managerial concerns for practical outcomes.

This was the mindset that Rost, an education studies academic, encountered within industrial-era leadership studies, and it may well have been the managerial imperative embedded within structural-functionalism that particularly annoyed Rost. Today, structural-functionalism remains the dominant mindset for leadership and organizational change understanding, as well as practice. Kotter (1996) and Bass and Riggio (2006) typify such thinking, both speaking to the practical challenges of transforming organizations, whilst maintaining and encouraging managerial imperatives and perspectives. The philosophical position of structural/functionalism underpins leadership studies and many of the other industrial leadership paradigm characteristics discussed below.

Rost's suggestion that management was the preeminent profession in the context of his leadership book is initially confusing. Partially, this characteristic was an extension of structural-functionalism and its emphasis upon managerial prerogative. However, Rost was troubled that management literature framed societies' understanding of leadership in a manner similar to Burns's (1978) dismay about the absence of artistic, intellectual, political or social leadership in processes of change. However, Rost (1993:133/134) was also signposting a persistent theme he encountered within the leadership literature, '. . .an attempt to label as leadership those management processes which produce excellence in organizational outcomes and which leave the meaning of management to include all the other management processes that produce less than excellent outcomes. Leadership is excellence management; management is doing anything less than excellence'. This belief appears to endure to this day. Whereas Rost encountered leadership being presented as good management, despite his fascination with leadership, he believed management was equally important within organizations. Rost (1993:140) captured this within his concerns about 'denigrating management to ennoble leadership.' Kotter (1996) in particular was symptomatic of denigrating management to ennoble leadership, but equally within Bass and Riggio's (2006) differentiation between transformational leadership and transactional leadership, there was hierarchical privileging of the former over the latter.

The personalistic focus on leaders and the self-interested and individualistic outlook evident in the leadership literature that Rost (1993) identified still exists and may even have increased. We certainly live in an age of heroic leaders, with critical leadership scholars (Alvesson and Spicer, 2011; Grint, 2005a; Tourish, 2013) challenging such societal beliefs. Whereas Kotter's (1996) *Leading Change* favoured a powerful guiding coalition over an individualistic leader, the book depicted leaders exceptionally heroically. Equally, Bass and Riggio's (2006) *Transformational Leadership* may be read as an updating, refreshing and repositioning of trait-based, individualistic approaches to leadership.

In the leadership literature, Rost (1993) found that the dominant objective was goal achievement; this orientation is closely aligned with the earlier discussion of structural-functionalism. The language of goals and achieving goals is very evident throughout the transformational leadership literature, and equally, Kotter (1996) repeatedly makes reference to goals and achieving goals. Critiquing the male model of life as characterised within the leadership literature highlights Rost (1993) being once again ahead of his time. In their study of gender and organizations, Alvesson and Billing (2009) critically acknowledged that cultural assumptions resulted in managers and leaders traditionally being constructed in masculine terms. In terms

of increasing opportunities for women to attain jobs and exercise authority in organizations, they identified four different positions: Equal opportunities, the meritocratic, the special contribution and the alternative values
position, with each position underpinned with different values and beliefs.
The special contribution position is interesting, as it speaks to a number
of the negative characteristics of leadership studies that Rost (1993) was
encountering.

> The leadership ideas and styles popular during recent years are not nec-
> essarily pro-women, but they accord ill with traditional ideas of the
> masculine character of the good manager: technocratically rational,
> aggressive, firm and just. At a minimum a masculine bias is reduced.
> Some organizations indicate that they are actually looking for certain
> new values which are associated with women, such as flexibility, social
> skills, team orientation, etc.
>
> (Alvesson and Billing, 2009:172)

Kotter's (1996) *Leading Change* certainly has a masculine tone, which is
less the case with Bass and Riggio's (2006) *Transformational Leadership*. It
is problematic, attributing a male model of life to an author's work when
we do not know fully the implicit mental model in use. However, Calas
and Smircich (1991:569), in their pioneering and influential analysis of four
famous leadership publications, demonstrated how organizational writing
about leadership '. . .maintains a specific set of practices and discourses in
place—the basic power relations network on which "leadership" has been
constituted and re-constituted.'

In reviewing the literature, Rost (1993) found that there was a preference for a utilitarian and materialistic ethical perspective. Rost's (1993:172)
concern with utilitarian ethics was that they suffer '. . .from doing a results
analysis before the results are in, from its counting inaccuracies, and from
its inability to focus on the common good.' Orthodox leadership literature
reflected a unitarist mindset, where all of the employees pull together in the
belief that organizational success and goal achievement will benefit everyone (ethics are revisited in the concluding section of this chapter). Unitarist
emphasis upon transformations as mutually beneficial is very evident within
the models of leadership that Kotter (1996) and Bass and Riggio (2006)
promoted.

Rost (1993) perceived the industrial leadership paradigm theory as being
characterised as rational, technocratic, linear, quantitative and scientific.
In reviewing a respected, American-based journal such as *The Leadership
Quarterly*, a predisposition to publish quantitative and scientific papers
depicting leadership processes as rational, technocratic and linear was evident. Whereas this is the orthodoxy, occasionally, qualitative accounts of
leadership were published that addressed the irrational, ambiguous and
non-linear aspects of leadership (see, for example, Yukl, 1999; Beyer, 1999).
In reviewing the transformational leadership literature, there appeared to

have been a conscious decision to model such studies on scientific principles, with a predisposition towards quantitative analysis. *Leading Change* (Kotter, 1996) neither cited original empirical work nor cited the work of other researchers. However, the eight steps offer a very rational, technocratic and linear vision of how to lead transformations.

In the next section, leadership is explained in terms of myths, social construction, language, discourse and frames. This section and subsequent sections should not be regarded as an extension of earlier leadership studies, but rather a reflection of the growing disillusionment with the leadership studies orthodoxy just discussed and a desire to describe, analyse and theorise leadership in new and more informative ways (see Marshak and Grant, 2008 for further discussion).

LEADERSHIP: MYTHS, SOCIAL CONSTRUCTION, LANGUAGE AND DISCOURSE AND FRAMES

Bryman (2004), in his critical but appreciative review of qualitative research into leadership, specifically looked at how leaders and change processes feature in research papers. He identified a recurring theme of leaders leading change needing to '. . .secure commitment to the change process, address multiple constituencies (external and internal), convey a sense of the need for change, and instill a vision of how change should be implemented and/or what the future state of the organization will look like' (Bryman, 2004:751). He subsequently discussed how such research emphasised '. . . the importance and significance of the leader as a manager of meaning who actively manipulates symbols in order to instill a vision, manage change, and achieve support for his or her direction' (Bryman, 2004:754). In the following section, myths, social construction, language and discourse and frames informing leadership that are believed to be particularly pertinent to understanding leadership and organizational change are featured.

Myths The ghost of Rost inevitably haunts this section, with Rost passionately believing that leadership scholars should clearly define what they meant and attend to the content of leadership, rather than what he referred to as the 'peripheral' aspects of leadership. Myths, social construction, language and discourse and frames offer a very different critical agenda to Rost's critique. However, Rost highlighted leadership as a mythological narrative, and his work offers the springboard into the more discursive debates featured in this section. Rost (1993:8) highlighted leadership as a mythological narrative, which explained the apparent success of the orthodox accounts of leadership: '[I]t has generated a mythological story of leadership that has been told over and over again and that almost everyone believes.' In developing the notion of this mythological narrative of leadership, Rost drew upon Edelman's (1971) symbolic theory of rewards in how leadership research and leadership scholarship are traditionally presented (see Figure 4.2).

1) The system of research has been working.
2) The leadership scholars have been doing what they are supposed to do—increasing our understanding of leadership.
3) There has been progress toward that objective, and as a result, both scholars and practitioners can rest assured that they have an increasingly sophisticated understanding of leadership.
4) This better understanding of leadership will help make organizations more productive and, in the end, will make the US and the world a better place to work and live.

Figure 4.2   The mythological leadership studies narrative

Rost (1993) did not favour this mythological narrative, but highlighted it because it limits alternative conceptualisations of leadership and keeps leadership studies within its outdated industrial paradigm. There are similarities here with Gemmill and Oakley (1992), who were writing at the same time and more radically depicting leadership as an alienating social myth that limits alternative conceptualisations of leadership as well as limiting participation in alternative organizational processes. These leadership myths reinforce existing social beliefs and structures about the need for both hierarchy and leaders within organizations at the expense of more collaborative conceptualisations. We tend to hope that our leaders enable transformations that are beneficial to wider societies, but a mythical perspective suggests it is the mythology of leadership itself that potentially enables transformations. Intriguingly, Gemmill and Oakley (1992) within their radical account of leadership as mythology highlighted how leadership exists to maintain the status quo. Rather than the contemporary preoccupations of leadership as enabling change, the primary role of leadership is to impede change within societies and institutions.

One further depiction of how leadership has been critically regarded as a myth surfaces within Kelly's negative ontology of leadership: '[L]eadership is arguably an empty signifier par excellence in that it has evaded attempts to confront its emptiness for hundreds of years' (Kelly, 2014:915). Kelly revisited Grint's (2005a) mythical association between leadership and the many-headed hydra of ancient Greece. In a manner similar to the hydra creating new heads after each head is severed, so too the empty signifier of leadership produces a surplus of meanings: '[T]here will always be the possibility of a better definition, research design, methodology, theoretical framework and so forth' (Kelly, 2014:918). In this exceptionally bleak and negative ontology, Gemmill and Oakley's (1992) and Rost's (1993) concerns that the prevalent leadership mythology limits alternative conceptualisations is echoed. However, it offers another provocative explanation for the mythology of leadership and organizational change, paraphrased as we currently do not fully understand this interrelationship, but if we work a bit harder, do more research and write more books, we will eventually succeed. Kelly's discussion of Grint encourages consideration of the social construction of leadership.

Social Construction Fairhurst and Grant (2010:175) acknowledge how extensive the social construction of leadership literature now is, having grown rapidly over the past 15 years with no signs of stopping. They (2010:175) identify two interrelated characteristics of social constructionist leadership approaches.

> First, they eschew a leader-centric approach in which the leader's personality, style, and/or behavior are the primary (read, only) determining influences on follower's thoughts and actions. . .Second, emphasis is given to leadership as a co-constructed reality, in particular, the processes and outcomes of interaction between and among social actors.

Both of these characteristics appear pertinent to the interrelationships between leadership and organizational change; shifting the focus away from a leader leading change towards a more participative process of changing enabled through a co-constructed reality amongst social actors. Acknowledging the significance of context has become an academic norm within management and organization studies (Hope-Hailey and Balogun, 2002). The assumption is that managers and/or leaders inside an organization are influenced by the external environment (context). In Grint's (2005b) social constructionist perspective, he suggests that a leader may construct a context and that '. . .we should pay more attention to the role of leaders and decision-makers in the construction of contexts that legitimates their intended or executed actions and accounts' (Grint, 2005b:1472). This offers a very different perspective from the leadership studies orthodoxy, which explains a strong leader and his or her actions as reactions to a very difficult operating context.

In Figure 4.3, Grint (2005b) differentiated between three types of problem that leaders may encounter, drawing upon Rittell and Webber (1973): Wicked, tame and critical problems. Grint then drew upon Etzioni (1964) to list the three types of power leaders could potentially apply: Coercive, calculative and normative. What is interesting about this creative typology is that it highlights command, management or leadership being appropriate for different types of problems. If the problem is critical, there may be a requirement for coercion, providing answers through command, rather than a collaborative resolution of the problem. If the problem is tame, calculative power may be more appropriate with management organizing processes. If the problem is wicked, normative power involving collaborative resolution

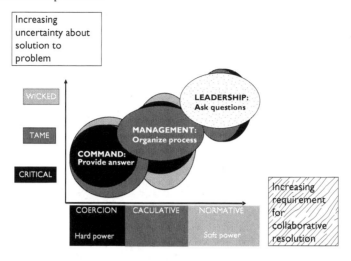

Figure 4.3   Graphic from problems, problems, problems: the social construction of leadership (Grint, 2005b)

Grint, K. "Problems, problems, problems: The social construction of leadership" *Leadership*, 58 (11). Page 1477, Copyright © 2005 SAGE. Reprinted by Permission of SAGE.

through leadership asking questions may be appropriate. Grint's (2005a) social constructionist account *Leadership: Limits and Possibilities* is the focus of the next section of this chapter.

An extensive social constructionist leadership literature now exists (Fairhurst and Grant, 2010), with competing accounts and explanations evident within this sub-field of leadership literature. There is never going to be a serene consensus amongst these scholars, and Bresnen's (1995) concerns with social constructionist accounts of leadership are worth revisiting. Bresnen (1995:500) regarded the problem with more radical social constructionist accounts as that, by default, '. . .they continue to conflate notions of leadership, management, and headship and, in so doing, inadvertently contribute to the confusion that continues to surround the concept.' Bresnen (1995), informed by research interviews with construction managers on three large construction projects, found considerable diversity in how these practicing managers constructed notions of leadership, as well as how critical academics constructed notions of leadership.

> At an individual level, the problem is heightened further to the extent that we each construct—from a complex set of phenomenological experiences—our own ideas of what leadership means to us.
>
> (Bresnen, 1995:500)

Bresnen (1995:501) posed an important question, still pertinent to today's engagement with social constructionist accounts of leadership: '. . .[T]o what extent and in what ways different constructions are put on leadership and how these are created, negotiated, emerge, and are sustained.' The implication is that the leader of the bank who socially constructs a difficult operating environment in order to justify bankers' bonuses shares similar reality construction processes to those who depict banking as led by greedy bankers, highlighted through the application of emancipatory Critical Theory.

Language and Discourse Pondy (1978:230) captures in the following quotation the centrality of language to leadership and the influence of leadership discourses: '[T]he real power of Martin Luther King was not only that he had a dream, but that he could describe it, that it became public, and therefore accessible to millions of people.' Earlier leadership orthodoxy was introduced and subsequently questioned in favour of more critical conceptualisations of leadership. However, within such reasoning, privileging the critical over the orthodox may miss an opportunity. Fairhurst (2008), in a paper introducing her new book, *Discursive Leadership*, presented a persuasive case for regarding discursive leadership and leadership psychology as alternating lenses that are neither superior nor derivative of each other.

Leadership psychologists have been very influential in explaining leadership in general and transformational leadership in particular. Figure 4.4, in differentiating the discursive and psychological lenses, informs understanding of both discursive explanations and psychological explanations. Leadership psychologists, in seeking to explain cognitions, emotions and behaviours, present leadership as mental theatre, whereas for discursive scholars, it is the discourse within leader-member interactions that is more significant. Leadership psychologists locate leadership within the leader,

	Discursive Leadership	Leadership Psychology
Object of study	Discourse	Mental Theatre
Ontology	Decentred subjects, thin actors	Essences
Power	Encompassing views, power and influence	Power and influence as dualisms
Agency	Reflexive agency	Untheorised/exaggerated agency
Analytic focus	Textual, contextual	Variable analytic
Communication	Primary	Secondary

Figure 4.4 Key differences between discursive and psychological lenses (Fairhurst, 2008)

whereas discursive scholars focus on socially constructed notions of leadership. Leadership psychologists tend to treat power negatively, whereas discursive scholars conceive power in both positive and negative ways. Leadership psychologists' treatment of leaders as agents is under-theorised, whereas discursive scholars emphasise the agency of leaders. Leadership psychologists address cause-and-effect, why questions concerning leadership, whereas discursive scholars are more interested in the contexts of leadership and the construction of unique discourses. Finally, for leadership psychologists, communication is a secondary consideration, whereas for discursive scholars, communication is the primary focus of their analysis. Fairhurst (2008) cites Bryman (2004:755), illustrating her 'alternating lenses' view at the level of leadership practice: '[W]hat is important is for leaders at the very apex of a hierarchy to be managers of meaning, especially in relation to the change process, but also to ensure that the more unexciting aspects of instrumental leadership get done.'

Marshak and Grant's (2008) account of discourse and organizational development is pertinent to both the organizational change focus of the previous chapter and the leadership focus of this chapter. They identify four key ideas: Create change by changing the discourse, create shared realities through negotiated narratives, power is central to the creation and change of discourses and new professional discourses are needed. Leaders may change their discourses in seeking to achieve organizational change; certainly there has been a dominant discourse of change leadership, with a marked change from the earlier change management discourses. Ideally, leaders socially construct new shared agreements and new mindsets about the reality of organizational change.

Framing The origins of framing attributed to Bateson (1955/1972) have been applied to many management and organization studies fields (see Cornelissen et al, 2011 for a comprehensive overview). Framing as specifically applied to leadership is an important outcrop of social constructionism, language and discourse. As framing potentially helps to explain the development of the sub-field of leadership and organizational change over the past 35 years, the concept is introduced and elaborated upon. When Fairhurst (2011:51) writes, 'in today's new market economies, recall that *leaders* are the architects of change, while *managers* are the everyday problem solvers,' she is framing a very particular hierarchical view of leadership and management, probably undertaken knowingly, given its context within her book on framing. There has been an understandable tendency for leadership researchers and scholars to focus on how leaders frame reality for followers, rather than more reflexively focusing on how leadership writers rhetorically construct realities for their readers. In Chapter Five, a framing analysis of *Leadership and Performance Beyond Expectations* (Bass, 1985) and *Leading Change* (Kotter, 1996) is undertaken to understand the framing of transformational leadership and leading change. However, first it is necessary to understand the theoretical background to today's interest in leadership framing.

> Leadership as managing meaning (Pondy, 1978) connects with earlier interest in social construction (Berger and Luckmann, 1966) and later interest in leadership discourses (Fairhurst, 2008) with the leader as manager of meaning (Bryman, 2004) unifying these different schools of thought.

Leadership is realised in processes whereby one or more individuals succeed in attempting to frame and define the reality for others. Leadership situations are those in which there exists an obligation or a perceived right on the part of certain individuals to define the reality of others (Smircich and Morgan, 1982:258).

This at that time radical explanation of leadership is now accepted within critical conceptualisations of leadership, although it is rarely acknowledged within leadership studies orthodoxy. Indeed, against the backdrop of the structural-functional philosophical assumptions underpinning leadership studies orthodoxy (Collinson, 2012; Rost, 1993), it is difficult to imagine the heroic conceptualisations that privilege leaders being replaced with far less potent depictions of leaders as managers of meaning.

Deetz et al (2000:67), in *Leading Organizations through Transition: Communication and Cultural Change*, highlighted the potential of framing and the potential of Gail Fairhurst's analyses, noting that 'people respond to the meanings they have for words and events rather than to the words and events themselves—the statement made is rarely the statement received.' Fairhurst's (Fairhurst, 2011; Fairhurst and Sarr, 1996) practically orientated books on framing leadership offer a framework to undertake the analysis of two practitioner-orientated leadership books (Bass, 1985; Kotter, 1996) (see Chapter Five). In the groundbreaking *The Art of Framing: Managing the Language of Leadership*, Fairhurst and Sarr (1996:3) described framing as an essential tool for the manager of meaning 'to determine the meaning of a subject is to make sense of it, to judge its character and significance.' The book benefitted from Gail Fairhurst being an established academic researching inside the organization in which Bob Sarr (her co-author) worked. They used an analogy of a gifted photographer focusing his camera and framing his subject so that a person viewing the photograph knew what the photographer intended, identifying three framing components: Language, thought and forethought.

Their discussion of goals is pertinent to the transformation and change themes of this critical review, suggesting that '. . .ambiguous language and generally framed goals often help facilitate organizational change' (Fairhurst and Sarr, 1996:37). Fairhurst and Sarr (1996) identified the tools used in designing memorable frames: Metaphors, jargon and catchphrases, contrast, spin and stories. When Fairhurst (2005) revisited *The Art of Framing* and its critical and practitioner reception, she acknowledged that practicing managers either really embraced the concept or struggled with it. In terms of those practicing managers embracing the concept, she noted that they '. . . seem to place a premium on communication especially regarding its role in organizational change' (Fairhurst, 2005:167).

The Power of Framing: Creating the Language of Leadership (Fairhurst, 2011) built upon *The Art of Framing: Managing the Language of Leadership* (Fairhurst and Sarr, 1996), but went deeper. Fairhurst (2011:2) offered six rules guiding the relationship between leadership and constructing reality (see Figure 4.5).

These rules of reality construction (see Figure 4.5) offer helpful and succinct insights into the construction of leadership realities through framing. More pragmatically, Fairhurst (2011) highlights framing skill components relating to cultural discourses, mental models and core framing tasks, and focuses on five types of memorable frames that are commonly used by leaders: Metaphorical, master, simplifying, gain and loss and believability. In terms of the leadership context of framing, Fairhurst (2011:184) offered the following succinct guidance: '[F]irst, you must focus on the "who, what, when, where, why" details of the situation at hand to discern framing at work. Second, you must figure out the design problem of the leader or leaders involved.'

In Figure 4.6, those framing questions derived from Fairhurst (2011) that are believed to be particularly applicable to the framing evident within the featured books of Bernard Bass and John Kotter are highlighted. The dilemma with framing, social construction and discourses is that leadership is made less real and more of a mythological narrative (Rost, 1993). It may even be perceived as an alienating social myth (Gemmill and Oakley, 1992).

---

1) Leaders often cannot control events, but they can control the context under which events are seen if they recognize a framing opportunity.
2) At its most basic framing reality means defining "the situation here and now" in ways that connect with others.
3) "Reality" is often contested and framing a subject is an act of persuasion by leaders, one imbued with ethical choices.
4) The uncertainty, confusion, and un-decidability of "the situation here and now" opens it up for interpretation, providing opportunities for leaders.
5) Leadership is a design problem and leaders must figure out what leadership is in the context of what they do and, through the framing and actions, persuade themselves and other people that they are doing it.
6) Effective framing requires leaders to control their own spontaneous communications.

Figure 4.5   Reality construction rules (Fairhurst, 2011)

1) What cultural discourse is being employed?
2) What is driving the framing of the specific situation (why, where, what and who questions)?
3) What mental model is being promoted?
4) How can leaders control the context under which events are seen if they recognise a framing opportunity?
5) Are metaphorical, master, simplifying, gain and loss and believability frames utilised?
6) What is leadership in the context of what leaders do and how do they persuade themselves and others that they are doing it (the design problem)?

Figure 4.6   Leadership framing questions (based on Fairhurst, 2011)

The very real and tangible leadership we perceive out there may largely be a social construction.

LEADERSHIP LIMITS AND POSSIBILITIES

The Commission on the Future of Management and Leadership (2014) recently reported how management and leadership needed to change by 2020 in order to deliver sustainable growth. The report presented research-informed insights into the contemporary experience of management and leadership, for example, that 'four fifths of workers don't think their manager sets a good moral example and less than a fifth are aware of their organisation's values' (2014:17). Equally, the Commission highlighted troubling inequalities and a need for far greater gender equality. The promising title of the report's opening chapter was *The state of UK management and leadership today*. However, what was noticeably missing was any engagement with the state of knowledge about leadership. The report illustrated the mythological leadership studies narrative (see Figure 4.2) that troubled Rost and many other critical leadership scholars. In mitigation, the Chartered Management Institute (CMI) is never going to sponsor a report challenging the status quo of existing leadership and management knowledge given their involvement in qualifications, certification and development. Equally, the CMI, in avoiding questioning the state of leadership knowledge, is not alone. However, denial about the real state of leadership knowledge has been a recurring theme within this critical review. Drawing upon Luke'ss (2005:28) radical three views of power, his three-dimensional view of power is informative '. . . for consideration of the many ways in which potential issues are kept out of politics, whether through the operation of social forces and institutional practices or through individuals' decisions.' Orthodox leadership knowledge becomes self-sustaining with alternative/critical explanations marginalised; the powerful remain powerful and notions of participative change and collaboration with implications of power sharing are never explored. This is, once again, a case of '. . .the more things change, the more they remain the same' (Calas and Smircich, 1991:568).

In engaging with possibilities of leadership and the resulting implications for leadership and organizational change, this section is organized around Grint's social constructionist account of leadership, specifically the account within his book *Leadership: Limits and Possibilities* (Grint, 2005a). Against this backdrop, whilst not espousing radical structuralism favoured by Lukes, Grint for over a decade has highlighted the limitations of leadership studies and equally the possibilities of how leadership and studies of leadership might evolve. *Leadership: Limits and Possibilities* (Grint, 2005a) commences with an innocent-looking fourfold typology, quickly disrupting the apparent consensus around leadership studies and highlighting possibilities for advancement. Rost would appreciate such a conceptualisation, although he would be troubled by the ambiguities that would inevitably be raised.

The following discussion elaborates on this fourfold typology (Figure 4.7), relating it to leadership and organizational change, with the acknowledgement that Grint's interests are far broader than leadership and organizational change.

Is it WHO 'leaders' are that makes them leaders? Grint highlighted how influential the notions of individual leaders had been within organizations and societies. A consequence of this orthodoxy had been the downplaying of the role of collaborators: '[I]f leadership cannot be reduced to a naked and individual human then we should start to consider both the collective and the hybrid nature of leadership' (Grint, 2005a:62). The tendency to over-emphasise individuals appears to be magnified in the context of organizational change, stereotyped as strong leaders make tough decisions which will not be popular, but are essential to the survival of XYZ Corporation. Huczynski (2006:114) acknowledged that the 1980s were an era of interest in leadership in the context of major corporate transformations, citing Anderson et al's (1985) study of 18 companies in which the championing leader was regarded as the major success factor. Provocatively, Huczynski suggested that this emphasis on leaders was driven by a desire to raise the self-esteem of individual leaders who often felt frustrated and ineffectual. Narratives within hero-manager biographies (see Collins, 2000 for further discussion) and, more recently, UK television programmes such as *The Apprentice* and *Dragon's Den*, depict leaders as they would like to be

---

Person: Is it WHO 'leaders' are that makes them leaders?
Result: Is it WHAT 'leaders' achieve that makes them leaders?
Position: Is it WHERE 'leaders' operate that makes them leaders?
Process: Is it HOW 'leaders' get things done that makes them leaders?

Figure 4.7   Leadership fourfold typology (Grint, 2005a)

socially perceived—although this is a socially constructed reality. The influential mindset of the potent individual helps to explain terminology such as a 'turnaround manager' or 'transformation leader.' There is now an expectation that individual leaders will deliver the desired change/transformation in public, voluntary and private sector contexts and if they do not, they will be replaced with individuals who can. The concept of individualised leadership never fails: It is only the individual leader who fails. On UK television, Alan Sugar is now infamous for his vulgar catchphrase 'you're fired,' and another wannabe leader quickly replaces the person fired, perpetuating the potent individual leader myth.

> Leadership has been treated as one of the ways in which people come to understand the cause of important organizational events and outcomes. Leadership appears to have been sanctified and been given a key role in our phenomenal constructs of organized activities and their outcomes.
>
> (Huczynski, 2006:115)

In the context of leadership and organizational change, a leader is socially constructed as a means of enabling organizational change, whereas unexceptional employees are disparaged as either 'resisting change,' patronised as important human resources/assets or marginalised through indifference. In 2015, this seems irrational, given that employees are the largest constituency of any organization; such beliefs are maintained and reinforced through mainstream academic literature, business literature, leader biographies and the wider popular media.

Is it WHAT 'leaders' achieve that makes them leaders? Grint (2005a:68) highlighted that the emphasis on results (goal achievement, in Rost terminology) typifies mainstream accounts of leadership to such an extent that '. . .those that fail to instigate change that is required or fail to stop change that is not required, are simply failed leaders.' Again, we are offered a glimpse into why an association between leadership and organizational change has proved so appealing for so many commentators. However, elsewhere, Grint (2005a:66) warns '. . .how quickly we attribute cause and effects, often with little or no evidence to support our attributions.' The unifying mantra of the science fiction television series *The X-Files* was, 'I want to believe,' and wanting to believe in the attributions of leaders appears equally applicable to the current state of leadership studies knowledge. I do want to believe that if the UK National Health Service parachutes one of its new super-leaders into a failing hospital, that hospital will quickly be transformed into a successful hospital. Unfortunately, leadership attributions do not necessarily result in organizational achievements. Beyond success and failure, there is a shadowy side of such beliefs. If for a moment, we attribute leaders with the capability of independently achieving successful organizational change, what about those leadership processes employed? The hospital is now depicted as successful, but this may be through the manipulation of waiting lists, the repeated cancellation of appointments and the expensive stop-gap employment of temporary staff—is this hospital leader still successful?

Is it WHERE 'leaders' operate that makes them leaders? In this question, Grint is concerned with processes of leadership and how, through leadership viewed as a reflection of community, leaders learn to lead. In order to understand this radical conceptualisation of leadership, it is useful to understand its opposite. In the following quotation, Grint does not refer to Kotter (1996), but Kotter's eight leadership steps prescribed in order to achieve a successful transformation (see Chapter Two) illustrate such a mindset.

> Hence, leaders are people who construct and implement innovative solutions to organization problems on the part of their subordinates—and in turn the subordinates learn little from the process except that the responsibility for problem—solving lies with the leaders.
>
> (Grint, 2005a:105)

Kotter's (1996) powerful guiding coalition emphasises a sense of urgency, developing a vision and strategy and then communicating that vision. It is only at the fifth step that they empower broad-based action to implement the guiding coalition's vision on behalf of the guiding coalition.

The where 'leaders' operate mindset is underpinned by two previous elements of Grint's typology (Figure 4.7), a common emphasis upon individual leaders and an emphasis upon leaders achieving results. It is always going to be difficult to disrupt this persuasive narrative, which explains why, despite the leadership failings at the heart of the 2008 global financial recession, there has been a continued appetite for strong leadership in organizations and societies. Grint's concern is that whilst strong leadership appealed to leaders, it may be neither in the interests of a leader nor those they lead.

> . . .where the relationship between leaders and followers is asymmetrical in either direction: weak/irresponsible leaders or weak/irresponsible followers, then success for the organization is likely to be short-lived because feedback and learning is minimized.   ╲
>
> (Grint, 2005a:105)

This isn't radical, but it does feel countercultural within the UK, where we are still encouraged to defer to the will of strong leaders (it may well be that in Scandinavian countries or Japan there is greater collaboration, let's hope so).

> What might be better would be an atmosphere of much greater trust (probably built around the removal of any assessment early on) when poor leadership is seen to fail and poor leaders are helped to understand

why they fail and how they might succeed by those affected by leadership failure.

(Grint, 2005a:135)

Whereas Grint (2005a) is interested in leadership in general, these
debates again appear particularly pertinent to leadership and organizational
change. In the previous chapter, change agency was discussed and an ongoing debate relates to where change agency is located—are the senior leaders
the most appropriate change agents, or could change agency be dispersed
to middle managers? There is never going to be a satisfactory generalised
answer, but where leaders operate certainly speaks to this debate, although
the power implications of dispersed change agency suggest that progress
towards shared/distributed leadership is likely to be limited.

Process: Is it HOW 'leaders' get things done that makes them leaders?
Grint acknowledged that since the end of the twentieth century, there had
been a shift away from assumptions about individuals 'leading' towards
more collective alternatives. The earlier discussions in this section offered
support for this shift in assumptions, although there still appears to be a
considerable cultural appetite for strong, individual leaders. Grint has highlighted the possibilities of distributed leadership as an example of a collective alternative, regarding distributed leadership as both a method and a
philosophy.

The latter implies for its supporters that Distributed Leadership is necessarily preferable to traditional leadership because it embodies decen-
tralization, social responsibility and collective learning; it encourages
subordinates to learn to lead and facilitates the growth of social capital.

(Grint, 2005a:144)

However, Grint cautioned that as a philosophy, distributed leadership
may be used for progressive liberal purposes such as the achievement of civil
rights in the US, but equally for undemocratic and illiberal purposes, such
as terrorism. Using leadership and organizational change as an illustration,
distributed leadership may be used to involve employees participatively
within organizational change. However, distributed leadership may be used
negatively by employees blocking change or leaders seeking to scapegoat
employees.

Each element within Grint's fourfold typology (see Figure 4.7) offers
choices. In the context of this chapter, they have been used as a counterpoint to leadership studies orthodoxy, which limits choices, identifying
constructive ways to advance leadership studies. Each element is not politically neutral: They are driven and supported by values and philosophies. As
Grint (1997:22/23) highlighted in his earlier writing on leadership studies,
'. . .[W]hether acts taken by anyone are acts of 'leadership' or not, and so

on are issues that are contingent on the power of persuasive accounts and not contingent on objective or rational analysis.' Even the most radical critical account of leadership is, in essence, a socially constructed, persuasive account seeking to influence collaborators; academic rhetoric is just framed using more sophisticated language, theories, models and concepts.

COLLABORATIVE LEADERSHIP

> . . .[T]he proof of leadership is not the emergence of a big new idea or the development of a vision for sweeping change. Rather, it is the capacity to convince others to contribute to processes that turn ideas and visions into reality that help to bring about change.
>
> (Haslam et al, 2011: 2)

> Leaders purportedly climb to the top of the mountain, gaze to the horizon, see the future, and come back down and share their vision with the troops who cannot see past the foothills.
>
> (Abrahamson, 2004:210)

Burns (1978) gave impetus to transformational leadership, but his landmark book was just as much a plea for leadership scholars to engage with followers through the adoption of more egalitarian and democratic forms of leadership. Burns wrote the foreword for Rost's (1993) survey of leadership, in which again the need to engage with followers as part of leadership studies was encouraged. In Rost's (1993) definition, leadership was an influence relationship among leaders and followers intending real changes reflecting their mutual purposes. Rost was reacting to the individualistic accounts he repeatedly found within industrial leadership paradigm studies, not just paying lip service to liberal language. He believed that you could not have leadership without a mutual purpose, and that influence relationships were integral to real, intended changes. However, Rost, in his extensive literature reviewing, encountered within industrial-era leadership studies a very disparaging picture of followers (see Figure 4.8).

Rost believed that a differentiation between leaders and followers was crucial, and just as he wanted leadership to be precisely defined. He also

---

1) Part of the sweaty masses and therefore separated from the elites.

2) Not able to act intelligently without the guidance and control of others.

3) Willing to let other people (elites) take control of their lives.

4) Unproductive unless directed by others.

Figure 4.8 Subordination of followers within industrial-era leadership studies (based on Rost, 1993)

encouraged clarity with regards to the concept of followers and their influence relationships with leaders.

What is intriguing about Rost's radical conceptualisation of leader-follower influence relationships is that the leaders are stripped of their usual fixed power and authority in specific situations. Rost was no anarchist: He still favoured the typical power and authority as residing with a managerial role and as necessary within that role, but believed that it was of limited value within post-industrial leadership, which emphasised real, intended change that reflected mutual purposes. The strong/powerful leaders we are often presented with today are the antithesis of how Rost envisaged leadership. Grint (2010) asked, with irony, what about the followers? Whereas followers have been underrepresented within leadership literature and research (Baker, 2007; Kellerman, 2013), there has been an increasing acknowledgement that leadership cannot really be understood without understanding followers and their relations with leaders. However, conceptualisations such as the heroic leader and the mythological leadership narrative marginalise followers (see Figure 4.8). A greater focus upon followers (collaborators) would mean less focus upon leaders, which explains why attempts to understand followers are limited in comparison to attempts to understand leadership and why mythological leadership narratives endure.

The logic of Grint's fourfold typology featured in the previous section was greater engagement with theorising and the practices of followers within leadership studies. Work organizations have been defined as '. . . arrangements involving relationships, understandings and processes in which people are employed or their services otherwise engaged to complete tasks undertaken in the organization's name' (Watson, 2006:53). As work organizations involve people in relationships completing tasks, organizational change is fundamentally about those people who make up the organizations changing. The common reification of organizations as 'things' independent of people is not helpful. However, leadership rhetoric often implies otherwise, with the attitude, 'I am going to change the culture around here!' So in the context of leadership and organizational change, there is a need

---

1. Only people who are active in the leadership process are followers.
2. Active people can fall anywhere on a continuum of activity from highly active to minimally active.
3. Followers can become leaders and leaders can become followers in any one leadership relationship.
4. In one group or organization, people can be leaders. In other groups and organizations, they can be followers.
5. Fifth, and most important, followers do not do followership, they do leadership, and there is no such thing as followership in the new school of leadership.

Figure 4.9 The new leadership school view of followers (Rost, 1993 summarised)

to understand the interface between leaders and followers, both in terms of how leaders influence followers and how followers influence leaders. Grint revisited the etymological origins of both management and leadership, although there is a need for caution, as different commentators favour different etymological explanations (see, for example, Rost, 1993). Grint's derivation is informative.

> If the English word 'management' derives from the Latin manus, the hand that controls, and 'leadership' from the Old German leader, to guide, to show the way, then the more leaders shift back into controlling the more likely followers are to resist.
>
> (Grint, 2005a:105)

In these etymological explanations, there appears to be support for leaders facilitating greater engagement of followers. However, equally, management in general and management control in particular are still necessary. The implication in the etymological explanation is that a controlling leader might not achieve the goals that they anticipate. Although the previous section critiqued the development of leadership studies, the cache of earlier progressive and linear accounts of leadership still remains with this orthodoxy, limiting and impeding development. As an alternative to the usual textbook treatment of leadership studies, Haslam et al's (2011:2) account of the old psychology of leadership looks back without the usual nostalgia, simultaneously critiquing earlier accounts and offering ways forward. They '. . .argue for a new psychology that sees leadership as the product of an individual's "we-ness", rather than his or her "I-ness." ' However, there are challenges in beginning such engagement. Grint (2005a:20) warned that 'negotiated' or 'distributed' or 'deep' leadership is often overlooked precisely because it remains informal and distributed amongst the collective, rather than emanating from a formal and individual leader.

Equally, understanding has been impeded by the semantics of followers and followership. Rost (1993) became disillusioned with the pejorative language of followership, which he believed connoted subordination, submissiveness, and passivity and, in the context of organizational change follower and followership terminology, may imply the problematic and naïve belief that everyone is willingly following the leader and embracing their favoured organizational change. One explanation offered for the lack of engagement with followership by leadership scholars is that for some, the term followership is not egalitarian enough, but for Rost, the problem was not with the word, but with the passive meaning attached to it.

In the post-industrial era that interested Rost, he did not regard followers and leaders as equal, but he did believe that the distinction between leaders and followers was crucial in advancing leadership.

In a manner similar to how inappropriate labels such as 'resistance to change' misrepresent the responses of individuals, groups and teams to organizational change (see Hughes, 2010), the well-intentioned references to followers and followership may do more harm than good. Once again, Rost's view is insightful.

> I tried to redeem the word *followers* in my book by reconstructing it with new meaning. But it didn't work. Everywhere I went to give seminars or speeches, the people attending them told me that *following* was essentially a passive concept and the word followers was not redeemable.
>
> (Rost, 1997:11)

Rost (1997) subsequently favoured collaborators, as he believed the denotation and connotation of the word fitted post-industrial values best. In the remaining sections and chapters, the term collaborator will be used instead of follower, except where a cited author is explicitly referring to followers. It is acknowledged that follower and followership are more easily understood, for reasons as discussed within the discourse, social construction and framing discussions. The word follower is more than a mere word: It has served an important limiting role within leadership studies to date.

THE FALL OF CHANGE MANAGEMENT AND THE RISE OF CHANGE LEADERSHIP

In this chapter and earlier chapters, a shift from change management towards change leadership has been acknowledged. This shift has now become leadership orthodoxy, with change leadership differentiated from change management and presented as superior (see Barker, 1997, although Barker appears to have been reporting upon the discourse he was encountering in his leadership studies). This privileging raises questions for this critical review with regards to the cultural aspects of this shift, the perceived deficiencies of change management and the historic publication milestones informing a shift towards change leadership. Consequently, in this section, three questions are addressed:

> What were the cultural aspects of the shift from change management to change leadership?
> What were the perceived deficiencies within change management that resulted in its decline?
> What has been the historical path of the rise of change leadership?

What were the cultural aspects of the shift from change management to change leadership? The cultural shift may be explained in terms of American national culture encouraging an emphasis on leadership and, secondly, on managers and leaders as significant cultural symbols within organizations ascribing meaning to organizational events. The American Dream contains powerful themes, '. . .but at its heart lies a view of America as the land of opportunity in which any individual, through hard work and self-improvement, can be a success' (Guest, 1990:390). Guest (1990) viewed the earliest articulation of the American Dream as the New Deal of the 1930s; the American Dream was not evident in the seventies, but re-emerged in the eighties under the political leadership of Ronald Reagan and notions of a Wild West frontier mentality. Guest (1990) cited Child (1969) when he referred to ideology justifying management roles and pre-scribing behaviour: Strong, individualised and anti-bureaucratic leadership was a manifestation of the ideology of the American Dream. Guest (1990) highlighted how human resource management fitted the American Dream, particularly in terms of leadership:

> A reinforcement of the importance of strong leadership, a kind of rug-ged entrepreneurial individualism reflected in and reinforced by a strong organizational culture.
>
> (Guest, 1990:391)

> A third feature of the American Dream is a belief that individualism and opportunity can be both reflected in industrial leadership and facilitated by enlightened leadership. . .These too are rugged individuals facing fearsome competitive odds but winning out through hard work and by seizing available opportunities.
>
> (Guest, 1990:392)

Another cultural explanation for the shift from change management to change leadership relates to the cultural meaning ascribed to the labels manager and leader. Central organizational roles such as leader and man-ager '. . .represent wishes and fears shared by organizational collectives; they are symbols which help to ascribe meaning to organizational events' (Czarniawska-Joerges and Wolff, 1991:530). In this way, the emphasis is shifted away from organizational requirements towards their cultural and symbolic significance, with an oscillation between leadership and manage-ment likely to occur over time. The political unrest of the sixties meant that in the seventies, managers introducing order and rationality were favoured and symbolized a return to stability. In the seventies, interest in leadership was in decline, as Harvard graduates saw the dark face of power behind the title of leader (Czarniawska-Joerges and Wolff, 1991). The authority figure of the unpretentious manager was in vogue. This was reversed in the neo-conservative eighties (Czarniawska-Joerges and Wolff, 1991). In terms of this critical review, the important insight is that 'the fashion of the day elevates one role above the other and then abandons it again. Now we need order, next we need change, and then we need to con-trol our fate' (Czarniawska-Joerges and Wolff, 1991:541). The role of the leader is symbolic in representing the personal causation of social events, attributing causality and confirming the feasibility of controlling events (Czarniawska-Joerges and Wolff, 1991).

What were the perceived deficiencies within change management that resulted in its decline? Practitioner-orientated organizational change literature encourages the belief in a 'burning platform' (Conner, 1998) and/or 'a sense of urgency' (Kotter, 1996) as catalysts for organizational change. So if this is the case, what were the catalysts, beyond the cultural drivers discussed in the previous section, for doubting the efficacy of change management? Two potential explanations may be offered. Firstly, management is associated with stability and leadership, with change a cultural norm, which is very evident within the following quotation: '[T]he function of leadership is to create change while the function of management is to create stability' (Barker, 1997:349). This dichotomy, which has proved popular and persuasive, remains problematic.

Kotter (1990), often regarded as a proponent of leadership over management, argued for a balance between leadership and management, noting that strong leadership without the counterbalance of management would be damaging for organizations. He wrote that 'transformation is not a process involving leadership alone; good management is also essential'(Kotter, 1996:129). Unfortunately and erroneously, the association between management and stability and leadership and change have stuck '. . .leaders 'make change happen' is a belief core to many assumptions about how organizational change works'(Ladkin et al, 2010:127).

Secondly, powerful discourses emerged suggesting that change management wasn't working, often couched in terms of change failure (Beer and Nohria, 2000; Kotter, 1995) and even the death of change (see Blanchard et al, 2009; Hughes forthcoming). Harvard Business School professors claimed that transformation efforts were failing (Kotter, 1995), asserting that 'the brutal fact is that about 70% of all change initiatives fail' (Beer and Nohria, 2000:133). Hughes (2011) questioned what was being reported and the way the available evidence was being misrepresented, but once influential Harvard Business School professors associated change management with failure, a very persuasive norm had been established. However, in revisiting these influential organizational change studies (Beer and Nohria, 2000; Kotter, 1995), change management was far more subtly being depicted as not working than the headline titles of these papers.

In Kotter's (1995) infamous critique, the role focus was on managers rather than leaders, despite the title of the paper referring to leading change. For example, 'a paralyzed senior management often comes from having too many managers and not enough leaders' (Kotter, 1995:60), '. . .management had a sense of direction, but it was too complicated or blurry to be useful' (Kotter, 1995:63), '. . .tedious quarterly management meetings. . .' (Kotter, 1995: 64) and 'a 60-year-old plant manager who has spent precious little time over 40 years thinking about customers'(Kotter, 1995:64).

The crisis of confidence in change management that was rhetorically constructed may have mirrored or been encouraged by cultural shifts away from management towards leadership (Czarniawska-Joerges and Wolff, 1991; Guest, 1990). In Beer and Nohria's (2000:133) *Harvard Business Review* article, again there was a subtle critique of managers and management embedded within their narrative. For example, '. . .few companies manage the process as well as they would like' (Beer and Nohria, 2000:133), '. . .managers end up immersing themselves in an alphabet soup of initiatives' (Beer and Nohria, 2000:133) and '. . .too often, managers try to apply theories E and O in tandem without resolving the inherent tensions between them' (Beer and Nohria, 2000:134). However, tellingly, Beer and Nohria (2000:133) referred to the role of leaders as the solution, writing that 'leaders need to crack the code of change' that would deliver successful organizational change. Alvesson and Sveningsson (2003:1435), in their account of the extra-ordinisation of leadership, highlighted depictions of leadership as '. . .very significant and something quite special.' Change leadership became significant and special, because, as much as anything, it was not change management.

What has been the historical path of the rise of change leadership? In Chapter Three, historiography was discussed, with reference to how the histories of organizational change are written and similar historiographical processes are at work with regards to the histories of leadership and management differentiations. In the following discussion, the most commonly cited publications differentiating managers and leaders are revisited. This discussion commences with one of the earliest accounts of leadership in an organizational setting (Selznick, 1957), as well as the frequently cited accounts of Zaleznik (1977) and Kotter (1988, 1990, 1995, 1996), differentiating management and leadership.

Leadership in Administration (Selznick, 1957) departed from the earlier classical studies of organization that emphasised management, administration and bureaucracy, instead differentiating organizations from institutions and administration from leadership, rather than today's preoccupation with differentiating management from leadership. As Perrow (1978) noted, Selznick's book was written for businesspeople as much as anyone. Selznick drew upon his earlier works *TVA and the Grass Roots* (1949) and *The Organizational Weapon* (1952), dealing with an innovative government agency and Marxist–Leninist ideology, respectively. His thesis was concisely stated early on: '[T]he executive becomes a statesman as he makes the transition from administrative management to institutional leadership' (Selznick, 1957:4). Selznick believed that large organizations had the potential to develop into institutions, with the institution leader acting as '. . .primarily an expert in the promotion and protection of values' (Selznick, 1957:28). In the final section of his book, within a concluding chapter entitled 'Creative Leadership,' Selznick (1957:151) wrote,

One of the most important of these techniques is the elaboration of socially integrating myths. These are efforts to state, in the language of uplift and idealism, what is distinctive about the aims and methods of the enterprise. . .

Selznick (1957) predated social constructionism (Berger and Luckmann, 1966) and pre-empted later interest in discourse accounts of leadership (Fairhurst and Grant, 2010). He gave impetus to the strategic leadership/ design school, developed and encouraged by Harvard Business School, although Harvard did not accord attention to the ethics and values that Selznick had originally emphasised (Grieves, 2010). Rost (1993) regarded Selznick's (1957) influence as being largely ignored by mainstream management writers.

Managers and Leaders: Are they Different? (Zaleznik, 1977) published in the practitioner magazine *Harvard Business Review* really fuelled the debate. Zaleznik answered his own question, differentiating leaders and managers in terms of their personalities and other traits, with his thesis subsequently developed into a book (Zaleznik, 1989). Rost (1993:74) regarded Zaleznik's (1989) subsequent book as symptomatic of the business and management-orientated leadership books of the 1980s in that '. . .it was filled with hundreds of paragraphs reflecting the view that leadership is doing what the leader wishes.' This insight highlights the potential darker side of the leadership and management differentiation, with the leadership imperative replacing the dated managerial prerogative with a new stronger and more rhetorical version (see O'Reilly and Reed, 2010). The dualism that began to be encouraged between leaders and managers is captured in this early exposition.

Leaders work from high-risk positions, indeed often are temperamentally disposed to seek out risk and danger, especially where opportunity and reward appear high. . .Managers prefer to work with people; they avoid solitary activity because it makes them anxious.

(Zaleznik, 1977:72)

Generalising leaders as seeking out 'risk and danger' and managers as becoming 'anxious' when left alone is amusing as well as stereotypical. What is more troubling is how frequently this silly magazine article is cited as evidence of leader/manager differentiations. It was the title that parroted the spirit of the times. Zaleznik cited the American billionaire J.D. Rockefeller in support of his differentiation. Rockefeller (1973) perceived organizations as impeded by the weight of tradition and inertia, with the deck stacked in favour of tried and proven ways of doing things, working against taking risks and striking out in new directions. Zaleznik (1977:68) differentiated managers from leaders for not being heroic, writing that 'it takes neither genius nor heroism to be a manager, but rather persistence, tough-mindedness, hard work, intelligence, analytical ability and, perhaps most important, tolerance and goodwill' (earlier discussions about the American Dream are very pertinent here). Leaders and managers were differentiated in terms of their orientations towards their goals, their work, their human relations and their selves. Zaleznik (1977:78) concluded his article thoughtfully with regards to the need for leaders to be open to being challenged: 'I am constantly surprised at the frequency with which chief executives feel threatened by open challenges to their ideas, as though the source of their authority, rather than their specific ideas, were at issue.' It is informative that both practitioners and academics enthusiastically adopted Zaleznik's (1977) leader/manager differentiation, yet neglected Zaleznik's encouragement for leaders to engage in a dialogue with subordinates and be open to challenge.

Kotter (1988, 1990, 1995, 1996) was the most influential contributor to the debates differentiating leaders and managers. It was *The Leadership Factor* (1988*)* and *A Force for Change: How Leadership Differs from Management* (1990) that generically emphasised the differences between leadership and management, with *Leading Change* (Kotter, 1996) subsequently emphasising change leadership. In *The Leadership Factor* (1988:20), management was defined simplistically as comprised of the processes of planning, budgeting, organizing and controlling. Whereas requirements for effective leadership in senior management jobs in complex business settings were identified as industry and organizational knowledge, relationships in the firm and industry, reputation and track record, abilities and skills, personal values and motivation (Kotter, 1988). In the opening statement of the book, Kotter cited American billionaire H. Ross Perot:

> Mr. Perot is also a man of strong convictions. Central among them is a belief that effective leadership is an enormously important factor in the world today, and yet a factor that is all too often missing. Commenting on the U.S. economic situation recently, he framed that conviction in the following way: "Our country cries out for leadership at the business level and the political level. Lack of leadership is the biggest problem we have in making this nation competitive."
>
> (Kotter, 1988:1)

Again, management was the problem responsible for America's malaise, and leadership was now the favoured solution. The scale of the problem gave legitimacy to the actions of strong/heroic leadership, and the leaders were perceived as acting for the greater good of America. *The Leadership Factor* benefitted from Kotter's extensive research with senior executives, with named leaders and named case study organizations. However, the book's deficiencies do require acknowledgement given its centrality to leader/management differentiations and this book still being cited in support of such differentiations.

> As research, the book falls short because terms are not defined or operationalized and self-reports are limited to senior executives. Since research is not Kotter's main concern, the research weaknesses are not critical to the importance of the book, although managers and management students reading it should be aware that the empirical evidence does not necessarily support Kotter's position.
>
> (Tucker, 1989:301)

It is troubling how much management and leadership writing rests upon Kotter's shaky self-referential reasoning. *The Leadership Factor* (Kotter, 1988) was really an aperitif for Kotter's (1990) main dish, *A Force for Change: How Leadership Differs from Management*. Early on, Kotter writes, '[T]hroughout the ages, individuals who have been seen as leaders have created change, sometimes for the better and sometimes not' (Kotter, 1990:4). Perversely, Kotter (1990:xi) recommended a reader '. . .who prefers seeing detailed conclusions. . .' read the postscript, although the postscript contained only boxed summaries of each chapter. In this book, Kotter references other leadership studies, describing the book in the preface as part of a research programme going back to his doctoral studies and with supporting references to earlier research projects. He cites named case studies throughout the book. In leadership studies, this was a milestone study and is still heavily cited to this day. However, in going back to the original source, and in fairness to Kotter's (1990:ix) original words, he never denigrated management as being inferior to leadership:

a) Leadership and management are both very important processes, and the notion that leadership is "good" and "management" is bad is most certainly wrong,

b) Despite differences that can create conflict, the two processes can work together very successfully, and furthermore, some people can be very effective leaders and managers,

c) For a variety of reasons, many firms today lack sufficient leadership, a deficiency that is increasingly costly, yet often correctable.

Corporate America and subsequently, Western economies, including public services, appear to have believed that the economic malaise of the eighties and nineties was a consequence of insufficient leadership. They may have lost sight of the importance of management. In this cultural shift, management came to be denigrated, but as Kotter observed, this idea was most certainly wrong. Leadership as a socially integrating myth (Selznick, 1957) was at work, although now unencumbered by the institutional leader's primary responsibility to promote and protect values. *Leading Change: Why Transformation Efforts Fail* (Kotter, 1995) restated that American corporate transformations were failing due to a lack of appropriate leadership, a view publically and explicitly encouraged by American billionaires J.D. Rockefeller and Ross Perot. Leadership was subsequently offered as a solution within *Leading Change* (Kotter, 1996), through taking eight steps towards a successful transformation.

When Spector (2014) revisited Lee Iacocca as the personification and embodiment of transformational leadership, he offered an intriguing historical perspective on the leadership and management differentiations discussed in this section. Spector acknowledged how difficult the seventies were for America, with a lack of leadership believed to be behind this malaise. As Spector (2014:364) observed, referring back to Zaleznik's (1977) article, '. . .[A] new hypothesis had emerged: American industry was suffering from an overabundance of managers and a paucity of leaders.' Spector acknowledged that the mandate to develop more leaders and fewer managers was picked up and popularised through Kotter's (1988, 1990) writings.

In this critical review, *Transformational Leadership* (Bass and Riggio, 2006) and Kotter's (1996) *Leading Change* have advanced independently of each other. However, Diaz-Saenz (2011:300) in his review of transformational leadership made an insightful contribution that is pertinent to the debates featured in this section.

> . . .The distinction that is drawn between transactional leadership and transformational leadership, as well the crucial role that transformational leadership plays in generating optimal performance, parallels the widely discussed distinction that has been drawn between management and leadership, most notably by Zaleznik in 1977 and Kotter in 1990.

Parallels between transactional/transformational leadership and management and leadership suggest that these debates may have been motivated by similar concerns, with Diaz-Saenz (2011:299) attributing the popularity of transformational leadership as follows:

> In accounting for its phenomenal popularity, Jay Conger (1999) pointed to the desperate desire on the part of American businesses to develop a heroic response to the threat of international competition during the 1980s and the need to foster empowerment in the context of organizational restructuring and an increasingly demanding educated work force.

This insight tends to echo earlier perceptions that increasing emphasis upon leader/manager differentiations was a solution to a perceived problem, rather than an outcome of social science inquiry. Two conclusions may be drawn from these discussions about a perceived shift from change management toward change leadership. Firstly, the shift has been cultural and socially constructed, rather than empirically informed. The shift, with its major proponents based in America, can be explained in terms of the American Dream (Guest, 1990) and oscillations between management and leadership (Czarniawska-Joerges and Wolff, 1991). History is written, and in revisiting the historical milestones informing the differentiations between management and leadership, despite Selznick (1957), Zaleznik (1977) and Kotter (1988, 1990) often being cited in support of such a differentiation between leaders and managers, each was primarily expressing an informed opinion, rather than reporting convincing empirical evidence.

Secondly, a (re)union of change management and change leadership would be theoretically and practically beneficial. 'Either/or' change management and change leadership thinking may be less useful to theory and practice than 'both/and' thinking, as highlighted in Chapter Three. A polarised shift from change management to change leadership has deliberately been featured, with management associated with stability and inertia and leadership associated with change (Barker, 1997). However, this dualistic 'either/or' thinking may mask the subtleties of what is happening and what needs to happen (Sutherland and Smith, 2013). Leaders have to deal with continuities and stability as well as change, with the popular dualisms of change or stability, leader or manager misrepresenting what is happening as false—although popular—rhetorical dichotomies.

LEADERSHIP STUDIES—OUT OF THE DARK AND INTO THE LIGHT

In reflecting upon his own extensive critical review of leadership studies, Rost (1993) highlighted how selective management academics had been in their reading of leadership literature, a criticism equally applicable to this chapter. What concerned Rost was the existence of a mythological leadership narrative (Figure 4.2) that constructed leadership studies as progressing through research and scholarship with this increasingly sophisticated understanding of leadership making organizations, the US and the world ultimately more productive. This narrative served what Rost referred to as the industrial paradigm, but he believed it would be inappropriate for the post-industrial paradigm of the 21st century. Now, looking back on the mythological leadership narrative, similarities with other critical scholars are evident. Gemmill and Oakley (1992) depicted leadership as an alienating social myth that limited alternative conceptualisations of leadership and reinforced existing social beliefs and structures.

Leadership becomes a little less mythological when its social construction is highlighted; we appreciate that heroic leaders responding to difficult environments may be responding to an environment they constructed themselves (Grint, 2005b). However, there is a need to be mindful that academics are equally engaged in social constructions of leadership (Bresnen, 1995). Leadership language and discourses structure our thinking in a manner similar to how a picture is framed: Leaders frame challenges for collaborators, and competing academic accounts frame leaders in both positive and negative ways. In this chapter, the intention was to revisit Rost's (1993) pioneering critique of leadership studies and highlight its compatibility with other critical and alternative conceptualisations of leadership studies. Understanding leadership and organizational change to date has largely been informed by practitioners (Parry, 2011). In beginning to further our understanding, we need to go beyond the orthodoxy of mainstream leadership studies, which will be the focus of the next chapter.

In reviewing this literature, what became apparent when considering leadership as a mythological narrative/alienating social myth was that these mythologies, as well as framing understanding limit alternative conceptualisations of leadership. So, this chapter concludes by revisiting the industrial leadership paradigm as characterised by Rost (1993) (see Figure 4.1) and Rost's hopes for a new school of leadership as well as more recent critical leadership writing in order to begin to reconceptualise leadership studies. This is in the hope that the darkness of the earlier critical discussions may be tempered with the light of how leadership might be represented and practised.

In Figure 4.10, Rost's original characteristics of industrial-era leadership studies are restated and adapted to allow the development of a three-column matrix.

Leadership Studies	Orthodoxy	Alternatives
View of Organization	Structural-functional	Radical Humanism
Preeminent Profession	Management	Political Science
Leadership Objective	Goal Achievement	Morally Uplifting
Leadership Focus/Outlook	Personalistic, Self-Interested/ Individualistic	Shared and Distributed Collaboration
Model of Life	Male	Female
Ethical Perspective	Utilitarian and Materialistic	Post-Industrial Paradigm Ethics
Rationality	Rational	Irrational
Linearity	Linear	Non Linear
Scientific Exemplar	Natural Science (Objective)	Social Science (Subjective)
Research Method	Quantitative	Qualitative (or combination)

Figure 4.10 Leadership studies—orthodoxy and alternatives (developed from Rost, 1993)

The first column (Figure 4.10) lists characteristics of leadership studies as identified by Rost (1993), and the second column reflects the orthodoxy of the industrial-era leadership studies that Rost (1993) encountered. The third column is illustrative of potential alternatives, rather than being comprehensive with regards to the many competing alternatives to leadership orthodoxy that now exist. In his concluding chapter, Rost (1993:183) wrote, '[L] eadership scholars in the future are going to have to think new thoughts about leadership, using post-industrial assumptions about human beings, organizations, societies and the planet earth.' In the following discussion, potential new (and not so new) thoughts about leadership feature.

The structural-functional view of an organization that Rost (1993) highlighted (see Figure 4.1) also underpins many of the other characteristics. Selznick (1957), cited earlier, was influential in merging sociological and managerial thinking, moving away from an earlier focus on bureaucracy towards a language of organizations and notions of the formal organization. Whereas many philosophies and paradigms of organizational analysis have subsequently been ventured, structural-functionalism remains very prevalent. As an alternative philosophical position, radical humanism underpins many of the social constructionist accounts of leadership cited earlier. Instead of the functionality, regulation and status quo of structural-functionalism, a radical humanist view highlights the inequalities that the status quo seeks to disguise, offering alternative and more radical purposes for leadership.

Rost's annoyance with management being the preeminent profession within leadership studies may partially have reflected his own academic background in education. He was aware of and even prescribed the need for different academic disciplines to inform our understanding of leadership. However, in reviewing the literature, he found 'that they leave out the stories of leadership theory from other academic disciplines. . .' (Rost, 1993:23). Political science is a good example of an academic discipline with the potential to enrich our understanding of leadership. More generally, interdisciplinary leadership studies enable the complexities of leadership to be understood through multiple lenses. However, unfortunately, management perspectives on leadership have a tendency to be very selective in what they take from other disciplines. The treatment of Selznick (1957) and Burns (1978) illustrates this view. Selznick, as a professor of sociology with interests in participation, regarded leaders as primarily experts in the promotion and protection of values, yet this emphasis was lost in the translation into management and organization studies leadership narratives. Similarly, Burns (1978) was a political scientist frequently commended for his differentiation between transformational and transactional leadership, with the significant intent behind this differentiation being the moral and egalitarian transformation of institutions and societies. However, Rost (1993:31) cited Avolio and Bass (1988), amongst others, as expanding Burns's (1978) concept of transformation '. . .to include any kind of significant change, not just changes that had a morally uplifting effect on people.' Management scholars favouring a structural-functional view of organizations will inevitably explain leadership in terms of goal achievement and this becomes magnified when the goal is changing organizations. However, leadership could have many other objectives, rather than the narrow and instrumental achievement of goals. As Selznick believed, leaders could be experts in the promotion and protection of values, or as Burns passionately argued, transformational leaders could transform institutions and societies so that they became morally uplifting.

Today's pejorative label 'heroic leader' has a much longer lineage, with such conceptualisations relating back to the 'Great Men' theories of leadership and more general accounts from history in which personal and individualistic accounts of a leader's achievements are celebrated. Both Zaleznik (1977) and Gemmill and Oakley (1992) related this yearning for leaders as heroic individuals to early parenting, and whatever the explanation, it has proved a popular and long-lasting conceptualisation of leaders. However, the downside of personalistic/individualistic accounts of leadership has been the discouragement of engagement with collaborators and shared and distributed leadership. The downside of celebrating the potency of individuals is that we lose sight of the potential of collective agency within organizations.

In reviewing leadership literature, Rost (1993) found a preponderance of male writers writing about male leaders; his concern was that women were being enculturated into a male model of leadership. Sinclair (2007) more recently appeared to share similar concerns when observing a leadership development programme for senior Australian managers, a group of which a good third were women. She tells the story of a master leadership teacher from a prestigious business school's contribution being based on cases of great men doing great deeds against enormous odds.

> Yet, in all the sessions, I couldn't recall a single woman leader being offered as an example in the discussions. The model of leadership with which the group was presented was both masculine and firmly heroic. Nobody seemed to notice this, let alone draw attention to it.
>
> (Sinclair, 2007:13)

Sinclair subsequently admits that it wasn't only the absence of women in these heroic stories, but the way leadership was being constructed and modelled by the leadership teacher that disturbed her. The shortcoming identified by Rost and Sinclair is not unique to leadership studies: Organizational scholarship has been criticised for being primarily a literature written by men, for men, and about men (Calas and Smircich, 1996). However, within leadership studies, a more particular seduction takes place: '. . . [L]eadership is seduction not by what it says but by what it does not say, or by the undecidability of what it may be saying. Once we make it openly sexualized, it loses its (sex) appeal as 'knowledge'' (Calas and Smircich, 1991:570). A recurrent theme of this chapter has been leadership talking the talk of change whilst simultaneously impeding change in the status quo.

In our analyses of organizational writings, we show how each text appears to promote change from prior works regarding what should be considered 'leadership' but each, at the same time, maintains a specific set of practices and discourses in place—the basic power relations network on which 'leadership' has been constituted and re-constituted.

(Calas and Smircich, 1991:569)

This insight helps to explain what was frustrating Rost and why he was no longer convinced about the rational and linear evolution of leadership studies, with Rost disparagingly referring to the mythological leadership narrative. He wanted a paradigm shift from what he called industrial-era leadership to post-industrial leadership studies, because only such a shift would result in a fundamental shift in how leadership was constituted.

Rost (1993) criticised Zaleznik's (1977, 1987) promotion of a view at this time of do what the leader wishes. Yet, Zaleznik (1977:78) claimed to be constantly surprised '. . .at the frequency with which chief executives feel threatened by open challenges to their ideas.' Industrial-era literature tended to depict leadership as rational and linear; again, this is a consequence of favouring a structural-functional view. If a leader does X, then Y will happen. In Chapter Two, Kotter's (1996) eight steps for leading change were featured. The implication and prescription within Kotter's account of leadership was that if you followed the eight steps in the order prescribed, your transformation would be successful. This type of change recipe is rational and linear in a manner similar to the recipe used to bake a cake. Whereas recipes are very useful, the dilemma relates to the application of rationality and linearity to all organizations and all diverse forms of organizational life. At the time of writing, no universal cake-baking recipe exists.

Industrial-era leadership studies have been characterised as utilitarian and materialistic (Rost, 1993). Materialistic speaks for itself, but Rost's perception of utilitarian ethics merits further elaboration. Rost (1993:168) acerbically paraphrased utilitarian ethics as 'judgements are made by a cost-benefit analysis of the probable effects of the proposed change on the people in the organization and society.' Rost wanted post-industrial leadership to move beyond utilitarian ethics, believing that utilitarian ethics suffered from four problems. Firstly, that cost-benefit evaluation will be most effective when undertaken retrospectively, whereas utilitarian ethics require gauging the consequences before leaders act. Secondly, effectively undertaking the quantitative and qualitative evaluation of the good and harm for a large number of people arising out of a leader's actions is problematic. Thirdly, it is impractical to evaluate good and harm for every stakeholder in a change, so choices and estimates have to be made. Fourthly, 'cost-benefit estimations of the ethical consequences that proposed changes will have on organizations and societies do not necessarily add up to a judgment based on the common good or on the public interest' (Rost, 1993:169).

In 1995, *Business Ethics Quarterly* devoted a special issue to leadership and ethics. Whereas a great deal has been written since then, what is interesting is that Rost (1995) contributed and Ciulla (1995), who had read *Leadership for the Twenty-First Century*, also contributed. Rost (1995) commences by highlighting the problems he perceived with the ethics of leadership, relating this to his leadership definition 'fetish' and to ethical concepts being more suited to explaining individuals rather than large organizations and governments, and the existence of plenty of literature about ethics or leadership, but the limited literature combining these fields. In what follows, Rost's communitarian beliefs become far more apparent than within his earlier book.

> The classical liberal philosophy, with its emphasis on rights, rules, individualism, positivism, scientism, competition and utility, may have served us well for 200 plus years, but increasingly it has become part of the problem rather than part of the solution. . .The liberal philosophy has bred a society that feeds on materialism and individualism and eschews spirituality and the common good.
>
> (Rost, 1995:138)

This was Rost's (1995) bleak diagnosis of the leadership problem, and his conclusion was even more nihilistic.

> It became very clear to me that the industrial theories of ethics (relativism, rule, social contract, utilitarianism and an updated version of virtue ethics) were of little use to leaders and collaborators intent on pursuing substantive and mutually agreed—upon changes in their organizations and communities. . .Our organizations and communities need a way out of the materialistic, individualistic, self-interested, short-term, pragmatic, cost-benefit driven, male-dominated, rational, management-oriented culture that is the primary cause of our present malaise.
>
> (Rost, 1995:141)

Rost's writings certainly provoke and they have been cited here as much as anything in order to disrupt the orthodoxy, in the belief that critical thinking will advance understanding. In Figure 4.10, the post-industrial paradigm ethics simply suggest the need for something else, and that something else still has to be confirmed. The downside of Rost's writings is that they are black and white: For somebody who believed passionately in relational theories of leadership and mutual purposes, in a few lines, he dismisses the whole field of ethics. Many of Rost's concerns about the ethics of leadership have been addressed and are being addressed (see, for example, By and Burnes, 2013). However, it is informative to read Ciulla's (1995) contribution to the same special issue as Rost. Whilst admiring Rost's contribution to leadership studies, Ciulla criticises and disagrees with Rost's provocative position on the state of ethics.

> The ultimate question is not "What is leadership?" but "What is good leadership?" The word good refers to both ethics and competence.
>
> (Ciulla, 1995:5)

Ciulla (1995) criticised Rost's (1993) treatment of ethics as informed by his limited and selective reading of the literature. In the leadership literature Rost (1993) reviewed, he encountered a predisposition towards scientific, quantitative research. This may be explained in terms of the preferences of American scholars at this time to advance management as a science and the prominence of psychology-based explanations of leadership (see Fairhurst, 2008). The field may be characterised as suffering from physics envy: If studies of leadership could employ similar objective and quantitative research methods as the natural sciences, the field would be more respected and more influential. There is real merit in objective and quantitative studies of leadership; however, once again, the orthodoxy limits other more qualitative and subjective approaches to leadership. The ideal is leadership studies informed by a combination of qualitative and quantitative research (Bryman, 1988), as all research designs have different strengths and weaknesses.

This chapter commenced with Rost's (1993) plea for the development of leadership studies through a large dose of critical thought and methodology. Rost (1993) would have probably been annoyed with the postmodern turn within critical leadership studies featured within this chapter. Rost favoured precise definitions and strongly opposed notions of leadership as something ambiguous/contradictory. However, the common ground is seeking to advance understanding of leadership studies through challenging leadership studies orthodoxy. Even if the eventual outcome is the realisation that leadership is really a socially constructed myth, that has to be better than propping up a spurious orthodoxy serving very narrow, sectional interests and perpetuating existing societal and workplace inequalities. In the next chapter, this critical account of leadership studies is drawn upon in combination with the critical account of organizational change featured in the previous chapter in order to evaluate the leadership and organizational change literature featured in Chapter Two.

REFERENCES

Abrahamson, E. 2004. *Change Without Pain: How Managers Overcome Initiative Overload, Organizational Chaos, and Employee Burnout.* Boston: Harvard Business School Press.
Alvesson, M., and A. Spicer, eds. 2011. *Metaphors We Lead by: Understanding Leadership in the Real World.* London: Routledge.

Alvesson, M., and S. Sveningsson. 2003. "Managers doing Leadership: The Extra-Ordinization of the Mundane". *Human Relations* 56 (12):1435–1459.

Alvesson, M., and Y.D. Billing. 2009. *Understanding Gender and Organizations*. London: Sage Publications Ltd.

Anderson, D.G., J.R. Phillips and N. Kaiable.1985. *Revitalising Large Companies*. *Working Paper*, Cambridge (MA): MIT Press.

Avolio, B.J., and B.M. Bass. 1988. "Transformational Leadership, Charisma and Beyond". In *Emerging Leadership Vistas*, eds. J.G. Hunt., B.R. Baliga, H.P. Dachler and C.A. Schriesheim, 29–49. Lexington MA: Lexington Books.

Baker, S.D. 2007. "Followership: The Theoretical Foundation of a Contemporary Construct". In *Discovering Leadership*, ed. J. Billsberry, 139–156. Houndmills: Palgrave Macmillan in association with OU.

Barker, R. 1997. "How Can We Train Leaders If We Don't Know What Leadership Is?" *Human Relations* 50 (4): 343–362.

Bass, B.M. 1981. *Stogdill's Handbook of Leadership*, rev. ed. New York: The Free Press.

Bass, B.M. 1985. *Leadership and Performance Beyond Expectations*. New York: Free Press.

Bass, B.M., and R.E. Riggio. 2006. *Transformational Leadership*, 2nd edition. Mahwah, NJ: Lawrence Erlbaum Associates Inc/Psychology Press.

Bateson, G. 1955/1972. *Steps to an Ecology of the Mind*. New York: Ballatine.

Beer, M., and N. Nohria. 2000. Cracking the Code of Change. *Harvard Business Review* 78 (3): 133–141.

Berger, P.L., and T. Luckmann. 1966. *The Social Construction of Reality: A Treatise in the Sociology of Knowledge*. Garden City, NY: Anchor Books.

Bennis, W. 1982. "Book Review of 'Leadership' by J.M. Burns." *American Journal of Sociology* 88 (1): 202–205.

Beyer, J.M. 1999. "Taming and Promoting Charisma to Change Organizations". *The Leadership Quarterly* 10 (2): 307–330.

Blanchard, K., with J. Britt. P. Zigarmi and J. Hoekstra. 2009. *Who Killed Change? Solving the Mystery of Leading People Through Change*. London: Harper Collins Publishers.

Bresnen, M.J. 1995. "All Things to All People? Perceptions, Attributions, and Constructions of Leadership". *The Leadership Quarterly* 6 (4): 495, 513.

Bryman, A. 1988. Quantity and Quality in Social Research. London: Routledge.

Bryman, A. 2004. "Qualitative Research on Leadership: A Critical But Appreciative Review". *The Leadership Quarterly* 15 (6): 729–770.

Burns, J.M. 1978. *Leadership*. New York: Harper Row Publishers.

Burrell, G., and G. Morgan. 1979. *Sociological Paradigms and Organizational Analysis*. London: Heinemann.

By, R.T. and B. Burnes, eds. 2013. *Organizational Change, Leadership and Ethics: Leading Organizations Towards Sustainability*. London: Routledge.

Calas, M.B., and L. Smircich. 1991. Voicing Seduction to Silence Leadership. *Organization Studies* 12 (4): 567–602.

Calas, M.B., and L. Smircich. 1996. "From the 'Womans' Point of View: Feminist Approaches to Organization Studies". In *Handbook on Organizations*, eds. S. Clegg., and C. Hardy, 212–251. London: Sage Publications Ltd.

Carey, M.R. 1992. "Transformational Leadership and Fundamental Option for Self—Transcendence". *The Leadership Quarterly* 3 (3): 217–236.

Child, J. 1969. *British Management Thought*. London: Allen & Unwin.

Ciulla, J.B. 1995. "Leadership Ethics: Mapping the Territory". *Business Ethics Quarterly* 5 (1): 5–28.

Collins, D. 2000. *Management Fads and Buzzwords: Critical—Practical Perspectives*. London: Routledge.

Collinson, D. 2012. "Prozac Leadership and the Limits of Positive Thinking". *Leadership* 8 (2): 87–107.

The Commission on the Future of Management and Leadership. 2014. *Management 2020: Leadership to Unlock Long-Term Growth*. London: Chartered Management Institute.

Conger, J. 1999. "Charismatic and Transformational Leadership in Organizations: An Insider's Perspective on these Developing Streams of Research". *The Leadership Quarterly* 10 (2): 145–179.

Conner, D.R. 1998. *Managing at the Speed of Change*. Chichester: John Wiley and Sons.

Cornelissen, J.P., R. Holt and M. Zundel. 2011. "The Role of Analogy and Metaphor in the Framing and Legitimization of Strategic Change". *Organization Studies* 32 (12): 1701–1716.

Czarniawska-Joerges, B., and Wolff, R. 1991. "Leaders, Managers, Entrepreneurs on and off the Organizational Stage". *Organization Studies* 12 (2): 529–546.

Deetz, S.A., S.J. Tracy and J.L. Simpson. 2000. *"Leading Organizations Through Transition: Communication and Cultural Change"*. Thousand Oaks, CA: In cooperation with Seton worldwide, Sage Publications Inc.

Diaz-Saenz, H.R. 2011. "Transformational Leadership". In *The SAGE Handbook of Leadership*, eds. A. Bryman, D. Collinson, K. Grint, B. Jackson and M. Uhl-Bien, 299–310. London: Sage Publications Ltd.

Downton, J.V. 1973. *Rebel Leadership: Commitment and Charisma in the Revolutionary Process*. New York: Free Press.

Edelman, M. 1971. *Politics are Symbolic Actions*. Chicago: Markham.

Evans, P., J. Hassard, and P. Hyde. 2013. *Critical Leadership: Leader-Follower Dynamics in a Public Organization*. Routledge Critical Studies in Public Management. London: Routledge.

Etzioni, A. 1964. *Modern Organizations*. Englewood Cliffs, NJ: Prentice Hall.

Fairhurst, G.T. 2005. "Reframing the Art of Framing: Problems and Prospects for Leadership". *Leadership* 1 (2): 165–185.

Fairhurst, G.T. 2008. "Discursive Leadership: A Communication Alternative to Leadership Psychology". *Management Communication Quarterly* 21 (4): 510–521.

Fairhurst, G.T. 2011. *The Power of Framing: Creating the Language of Leadership*. San Francisco: Jossey Bass, Wiley Imprint.

Fairhurst, G.T., and D. Grant. 2010. "The Social Construction of Leadership: A Sailing Guide". *Management Communication Quarterly* 24 (2): 171–210.

Fairhurst, G.T., and R.A. Sarr. 1996. *The Art of Framing: Managing the Language of Leadership*. San Francisco: Jossey Bass Inc.

Fayol, H. 1916 translated 1949. *General and Industrial Management*. London: Pitman.

Gemmil, G., and G. Oakley. 1992. "Leadership: An Alienating Social Myth". *Human Relations* 45 (2): 113–129.

Gill, R. 2011. *Theory and Practice of Leadership*. London: Sage Publications Ltd.

Grieves, J. 2010. *Organizational Change: Themes and Issues*. Oxford: Oxford University Press.

Grint, K. 1997. "Reading Tolstoy's Wave". In *Discovering Leadership*, ed. J. Billsberry, 15–23. Houndmills: Palgrave Macmillan in association with OU.

Grint, K. 2005a. *Leadership: Limits and Possibilities*. Houndmills: Palgrave Macmillan.

Grint, K. 2005b. "Problems, Problems, Problems: The Social Construction of 'Leadership'". *Human Relations* 58 (11):1467–1494.

Grint, K. 2010. *Leadership: A Very Short Introduction*. Oxford: Oxford University Press.

Guest, D. 1990. "Human Resource Management and the American Dream". *Journal of Management Studies* 27 (4): 377–397.

Haslam, S.A., S.D. Reicher and M.J. Platlow. 2011. *The New Psychology of Leadership: Identity Influence and Power*. Hove: Psychology Press.

Hope Hailey, V., and J, Balogun. 2002. "Devising Context Sensitive Approaches to Change: The Example of Glaxo Wellcome". *Long Range Planning* 35 (2): 153–178.

Huczynski, A. 2006. *Management Gurus*, rev. ed. Abingdon: Routledge.

Hughes, M. 2010. *Managing Change: A Critical Perspective*. London: CIPD Publishing.

Hughes, M. 2011. "Do 70 Per Cent of All Organizational Change Initiatives Really Fail?". *Journal of Change Management* 11 (4): 451–464.

Hughes, M. forthcoming. "Who Killed Change Management?" *Culture and Organization*.

Kellerman, B. 2013. "Leading Questions: The End of Leadership—Redux". *Leadership* 9 (1): 135–139.

Kelly, S. 2014. "Towards a Negative Ontology of Leadership". *Human Relations* 67 (8): 905–922.

Kotter, J.P. 1988. *The Leadership Factor*. New York: Free Press.

Kotter, J.P. 1990. *A Force for Change: How Leadership Differs from Management*. New York: Free Press.

Kotter, J.P. 1995. "Leading Change: Why Transformation Efforts Fail". *Harvard Business Review* 73 (2): 259–267.

Kotter, J.P. 1996. *Leading Change*. Boston: Harvard Business School Press.

Ladkin, D., M. Wood and J. Pillay. 2010. "How Do Leaders Lead Change?" In *Rethinking Leadership: A New Look at Old Leadership Questions*, ed. D. Ladkin, 127–152. Cheltenham: Edward Elgar.

Lukes, S. 2005. *Power: A Radical View*. Houndmills: Palgrave Macmillan published in association with the British Sociological Association.

Marshak, R.J., and D. Grant. 2008. "Organizational Discourse and New Organization Development Practices". *British Journal of Management* 19, Special Issue: S7–S19.

O'Reilly, D., and M. Reed. 2010. " 'Leaderism': An Evolution of Managerialism in UK Public Service Reform". *Public Administration* 88 (4): 960–978.

Parry, K.W. 2011. "Leadership and Organization Theory". In *The SAGE Handbook of Leadership*, eds. A. Bryman, D. Collinson, K. Grint, B. Jackson and M. Uhl-Bien, 53–70. London: Sage Publications Ltd.

Perrow, C. 1978. *Complex Organizations: A Critical Essay*. Glenview, Illinois: Scott Foresman and Company.

Pondy, L.R. 1978. "Leadership Is a Language Game". In *Readings in Managerial Psychology*, eds. H.J. Leavitt, L.R. Pondy and D.M. Boje, 224–233, 1989. Chicago: University of Chicago Press.

Rittel, H., and M. Webber. 1973. "Dilemmas in a General Theory of Planning". *Policy sciences* 4 (2): 155–169.

Rockefeller, J.D. 3rd. 1973. *The Second American Revolution: Some Personal Observations*. New York: Harper-Row.

Rost, J.C. 1993. *Leadership for the Twenty-First Century*. Westport, CT: Praeger.

Rost, J.C. 1995. "Leadership: A Discussion about Ethics". *Business Ethics Quarterly* 5 (1): 129–142.

Rost, J.C. 1997. "Moving from Individual to Relationship: A Post-Industrial Paradigm of Leadership". *The Journal of Leadership Studies* 4 (4): 3–16.

Salaman, G., and P. Thompson, eds. 1973. *People and Organisations*. London: Longman.

Selznick, P. 1949. *TVA and the Grass Roots*. Berkeley and Los Angeles: University of California Press.

Selznick, P. 1952. *The Organizational Weapon*. New York: McGraw Hill.

Selznick, P. 1957. *Leadership in Administration: A Sociological Interpretation*. Berkeley: University of California Press.

Simola, S.K., J. Barling and N. Turner. 2010. "Transformational Leadership and Leader Moral Orientation: Contrasting an Ethic of Justice and an Ethic of Care". *The Leadership Quarterly* 21 (1): 179–188.

Sinclair, A. 2007. *Leadership for the Disillusioned: Moving Beyond Myths and Heroes to Leading that Liberates*. Crows Nest (NSW): Allen and Unwin.

Smircich, L., and G. Morgan. 1982. "Leadership: The Management of Meaning". *The Journal of Applied Behavioral Science* 18 (3): 257–273.

Storey, J., ed. 2011. *Leadership in Organizations: Current Issues and Key Trends*, 2nd ed. London: Routledge.

Spector, B. 2014. "Flawed from the 'Get-Go': Lee Iacocca and the Origins of Transformational Leadership". *Leadership* 10 (3): 361–379.

Sutherland, F., and A.C.T. Smith. 2013. "Leadership for the Age of Sustainability: A Dualities Approach to Organizational Change". In *Organizational Change, Leadership and Ethics: Leading Organizations Towards Sustainability*, eds. R.T. By and B. Burnes, 216–239. London: Routledge.

Taylor, F.W. 1911. *The Principles of Scientific Management*. New York: Harper.

Tourish, D. 2013. *The Dark Side of Transformational Leadership*. Hove: Routledge.

Tucker, S.A. 1989. "Book Review: 'The Leadership Factor' by J.P. Kotter". *Academy of Management Review* 14 (2): 297–301.

Watson, T.J. 2006. *Organising and Managing Work*, 2nd ed. Harlow: FT Prentice Hall.

Yukl, G. 1999. "An Evaluation of Conceptual Weaknesses in Transformational and Charismatic Leadership Theories". *The Leadership Quarterly* 10 (2): 285–305.

Zaleznik, A. 1977. "Managers and Leaders: Are They Different?" *Harvard Business Review* 15 (3): 67–84.

Zaleznik, A. 1989. *The Managerial Mystique: Restoring Leadership in Business*. New York: Harper and Row.

5 A Critical Evaluation of Leadership and Organizational Change

INTRODUCTION

Leaders have been defined as ' . . . agents of change. . .' (Bass, 1981:16) and, more recently, Ladkin et al (2010:127) wrote that 'for many leadership theorists, leadership and change are almost synonymous.' The interrelationship between leadership and organizational change has also caught the imagination of practitioners: '[I]n business organizations and government, we hear a constant murmur on the lips of executives of all stripes and persuasions about "the necessity of change", "the imperative of effecting major transformations"'(O'Toole, 1995:xi). This imperative to lead change spawned large volumes of practitioner-orientated literature (see, for example, Kotter, 1996; Kanter, 1999; Tichy and Devanna, 1986; Wagner et al, 2010). This literature has given emphasis to the involvement of leaders in transformation and change over many decades.

These discourses simultaneously define intractable problems as tractable and offer leadership as the solution. This is not a new phenomenon, with Abrahamson and Fairchild (1999) explaining quality circles through articulating a problem discourse, a solution discourse and a bandwagon discourse; such discourses remain very persuasive. All of this activity is predicated upon an assumption that leadership applied to organizational change results in successful change, which, it is believed, is underpinned by a body of research-informed cumulative leadership and organizational change evidence. However, as Chapter Two highlighted, the anticipated research and scholarship informing understanding about leadership and organizational change interrelationships was lacking (see also Parry, 2011; Ford and Ford, 2012).

In this critical review, the focus has neither been upon the enthusiastic expectations practitioners place upon the leadership of organizational change, nor gathering, quantifying and/or deconstructing such discourses. Instead, the focus has been on the expectation that such activities would be informed by authoritative knowledge based upon research and scholarship that results in the development of convincing theories, models and concepts. In this spirit, the chapter draws upon earlier chapters, in order to take critical stock of the state of the sub-field of leadership and organizational change.

The *International Journal of Management Reviews* (IJMR) key principles for literature reviewing (see Figure 5.1) offer a structured means of evaluating management and organization studies literature in general, representing best practice as prescribed by a relevant and respected double-blind, refereed journal. In the context of this chapter, these key principles are highly applicable to critically evaluating the state of the sub-field of leadership and organizational change, the quest that is at the heart of this critical review.

The application of these key principles (Figure 5.1) encourages further engagement with the fields of leadership studies and organizational change, as well as with the sub-field of leadership and organizational change. The question ordering of the key principles in this chapter has been changed to fit the discussions featured here, with the final two questions carried over into the concluding chapter. The evaluation of the sub-field of leadership and organizational change is organized around these IJMR questions, which serve as the main sections of the chapter: The boundaries of the sub-field, the maturity of the sub-field, the major categories of the sub-field, contrasting methodologies and evaluating the research of the sub-field. This leads into a final discussion focused upon gauging the synthesis and accumulated state of knowledge of the sub-field of leadership and organizational change. The discussion is facilitated through a summary of earlier findings, resulting in four related themes: Divergence, dissensus, discourse and disappearance.

- Is the choice of a field or sub-field in management and organization studies mature enough to warrant a literature review?
- Are details provided of how the boundaries to that field have been defined to include specific details of what is included and excluded, and why?
- Is there a synthesis and evaluation of the accumulated state of knowledge in that field, summarising and highlighting current and emerging insight, while stressing strengths and weaknesses of prior work?
- Does the review include consideration of how research has developed in the field into sub-categories, concepts or themes that can provide a more holistic interpretation and (re)categorisation of that field?
- Is there a complete analysis of the literature surveyed in terms of discussions of any contrasting methodologies used in the literature, the strength and weakness of particular approaches to studying the subject under review, the quality of the studies in the field, with the general conclusions to be drawn from the literature (for example, the current agreements and disagreements contained within the field) providing a thorough discussion of where the literature is now?
- Are there reasoned and authoritative conclusions as to where the literature is, or perhaps should be going, and what important questions or gaps still exist in the field?
- Is there a clear statement about what contribution the review makes to theory, practice and/or research?

Figure 5.1 *International Journal of Management Reviews* key principles

THE BOUNDARIES OF LEADERSHIP AND ORGANIZATIONAL CHANGE AS A SUB-FIELD

As the sub-field of leadership and organizational change draws upon two separate fields of study (leadership studies and organizational change studies) explanations which lack either understanding of leadership or organizational change are flawed through their partiality. This intersecting sub-field boundary includes scholars with knowledge of both fields, but equally excludes the majority of scholars, pragmatically choosing to focus either upon leadership studies or upon organizational change studies. In reviewing leadership and organizational change literature over 35 years, the intellectual boundary of a scholar's favoured field of study should not be underestimated, as it acts potentially as the greatest impediment to advancing knowledge about leadership and organizational change. In seeking to understand the boundaries of the sub-field of leadership and organizational change, it was telling that in the academic handbooks of both the fields of leadership studies and organizational change studies (see Chapter Two), neither field appeared to take ownership of this sub-field. It almost seemed as if advancing knowledge was being left to the scholars in the other field.

More pragmatically, the boundaries of these separate fields are themselves problematic, with both leadership studies and organizational change studies informed by different academic disciplines that draw upon very different philosophies and methodologies. In the halcyon days of the 1950s, the anticipation was that management and organization studies would develop into an integrated, coherent and relevant 'science of management,' but instead, multiple fields and sub-fields with differing goals, problems and research approaches developed (Whitley, 1984, 2000). Whilst functional and rational approaches have become the mainstream orthodoxy of both leadership studies and organizational change studies, the divergence and dissensus of these fields may prove to be strengths in advancing knowledge, rather than weaknesses (see Chapters Three and Four for further discussion). However, the issue remains that there is an absence of tightly delineated boundaries around leadership studies and around organizational change studies, with the acknowledgement of divergence only increasing such boundary challenges. One way forward would be through precise and consistent definitions of key terminology.

However, despite the terminology of leadership and organizational change being in everyday use, within academic debate, definitions and meanings contrast greatly. In Chapter One, the failing of leadership studies academics to define leadership was highlighted (Rost, 1993), and more recently, Grint (2005a) warned that we have yet to establish what leadership is. Kelly (2014) was even more sceptical, regarding leadership as an empty signifier par excellence, evading attempts at definition. The ambiguity of leadership is mirrored within the definitions of organizational change, with organizational change taking on many different guises, including 'transformation, development, metamorphosis, transmutation, evolution, regeneration, innovation, revolution and transition . . .' (Stickland, 1998:14). It has been described as a container concept, as allowing a range of meanings (De Caluwe and Vermaak, 2003), ranging from macro to micro, from small scale to large scale, from human resource-orientated to operations management-orientated (Frahm, 2007).

In this critical review, Rost's (1997:11) definition was favoured: '[L]eadership is an influence relationship among leaders and collaborators who intend real changes that reflect their mutual purposes.' The definition potentially offers a boundary around the sub-field, as it combines leadership and organizational change. However, the boundary-defining weakness is that it would exclude the majority of the literature cited here. In looking towards practices of leadership and organizational change, they rhetorically imagine organizational futures with certainty in order to inspire and motivate employees, despite the uncertainties and ambiguities of the processes of organizational change (see Dawson 2003, 2014; March 1981). In practice, the boundaries of unknown futures may be intentionally imprecise, again with implications for academic boundary defining.

Another means of understanding the boundaries of the sub-field is to look to significant contributors, such as John Kotter and Bernard Bass, which will be the focus of a later section of this chapter. In the interim, the cautionary boundary-defining note is that in *Leading Change*, Kotter (1996) referred to change in the title, but largely related leadership to transformations within the book without ever clarifying what he meant by transformation. In *Transformational Leadership*, Bass and Riggio (2006) focused on leaders transforming followers' attitudes and motivations, with implications for their subsequent behaviours. Unfortunately, the potential transformation of followers has been misinterpreted as transforming organizations (Haslam et al, 2011). The application of specific inclusive and exclusive boundaries may be a natural science preoccupation, caught up in the belief that the goal of a field is movement towards the convergence of a unified science of an academic discipline. However, Grint (2000), cited in Chapter One, warned against leadership being regarded as a science that could be reduced down to a parsimonious set of rules.

The sub-field of leadership and organizational change, in drawing upon two separate fields that are informed by multiple and different academic disciplines, potentially explains why defining leadership and organizational change is problematic and why the boundaries appear so permeable. The implication of this divergence and dissensus is that reasonable questions about what to include and exclude are complicated, counting against this sub-field when evaluated against the IJMR criteria. Fields and disciplines characterised by divergence and dissensus rather than convergence and consensus result in a whole range of competing paradigms, philosophies and perspectives. The implication is that multiple explanations will exist, with favoured explanations a consequence of favoured paradigms, philosophies and perspectives. The prevalence of this pluralism was captured within Smith and Graetz's (2011) *Philosophies of Organizational Change*, which favoured a dualities-aware approach invoking very different, even contradictory explanations of leadership and organizational change (see the 'Methodologies Contrasted' section for further discussion).

THE MATURITY OF LEADERSHIP AND ORGANIZATIONAL CHANGE AS A SUB-FIELD

Leadership narratives within societies feature stories about the role of great leaders making history and initiating change going back a long way (Haslam et al, 2011). Grint (2008), although critical of such conceptualisations, highlighted the popularity of the 'Great Men' accounts of leadership in the 1800s and 1900s. However, the problematic mindset of leadership as masculine, heroic, individualist and normative (see Rost, 1993) may still be at work in people's conceptualisations of leadership and organizational change. In this sense, leadership and organizational change is very mature in its lineage, yet remains problematic with regards to the historic masculine and heroic leadership such archetypes evoke.

Gouldner's (1971:29) discussion of background assumptions was highly influential in formulating social theory: '. . .[A] social theory is more likely to be accepted or rejected because of the background assumptions embedded in them.' In this way, the acceptance or rejection of explanations of leadership and organizational change relate back to background assumptions. This has the unfortunate hierarchical implication that newer explanations are immature and older explanations are mature. Gouldner suggested that something far more intrinsic than the normal criteria applied to evaluating research and theory were at work. We refer to the background assumptions of the authors we cite. The background assumption that great leaders make history and initiate change (Haslam et al, 2011) is very persuasive, even if the research evidence is less persuasive. Attempting to surface background assumptions is informative in seeking to explain leadership and organizational change, or any other field or sub-field.

> What makes a theory intuitively convincing? One reason is that the background assumptions coincide or are compatible with, consensually validate or bring to psychic closure, the background assumptions held by the viewer.
>
> (Gouldner, 1971: 30)

The implication is that certain explanations of leadership and organizational change are going to prove intuitively more appealing than others, probably informed by the favoured *Philosophies of Organizational Change*

(Smith and Graetz, 2011). The theories we choose to critique and seek to supersede may also be understood in terms of background assumptions.

> The most basic changes in any science commonly derive not so much from the invention of new research techniques but rather from new ways of looking at data that may have long existed. Indeed, they may neither refer to nor be occasioned by "data," old or new.
>
> (Gouldner, 1971:34)

Maturity implies development in a manner similar to a chronological life cycle, but the background assumptions suggest that cultural factors may offer better explanations for shifts in thinking, rather than chronology. In the next section, the appeal of transformational leadership (Bass, 1985) and leading change (Kotter, 1996) are explained in terms of framing leadership (Fairhurst, 2005), highlighting their appeal as cultural responses to the anxieties of corporate America in the eighties and nineties. Solutions are favoured, and if they intuitively appeal to sufficient people, they became orthodoxies. The implication is that it is not necessarily as we imagine the quality of an explanation and its empirical and theoretical rigour; instead, it may merely be the right explanation at the right time. Hopefully, understanding leadership and organizational change will be informed by future empirical work that will be rigorously undertaken. However, revisiting Gouldner's (1971) work from forty years earlier encourages exploration of the background assumptions of leadership and organizational change as a sub-field. By definition, background assumptions are intangible, but those evident when reviewing the literature are discussed below.

Huczynski (2006), in his account of management gurus, posed the question: What accounts for high levels of interest in leadership? He offered a number of plausible explanations, including leadership raising the self-esteem of individuals and having the ability to explain the inexplicable. He identified the meta-assumption as leadership is beneficial, which is likely to underpin all leadership and organizational change assumptions. In reviewing the leadership and organizational change literature, at least six more specific background assumptions appeared to be at work (see Figure 5.2).

---

1) A consensus definition/understanding of leadership exists
2) A shared explanation of how organizations change exists
3) Leadership and management can/should be differentiated
4) Leading change is superior to managing change
5) Leadership potentially results in organizational change
6) Leadership + Organizational Change = Successful Change

Figure 5.2 Leadership and organizational change background assumptions

In the text, the numbers refer back to the listing and numbering of the background assumptions in Figure 5.2. They are closely interrelated and discussed separately only to aid their exposition, with relevant illustrative literature included where possible.

There is a background assumption that a consensus leadership definition and understanding exists (1). This critical review of leadership studies (see Chapter Four) revealed the existence of a mythical leadership narrative (Rost, 1993), yet the more you study leadership, the less of a consensus there appears to be (see Grint, 2005a). The conceptualisations of leadership and organizational change did not draw upon such critical literature, instead assuming that an authoritative understanding of leadership had developed over hundreds of years of theory development and theory testing (see Kotter, 1990). Leadership was assumed to be the universal panacea for dealing with the problems and challenges that organizational change raised. The studies of leadership are, at best, a work-in-progress, with the dissensus of competing explanations acknowledged (Burns, 1978; Grint, 2005a; Kelly, 2014; Rost, 1993), yet a background assumption endures that a consensus definition/understanding of leadership exists.

In parallel to assuming a leadership consensus, there is a background assumption about the existence of a shared explanation of how organizations change (2). Studies of organizational change are a far more recent development than leadership studies. Whereas its origins may be traced back to the pioneering writings of Kurt Lewin (1947), the first change management textbooks only appeared in 1990 (Carnall, 1990) and 1992 (Burnes, 1992). In this sense, the studies of organizational change engage with new frontiers, in comparison to leadership studies. Each of Smith and Graetz's (2011) philosophies of organizational change highlights different approaches to explaining organizational change (see also Van de Ven and Poole, 1995 and Eisenhardt, 2000). Despite such divergence, a background assumption appears to endure that a shared/unitarist explanation of how organizations change exists.

The background assumption that leadership and management can/should be differentiated has significantly influenced management and organization studies in recent decades (3). The simplistic assumption is that people can be labelled as either managers or leaders and/or that their leadership and management roles can be disentangled or differentiated. This assumption is not unique to organizational change. In Chapter Four, the expected literature supporting this differentiation was critically reviewed and found to be lacking. The management and leadership differentiation may subsequently receive empirical support, or it may prove simply to be an aspiration grounded in the troubles of corporate America in the eighties and nineties (see Chapter Four). However, the assumption relates to the differentiation being real, evidence-based and beyond doubt.

The assumption that leading change is superior to managing change (4) rolls out of the logic of the previous assumption. Bass (1985) drew upon

Burns's (1978) conceptualisation of transformational leadership to develop his own organizational differentiation between transactional leadership (stability) and transformational leadership (change). However, Bass neglected Burns's (1978:416) belief in the interplay between continuity and change, writing that 'the vast proportion of the decisions of decision makers, high and low, is readjustment that maintains the equilibrium of the status quo.' Similarly, Kotter (1990) argued for a balance between leadership and management, noting that strong leadership without the counterbalance of management would be damaging for organizations. Even in *Leading Change*, Kotter (1996:129) conceded that 'transformation is not a process involving leadership alone; good management is also essential.' Despite these caveats, there has been a perceivable shift away from managing change towards leading change (discussed in Chapter Four), based upon the very dubious background assumption that it is more beneficial to lead change rather than to manage change.

The perceived superiority of leadership over management informs the next assumption, which is that leadership potentially results in organizational change (5). As Ladkin et al (2010:127) noted, '. . .[L]eaders "make change happen" is a belief core to many assumptions about how organizational change works.' Any attempt to understand how the agency of a leader results in organizational change is a very narrow conceptualisation, privileging psychological/sociological explanations that may be too narrow, particularly given the interdisciplinary nature of both leadership studies and organizational change studies. Ford and Ford (2012), in their review of the recent empirical evidence with regards to leadership and organizational change, highlighted the lack of empirical evidence that would confirm that leadership does impact upon organizational change, or even how leadership would impact upon organizational change. Barker (1997) critically questioned the goal of determining cause-effect relationships with regards to leadership, which would lead to some level of predictability and control. This appears magnified when studying how leadership results in organizational change. The quest to understand interrelationships between leadership and organizational change at best may result only in partial explanations, and at worst, the interrelationship may prove to be a rhetorical illusion.

Assumptions around leadership and organizational change are not just about the application of leadership resulting in organizational change: They assume that organizational change that is lead will be successful. This assumption may be depicted as a simple equation:

Leadership + Organizational Change = Successful Change (6)

Success rather than failure tends to be the goal for most individuals and organizations. The implication that combining leadership and organizational change will result in successful change (see Tichy and Devanna, 1986; Wagner et al, 2010) is understandable. The framing of such thinking may be attributed to Kotter, although this may not have been his intention. Kotter's (1995) *Harvard Business Review* paper *Leading Change: Why Transformation Efforts Fail* asserted that transformations failed due to a lack of leadership, and Kotter's (1996) subsequent *Leading Change* book asserted that with added leadership, transformations would succeed. These publications, although not based upon new empirical work, were highly influential (if gauged by academic citations) and may have influenced simplistic mental models that have subsequently proved difficult to escape:

Organizational Change (–) Leadership = Failure (Kotter, 1995)

Organizational Change (+) Leadership = Success (Kotter, 1996)

The assumption is problematic, given the dearth of empirical evidence to support Kotter's original assumption or subsequent evidence; however, the assumption remains intuitively appealing (see Gouldner, 1971). There is another assumption nested within this assumption, that organizational change success or failure is easily discernible. Academic claims that 70% of all change initiatives fail (Beer and Nohria, 2000) may have unintentionally given impetus to such assumptions about failure. Equally, practitioners optimistically believed that with the right recipes, tools and techniques, their change initiatives would succeed. However, there are reasons to question both these positions in terms of the variability of organizational change initiatives, their different contexts and the problematic nature of evaluating organizational change initiatives (see Hughes, 2011). Whereas the prevalence of these leadership and organizational change background assumptions may imply a maturing sub-field, this perception may misrepresent leadership and organizational change understanding, rather than inform the sub-field.

Political scientists such as Burns (1978) made connections between historic, reoccurring political and societal beliefs relating leading and changing to transforming societies, institutions and organizations. These scholars were clear on the relational nature of transformational leadership, with Burns (1978:4) writing, '[M]oral leadership emerges from, and always returns to, the fundamental wants and needs, aspirations, and values of the followers.' Rost (1993:4), a student of Burns (1978), shared a similar belief in '. . .leadership viewed as a dynamic relationship.' The centrality of such relationships is missing from today's debates about leadership and organizational change. O'Toole (1995), in a similar manner to Burns and Rost, explicitly drew upon history and moral and political philosophy; however, possibly due to the era in which he was writing, he was far more critical of how leading change was being conceptualised. He highlighted a paradox that '. . .we still long for the "strong leader," even as we rebel against anyone who dares to tell us what to do' and that 'as a society we celebrate leaders who in a corporate setting betray the very values that we espouse in our churches, homes and communities' (O'Toole, 1995:5/6). Burns and Rost's belief in morally and politically grounded leadership was shared by O'Toole, but O'Toole (1995:15) also appeared to react to what he was witnessing in American corporations '. . .having the will of others imposed on us.' The sub-field of leadership and organizational change is mature enough to merit a literature review; however, despite the best efforts of many capable academics, in many ways it remains very immature. Only certain elements of the sub-field have been nurtured and developed, resulting in a dysfunctional celebration, reification and solidification of the centrality of individual leaders within organizations and their agency and will to make change happen. In reviewing the *Journal of Change Management*, it was found that contributors most commonly focused on competencies, capabilities and the development of change leaders, and in reviewing *The Leadership Quarterly*, it was found that contributors most frequently addressed transformational leadership, possibly to the detriment of competing conceptualisations (see Chapter Two for further discussion). The considerable relational potential to engage with the majority of people comprising any organization remains very immature. The potential of such collaborators integral to any meaningful organizational change process appears intentionally diminished. Today, academics venturing critiques of the prevalence of the imposition of the leader's will are subjected to censure. Throughout 2014, *Times Higher Education* highlighted the suspension by the University of Warwick of Professor Thomas Docherty. Docherty (2014:43) expressed his frustrations within a *Times Higher Education* article as follows:

> The possibilities for participation in democratic change are denied, because everything, including dissent, is managed and circumscribed to keep existing authority in power. Institutionally, it's called "change-management". We are perilously close to a position where the unquestioned power of management is declaring war on the academic community, the university itself: civil war in academia.

This is one explanation of the evolving narrative of leadership and organizational change, as an emphasis upon the importance of the will of an elite and privileged minority of leaders over the majority of collaborators within any organizational change process. The analogy of the sub-field of leadership and organizational change resembling a very noisy, very stroppy teenager comes to mind. This was the level of maturity encountered here and unfortunately, over time, this teenager has shown no signs of growing up and out of this selfish stage of development. Despite encouragement, it was their will that always had to prevail. Doors metaphorically and literally slammed shut on debates about organizational change democratically facilitated through engagement with the majority, rather than with the powerful minority. The considerable potential of democratically engaging with the majority of people who constitute any organization remains very immature. This begs the question: How has our understanding of leadership and organizational change been framed in terms of the supremacy of strong/individualistic leadership?

CATEGORIES OF LEADERSHIP AND ORGANIZATIONAL CHANGE AS A SUB-FIELD

In this section, the focus is on the categorisations evident when reviewing the sub-field. Framing analysis (Fairhurst, 2011; Fairhurst and Sarr, 1996) is used to understand how two of the most influential writers (Bernard Bass and John Kotter) influenced the sub-field. Secondly, metaphors applied to leadership and to organizational change as categorisations potentially inform the sub-field of leadership and organizational change.

Who framed leadership and organizational change? In Chapter One, Burns's (1978) polemical classic *Leadership* was introduced. Burns accused leadership studies of suffering from intellectual mediocrity, subsequently encouraging serious engagement with the transformative capabilities of leadership, with a view to transforming societies and institutions. His relatively straightforward vision was informed by and illustrated with extensive examples from political science. What happened over the next 35 years was not what Burns advocated, although oddly he may have anticipated it, given his dismay about the absence of artistic, intellectual, political or social leadership in processes of change (see also Rost's (1993) concerns about the excessive influence of management writers on leadership studies).

In terms of management and organization studies, what transpired were two completely different categorisations of how organizations might be transformed through leadership as gauged through the citation counts (see Appendices One and Two). Transformational leadership (Bass and Riggio, 2006) encouraged and promoted by Bernard Bass has, over the past 30 years, been the single most-studied and debated idea within the field of leadership studies (Diaz-Saenz, 2011). In parallel, Kotter's (1995, 1996) practitioner-orientated prescriptions for leading change were by far the most-cited leadership and organizational change citations (see Appendix Two). Earlier in this chapter, the sub-field was characterised as being strong on rhetoric, yet weak on definitions and/or boundary precision. In terms of advancing knowledge, two very different categorisations of leadership and organizational change are now highlighted.

Both approaches are critiqued later in the chapter. At this stage in evaluating the sub-field, they appear to have had a significant, potentially disproportionate influence upon understanding leadership and organizational change. Leadership is realised when one or more individuals successfully frame and define the reality for others (Smircich and Morgan, 1982) and today, there is an extensive social construction of leadership literature that explains leadership as a co-constructed reality (Fairhurst and Grant, 2010). Frame analysis as introduced in Chapter Four offers another means of explaining the influence of Bernard Bass and John Kotter upon the sub-field of leadership and organizational change. Gail Fairhurst's (Fairhurst, 2011; Fairhurst and Sarr, 1996) practically orientated books on framing leadership offer a framework to undertake the analysis of two influential, practitioner-orientated leadership books. *Leadership and Performance Beyond Expectations* (Bass, 1985), as one of Bass's earliest expositions of transformational leadership, is pertinent to understanding the framing of the original conception. *Leading Change* (Kotter, 1996), as by far the most-cited publication within the sub-field of leadership and organizational change, merits analysis in terms of its influence upon the sub-field.

Bernard Bass's transformational leadership The frame analysis reported here is informed by and organized around the six framing questions introduced in Chapter Four (see Figure 4.5), which are believed to offer new insights into the construction of this particular account of transformational leadership.

What cultural discourse is being employed? In the preface of *Leadership and Performance Beyond Expectations* (Bernard Bass, 1985), cultural reference points were immediately apparent: President John F. Kennedy, Theodore Roosevelt, Mahatma Gandhi. Bass's discourse, however, was one of change rather than continuity. He wrote that 'a shift in paradigm is in order. Another concept is required to go beyond these limits. To achieve follower performance beyond the ordinary limits, leadership must be transformational' (Bass, 1985:xiii). Bass (1985) acknowledged the centrality of promoting change for individuals, groups and organizations; he regarded the social and political situation in the US at that time as conducive to the emergence of transformational leadership.

What is driving the framing of the specific situation (why, where, what and who questions)? In terms of why does America require transformational leaders, the answer was in order to complement existing transactional leaders. In terms of where are American organizations heading, it was towards more change and environmental turbulence. In terms of what, Bass (1985) encouraged moral leadership for the well being of organizational life, with profit-maximisers disparaged for being transactional, whereas quality of life managers were applauded for being transformational. In terms of who, Bass (1985:24) believed that 'the transformational leader changes the social warp and woof of reality.' This may be read as an early precursor to the later interest in socially constructed leadership (see Fairhurst and Grant, 2010).

What mental model is being promoted? Bass's mental model underpinning his book was that a particular form of leadership, transformational leadership, would result in transformation. Transformational leadership subsequently became the mental model for Bass and his readers. The book concluded with Bass (1985:230) declaring some confidence in '. . .the transformational factors of charismatic leadership, individualized consideration, and intellectual stimulation, and the transactional factors of contingent reward and management-by-exception.' The book offered the preliminary testing of his mental model.

How can leaders control the context under which events are seen if they recognise a framing opportunity? Although not a postmodernist, Bass (1985:4) explicitly acknowledged the role of the leader in changing the context.

> More quantity is no longer enough; quality must improve dramatically. Leaders may help in bringing about a radical shift in attention. For instance, groups oriented toward traditional beliefs will be shifted so that they come to value modern approaches. The contextual framework may be changed by leaders.

The leader is tasked with changing the context, and through the reification of transactional leaders and transformational leaders, the context of both leading and following is framed.

Are metaphorical, master, simplifying, gain and loss and believability frames utilised? The book is divided into six parts, with each part introduced with a short vignette. In terms of framing, these vignettes may be regarded as metaphorical frames, transferring meaning between entities, and/or as simplifying frames, offering illustrations before the more complicated discussion of concepts. The master frame repeatedly invoked throughout the book is the explanation of transformational leadership as differentiated from transactional leadership. This contrasting features prominently in Fairhurst and Sarr (1996:111): '. . .[C]ontrast is very useful because sometimes we can say what our subject is not more easily than we can say what it is.' Gain and loss framing is also applicable to such differentiations between transformational leadership and transactional leadership. There will be gains or losses if the most appropriate form of leadership is/is not applied to a particular situation. Finally, in terms of believability framing, credibility is gained through the use of extensive supporting references. Bass's (1985:xiv) refers to '. . .studying leadership behaviour over the past 35 years. . .', suggesting a quest that is far more than a whim.

What is leadership in the context of what leaders do and how do they persuade themselves and others that they are doing it (the design problem)? Focusing back to *Leadership and Performance Beyond Expectations* (Bass, 1985), the book speaks directly to the design problem, explaining the requirement for transactional leadership as well as, transformational leadership, and explaining the purpose of leadership to a reader who can relate it to their own context. The transformational leader is succinctly described '. . .as one who motivates us to do more than we originally expected to do' (Bass, 1985:20). Transformational leadership offers a design of what leaders do, as well as signposting to followers and other stakeholders what leaders should be doing—transformational leadership.

John Kotter's leading change The frame analysis reported here is informed by and organized around the six framing questions introduced in Chapter Four (see Figure 4.5), which are believed to offer new insights into the construction of this particular account of leading change.

What cultural discourse is being employed? *Leading Change* (Kotter, 1996) commences with an anxiety-provoking first chapter—'Transforming Organizations: Why Firms Fail.' This is a depressing way to begin a book, but very much in tune with the cultural discourses of the day, questioning the efficacy of managing change (Beer et al, 1990) after businesses looked to the East as a competitive threat as well as a potential cultural solution in terms of managing cultures (Peters and Waterman, 1982).

What is driving the framing of the specific situation (why, where, what and who questions)? Why had American organizations arrived at the situation that Kotter was framing? Because they had overemphasised management at the expense of leadership (see Chapter Four). Where were organizations heading? Towards far more uncertain and turbulent operating environments. What really counts in organizations? Leading change. Who are we, relates to two of Kotter's eight steps, with the second step encouraging the creation of a guiding coalition. In this way, instead of individualistic leadership, there was an emphasis on a powerful leadership grouping. The fifth step empowered employees within broad-based action, implying that everyone was potentially involved within a change process.

What mental model is being promoted? In many ways, *Leading Change* was a change-orientated extension of Kotter's influential thinking around differentiating leadership and management (Kotter, 1988, 1990). Kotter's writing reflected his mental model of leadership, with *Leading Change* (Kotter, 1996) prescribing an eight-stage process: Establishing a sense of urgency, forming a powerful guiding coalition, creating a vision, communicating the vision, empowering others to act on the vision, planning for and creating short term wins, consolidating improvements and producing still more change and institutionalizing new approaches. It is likely that this model became the mental model of change leadership for many leaders and academics even if it had not been attributed to John Kotter; certainly, the language of the eight steps pervades organizations to this day.

How can leaders control the context under which events are seen if they recognise a framing opportunity? Kotter (1996:3) begins his introductory chapter with the following sentence: '[B]y any objective measure, the amount of significant, often traumatic, change in organizations has grown tremendously over the past two decades.' Kotter constructs a particular account of a turbulent context that potentially frames the context in which leaders operate, and offers leaders a ready-made context with which to justify their leadership actions, which may be paraphrased as 'the traumatic context which we face necessitates these strong leadership actions!'

Are metaphorical, master, simplifying, gain and loss and believability frames utilised? Kotter's (1996) writing is rich in metaphors (see the next sub-section of this chapter), with the most obvious being the metaphor of a step within his eight-step leadership process for successful transformation. Steps literally describe steps, but equally imply a rational, linear and sequential process for leaders to lead successful change. The master frame emphasises leading change rather than managing change, although (often overlooked) Kotter does acknowledge that management is as important as leadership (see Chapter Four). Kotter's eight steps themselves and how they are depicted may be seen as simplifying frames, with the book containing many case studies of anonymous leaders working in anonymous organizations, again simplifying the concepts under discussion. Gain and loss is one of the main ways leading change is framed, with transformation efforts depicted as failing as a consequence of leadership errors (Kotter, 1995). In *Leading Change*, the eight errors are reversed into a proactive means of leading change, with the gain being successful transformation. The believability framing is very different from the work of Bernard Bass in that Kotter gains credibility from the many published senior leader endorsements adorning the book. Kotter's track record of working as a consultant with large corporations, his leadership publications and earlier research projects also give the book legitimacy.

What is leadership in the context of what leaders do and how do they persuade themselves and others that they are doing it (the design problem)? *Leading Change's* (1996) inclusion in TIME's (2014) 25 most influential business management books highlights its continuing practitioner appeal. The book offers an account of what a leader does in the context of change, and is unusually endorsed both by practitioners and academics (through 6000+ citations). If leaders follow these eight steps, they have a rationale for doing change leadership, a justification for how they do change leadership and a methodology for doing change leadership. This is an approach to leadership that is likely to be persuasive for themselves and for those around them.

Leadership framing normally focuses on leadership/leaders doing the framing (Fairhurst, 2011; Fairhurst and Grant, 2010). However, here, the focus has been on how the sub-field of leadership and organizational change appears to be framed (either unintentionally or intentionally) by leadership writers. In contrasting Bernard Bass's and John Kotter's contributions, there is a second and not mutually exclusive explanation for their influence upon the field. This is in terms of the 'Matthew Effect,' particularly in terms of the frequency with which these authors are cited and the longevity of being cited. If Kotter's (1996) *Leading Change* was a management fad (see Collins, 2000), you would expect it to have gone 'off the boil' by now. Podsakoff et al (2008) favoured citation counts as a measure of influence, citing Robert Merton's (1968, 1988) work on the diffusion of ideas through scientific communities. Merton highlighted how the distribution of citations tends to be skewed towards a small number of scholars, with these scholars accounting for the majority of citations; this phenomenon he labelled the 'Matthew Effect.' This appears to be highly applicable to the concentration of leadership and organizational change citations referring to either Bernard

Bass or John Kotter, with the implication that this distribution becomes self-sustaining (see Appendices One and Two).

Metaphors of leadership and organizational change Metaphors are another means of categorising the explanations of leadership and organizational change. Leaders, managers and academics invoke metaphors both knowingly and unknowingly, implicitly and explicitly; '. . .human thought processes are largely metaphorical' (Lakoff and Johnson, 1980:6). Kotter's (1996) *Leading Change* is illustrative of such use of metaphors. In Kotter's (1996) explanation of his first leadership error, allowing too much complacency, his use of metaphors is very apparent (see Figure 5.3).

Kotter explaining leadership through metaphor (see Figure 5.3) is not atypical. Spicer and Alvesson (2011:45) highlighted that many studies have focused on the senior manager/leader metaphors in use, suggesting that '. . .the more and better the metaphors, the better the leadership. It is as if leaders are poets dwelling in the boardroom who are able to spin appealing metaphors.' Metaphors and metaphorical analysis was given impetus by Morgan (1986) and has subsequently caught the imagination of management and organization studies academics, with specific leadership examples including Amernic et al (2007), Spicer and Alvesson (2011) and Collinson (2012), and organizational change examples including Marshak (1993), Palmer and Dunford (1996) and Cornelissen et al (2011).

In terms of metaphorically understanding leadership and organizational change, the metaphors identified in previous studies are considered as potential categorisations informing leadership and organizational change. Spicer and Alvesson (2011) cite Pinder and Bourgeious (1982), acknowledging that metaphors can be very helpful in developing knowledge about a novel or under-investigated phenomenon. Metaphors of leadership and organizational change disrupt superficial understanding by presenting competing ways of understanding leadership and organizational change. Hatch et al (2006) metaphorically highlighted the three faces of leadership as manager, artist and priest, based upon interviews with famous chief executive officers (CEOs) featured in the *Harvard Business Review*. Amernic et al (2007) in

---

. . .Adrien watched initiative after initiative sink in a sea of complacency. (Page 4)

A reorganization was talked to death by skilled filibusters on his staff. (Page 4)

. . .a subtle battle played out over another two years. . . (Page 5)

. . .drive people out of their comfort zones. (Page 5)

They become paralyzed with the downside possibilities associated with reducing complacency. . . (Page 5)

. . .push people even deeper into their foxholes. . . (Page 5)

. . .reengineering bogs down. . . (Page 5)

Figure 5.3 Metaphors used to convey too much leadership complacency (Kotter, 1996)

their analysis of Jack Welch's CEO letters, identified five root metaphors of a transformational leader as: Pedagogue, physician, architect, commander and saint. Amernic et al (2007:1842) suggested that transformational leaders

> . . .use a variety of theatrical and rhetorical devices to encourage followers to believe in the leader's ability to exercise unique and extraordinary insight into the environment around them, to diagnose organizational ailments accurately, to prescribe effective treatment regimes, and to render organizational transformation.

Each of these five root metaphors merits clarification, offering alternative explanations of leadership and organizational change. In the CEO letters, the leader as a pedagogue was revealed, in which Welch adopted the guise of teacher. The leader as a physician focused on diagnosing health and prescribing solutions for ailments. The leader as an architect emphasised Welch's interest in the social architecture of General Electric and a need to engage with every mind in the company. The leader as a commander drew upon a military metaphor, portraying Welch as undertaking major moves using the language of winners and losers, brutal environments and strong positions. Finally, the leader as a saint highlighted Welch's saintly virtues of compassion at General Electric. Western's (2013) application of metaphors of leaders as controller, therapist, messiah and eco-leadership highlighted different leadership discourses, creatively fusing leadership studies with organization studies (see Figure 5.4).

What is interesting about Western's approach is that different leadership discourses are related to a timeline and generic approaches to management (see discussion of management idea families in Chapter Three). The leader as a messiah is exemplified by transformational leadership, with Western (2013) arguing that the discourse has strong links with the heroic leaders of earlier ages. Although for Western (2013), there were similarities with earlier 'Great Men' conceptualisations of leadership, there was a difference in that the leader as a messiah emphasised a strong collectivist culture. In terms of the discussions in this sub-section, leadership working with four different organizational metaphors is pertinent, as there is likely to be a hybrid of these metaphors at work in the explanations of leadership and organizational change presented within this critical review. Alvesson and Spicer (2011), within their edited reader, offered six further metaphors for the leader as a gardener, buddy, saint, cyborg, commander and bully.

O'Reilly and Reed (2010:964) dealt with leadership metaphors in a slightly different way using the lens of leaderism, the 'belief that many core aspects of social life can and should be co-ordinated by one or more individuals who give direction and/or purpose to social activity conducted by themselves and others.' Leaderism as a development of managerialism is evident within the policy discourses of public service reform in the UK. Leaderism was composed or supported by a series of framing metaphorical narratives:

	Controller Discourse	Therapist Discourse	Messiah Discourse	Eco-Leader Discourse
Mantra	Controlling resources to maximise efficiency	Happy workers are more productive workers	Visionary leaders and strong cultures	Connectivity and ethics
Key Words	Science, Rationality, Control, Efficiency, Productivity, Task and Functionalism	Relationships, Motivation, Teamwork, Personal Growth, Therapeutic Culture, Emotions, Subjectivity	Transfor- mational Leaders, Charisma, Vision and Belief, Strong Cultures, Loyalty, Conformist Cultures, Dynamic Engagement	Ecosystems, Distributed and Ethical Leadership, Networks, Connectivity, Interdepen- dence, Globalization, Technology, Sustainability
Prevalent Era	1900s to 1940s	1940s to 1980s	1980s to 2000	2000 and Beyond
Organizational Metaphor	Organization functions like a machine	Organization is like a therapeutic clinic	Messiah leads a community	Organization as an ecosystem within ecosystems

Figure 5.4 Four leadership discourses (based upon Western, 2013)

- Endemic situations of competition, survival and progress require social co-ordination.
- Social co-ordination is best achieved through single or small groups of specially gifted and/or positioned individuals who lead.
- Individuals that lead use particular moral, intellectual, interpersonal, conative, material or politico-cultural resources in order to achieve social co-ordination.
- Such social co-ordination by those who lead places them in a pre-eminent role.
- To perform, leaders must be empowered by giving them sufficient room to manoeuvre the 'right,' or authority, to lead (adapting Pollitt, 1993:2–3).
- Those who lead require effort and commitment from those being led.
- Such social co-ordination leads to progress, which benefits all of those involved.

Figure 5.5 Metaphorical narratives framing leaderism (based upon O'Reilly and Reed, 2010)

In Figure 5.5, discourses of leaderism believed to influence public services are metaphorically framed. In this depiction, overlaps between philosophies, framing, background assumptions and metaphors as featured in this chapter become apparent. Leaderism as a practice is underpinned by entrepreneurial and cultural management ideologies (philosophies), metaphorically framed (see earlier discussion in this section) and working with background assumptions (see previous section) about the best way to achieve public service reform. Equally, though O'Reilly and Reed's (2010) leaderism may be critiqued in terms of their philosophies, framing, background assumptions and metaphors. In their overview of the role of metaphor in processes of organizational change, Oswick and Marshak (2011) highlighted two dominant metaphors: The notion of change as a journey and a deeply embedded health metaphor. They juxtaposed these traditional discourses of change with recently emerging discourses based upon metaphors of 'change as a conversation' and 'organization as a mystery.' However, they subsequently warned against clearly delineating the four metaphors and also privileging emerging metaphors over earlier metaphors.

Spicer and Alvesson (2011) believed that using metaphors encourages critical scrutiny, pushing us to explore the basic assumptions underlying our conceptualisations. In the previous two sub-sections, background assumptions and metaphors as categorisations have surfaced and in many ways, they are closely related, although not necessarily consistent.

LEADERSHIP AND ORGANIZATIONAL
CHANGE—METHODOLOGIES CONTRASTED

Another means of evaluating the sub-field of leadership and organizational change as encouraged through the application of the IJMR key principles is through contrasting the methodologies used within the literature. In Chapter Three, *Philosophies of Organizational Change* (Smith and Graetz, 2011) offered a means to explain competing philosophies within organizational change, consciously avoiding privileging a single paradigm or perspective-based explanations (Demers, 2007; Eisenhardt, 2000; Van de Ven and Poole, 2005). Smith and Graetz (2011) identified the following philosophies of organizational change: Rational, biological, institutional, resource, psychological, systems, cultural, critical and dualities. These social science-orientated philosophies are equally applicable to leadership studies in general and leadership and organizational change in particular. For example, rational and psychological philosophies appear to have informed research and scholarship into transformational leadership (see Fairhurst, 2008 for further discussion), whereas more recently, the accounts of leadership have reflected a critical philosophy (see Collinson, 2011). Each philosophy offers a means of contrasting the different methods and methodologies informing accounts of leadership and organizational change. Leadership and organizational change as a sub-field is likely to be comprised of different communities of scholars who favour competing methods and methodologies as a means to advance knowledge about leadership and organizational change. In Figure 5.6, Smith and Graetz's (2011) philosophies are applied to leadership and organizational change in order to contrast the different philosophies at work.

Philosophy (Smith and Graetz, 2011)	Philosophy summarised	*The Leadership Quarterly* illustrations	Leadership and organizational change in terms of. . .
Rational	Planned and directed change with strategy and planning emphasised	Berson and Avolio (2004)	Leadership style and effectiveness of conveying organizational goals
Biological	Ecological, organic and evolutionary change, emphasis upon life cycles	Reichard et al (2011)	Adolescent personality, intelligence and transformational leadership
Institutional	Emphasis on industry influence gauged through standards and benchmarks	Currie et al (2009)	Examination of leadership in the context of institutional change
Resource	Emphasis upon resource access determining change	Zhu et al (2005)	The mediating role of HRM in transformational leadership
Psychological	Change embedded within the minds of those affected	Rubin et al (2009)	Outcomes of leader organizational change cynicism
Systems	Emphasis upon interconnected nature of organizations	Avolio et al (2014)	Leadership and advanced IT transforming organizations
Cultural	Emphasis upon entrenched values and beliefs	Menges et al (2011)	Transformational leadership climate as an organizational level construct
Critical	Emphasis upon power, genuine empowerment and emancipation	Boje and Rhodes (2006)	Ronald McDonald as a transformational leader

Figure 5.6 Explaining leadership and organizational change through the application of a philosophies-based approach (Smith and Graetz, 2011)

The illustrative examples in Figure 5.6 are drawn exclusively from papers identified through reviewing *The Leadership Quarterly* (see Appendix Three). In particular, these leadership papers in a respected, refereed leadership journal engage with and offer insights into either transformation or change. This framework is equally applicable to the other publications cited in the earlier chapters, but focusing upon a single unified journal enables the contrasting of the diversity of explanations evident even within a single journal source. Contributors and readers of *The Leadership Quarterly* will have preferences for particular papers reflecting particular philosophies, with each philosophy sufficient that an academic could undertake all their research and scholarship within a single philosophy or within a pairing of philosophies. The following discussion briefly summarises the methodologies and conclusions contained within each of these illustrative examples (see Figure 5.6). It is likely that more than one philosophy is at work within each paper, but to aid exposition, only the major one has been highlighted.

The rational philosophy was evident in many of *The Leadership Quarterly* papers, with Berson and Avolio (2004) chosen as an illustrative example. The authors examined top- and middle-level manager style in a telecommunications firm with regards to how effectively strategic organizational goals were conveyed. Their explanatory analysis suggested that managers directly reporting to transformational leaders tended to have higher agreement with strategic organizational goals. Whereas biological philosophies often work with a biological metaphor of an organization, in the case of Reichard et al (2011), they studied the emergence of transformational leadership over a twelve-year span from adolescence. They found a significant relationship between adolescent extraversion and adult leader emergence and transformational leadership.

Currie et al (2009) were illustrative of the institutional philosophy at work, in their case, the study of leadership within English secondary schools. They highlighted how leadership is embedded within a societal context and influenced by institutional environments. Their approach allowed them to contrast results-oriented leadership with value-based leadership. Zhu et al (2005) studied 170 firms in Singapore, illustrating a resource philosophy at work and specifically testing an integrated model of CEO transformational leadership, human resource management (HRM) and organizational outcomes. They found that HRM fully mediated the relationship between CEO transformational leadership and subjectively assessed organizational outcomes. Psychological philosophies were very evident in *The Leadership Quarterly* papers, for example, Rubin et al (2009) researched the rarely examined impact of leader cynicism upon organizations using data from 106 manufacturing managers. They found that leader cynicism about organizational change negatively influenced both leader and employee outcomes, whereas transformational leadership leader behaviour mediated these relationships.

Avolio et al (2014), whilst interested in advanced IT systems, also applied systems theory within their paper (Katz and Kahn, 1978). In their review, they re-examined how theory, research and practice domains had evolved with reference to e-leadership, referring back to an earlier study by Avolio et al (2001). They provided a detailed set of conclusions within their paper, although they concluded rather obliquely that '. . .although the term e-leadership was introduced into the literature now more than a decade ago, the sun is still rising and shedding light on the earliest developments in this area, with much more to go before it hits its zenith' (Avolio et al, 2014:126).

Menges et al's (2011) study, which focused upon transformational leadership climate within 158 German small- to medium-sized enterprises, is illustrative of cultural philosophy at work. The transformational leadership climate referred to the degree to which leaders engaged in transformational leadership behaviours throughout an organization. They found a pattern of moderated mediation for overall employee productivity and employee's aggregate task performance behaviour with transformational leadership climate indirectly related to these outcome variables under a high trust climate, but not under a low trust climate.

Critical philosophies were not the norm in *The Leadership Quarterly*, but Boje and Rhodes's (2006) critique stands out for its audacious critical deconstruction of transformational leadership. They depicted the McDonald's clown Ronald McDonald as a transformational leader (this was in the context of a journal that had done so much to advance the concept of transformational leadership).

> This clown persona has enabled Ronald to emerge as a leader along two interrelated lines of organizational stylistic transformation: from epic to novelistic corporation and from purveyor of unhealthy foods to a nutrition-fitness enterprise.
>
> (Boje and Rhodes, 2006:94)

Smith and Graetz (2011) argue that each philosophy contributes in different ways to understanding, with no single philosophy fully encapsulating an explanation. The implication for this critical review of leadership and organizational change is that different philosophies inform the sub-field of leadership and organizational change in different ways. Sutherland and Smith (2013) subsequently outlined a dualities-aware approach towards leadership and organizational change, which was introduced in Chapter Three, where the following quotation was cited:

> Effective change leadership means appreciating how dualistic forces can shape and enable change. By adopting a dualities aware perspective, leaders can come to terms with the intuitive desire to resolve contradiction by instead managing the complementarities within contradictory forces.
>
> (Sutherland and Smith, 2013:220)

They are referring in this quotation to the practical implications of a dualities-aware approach, but their approach is also applicable to academic explanations. Sutherland and Smith (2013) highlighted five duality characteristics: Simultaneity (both/and thinking), relational (interdependence), minimal threshold (minimum required), dynamism and improvisation. What they propose is the antithesis of best practice, of the one-best-way conceptualisations of leadership and organizational change. Instead, they encourage avoiding 'either/or' thinking (manager or leader, change or continuity) in favour of 'both/and' thinking, for example, acknowledging a leader's involvement in both organizational changes and inevitable (although often unacknowledged) organizational continuities. Change leaders need to be relational, for example, encouraging collaborators to work both independently and within teams. Change leaders need to ensure minimal thresholds, for example, assuring job security for employees taking risks. Change leaders need to acknowledge and work with the dynamic interactions between duality poles such as integration and differentiation. The five leadership duality characteristics of simultaneity, relational, minimal threshold, dynamism and improvisation have implications for how leadership and organizational change is researched and explained, emphasising the need to draw upon varied insights of different philosophies (see Figure 5.6). In this way, the divergence of alternative explanations may be regarded as strengths rather than weaknesses.

CHALLENGES AND CRITIQUE OF LEADERSHIP AND ORGANIZATIONAL CHANGE

This section is organized around acknowledging research design and the methodological challenges raised in researching leadership and organizational change and critiques of the concepts of transformational leadership (Bass and Riggio, 2006) and leading change (Kotter, 1996).

Research design challenges A unifying theme of this critical review has been that the rhetoric of leadership and organizational change does not match the empirical reality. However, researching leadership and organizational change raises significant research design challenges, particularly in terms of ambiguity, contexts, dynamism and evaluation. As this chapter has acknowledged, boundaries around leadership and organizational change are very permeable, with considerable ambiguity around independent components of leadership and organizational change even before they are combined. Both leadership and organizational change speak to unknown futures, with leadership rhetoric and organizational change rhetoric implying certainties that only the passage of time can confirm (see Dawson 2003, 2014; March 1981). Questionnaire surveys, interviews, participant observation or documentary research have to address these ambiguities within their research designs. Unless the research was processual and longitudinal (see

Pettigrew et al, 2001), any forward-looking insights would inevitably be speculative. At present we can only assert the future, and we cannot predict the future with certainty.

Another challenge is contextual (see Pettigrew et al, 2001), as empirical findings from research into leadership and organizational change will be particular to their sector and/or national cultural context. In Chapter Two, fragmented insights into leadership and organizational change were offered. The identification of these insights informs our understanding of the influence of leadership on organizational change, although these insights may also reflect the influence of particular sectors and national contexts. Even within a single specific organization, leadership and organizational change interrelationships may vary at different organizational levels and within different functionalisms/specialisms. As Beyer (1999:318) warned, '[I]t seems a romantic oversimplification to describe organizations as if they had only one leader as a source of leadership.'

Whereas research designs such as questionnaire surveys, interview research, participant observation or documentary research might take a cross-sectional view of leadership and organizational change at a single moment in time, both leadership and organizational change are best understood dynamically. Leadership and organizational change are processes, rather than things (Van de Ven and Poole, 2005), thus requiring the research designs to address the processual and emergent nature of leadership. The dynamism of both leadership and organizational change is challenging, but in combination, particularly challenging. It is pragmatically understandable why there is a predisposition to quantitative questionnaire surveys (see, for example, contributions to *The Leadership Quarterly*). Process theories, as discussed in Chapter Three, have had a significant impact upon management and organization studies in general and organizational change in particular (see Langley et al, 2013), emphasising the prevalence of fluidity, emergence and becoming.

Grint (2005a) highlighted claims of leadership as critical to all organizational success (and failure) being as commonplace as claims to have discovered the recipe for success. Despite the management rhetoric, it is extremely difficult to empirically establish the successful achievement of organizational change. Success is often taken for granted or masked within the organization histories written by leaders celebrating how they successfully transformed their organizations (see Collins, 2000 and Huczynski, 2006 for further discussion). Writing with specific reference to transformational leadership, Tourish (2013:28) sceptically noted that 'success is due to the correct application of the transformational leadership model. Failures are due to external factors beyond its control.' This reasoning simultaneously creates a rationale for more transformational leadership and limits critique of transformational leadership. Whilst there is considerable rhetoric about leading change success (Kotter, 1996) and failure (Kotter, 1995), researching such success and failure is empirically challenging. This is partially explained in terms of the ambiguities, contexts and dynamism of leadership and organizational change already discussed, but also issues of perception complicate evaluations of leadership and evaluations of organizational change, with the success or failure likely to be in the eye of the beholder. The cause-and-effect relationships that the discourses of leadership and organizational change imply are problematic (see Barker, 1997). A satisfactory research design would need to isolate leadership from other explanations of why an organizational change has occurred, such as management, a particular organizational change methodology or the context/economic environment in which an organization was operating. Equally, instead of an implied linear and one-way cause-and-effect interrelationship, two-way interrelationships will be at work, requiring an effective research design to accommodate how organizational change influences as well as impacts leadership, and vice versa (see Hughes, 2011 for further discussion about evaluating organizational change).

These research design challenges do not negate the need to research leadership and organizational change, but they do highlight the problematic nature of making empirical advances in this area. The absence of anticipated research within the fields of leadership studies and/or organizational change studies into leadership and organizational change may be far more knowing than this critical review has implied.

Critiques of transformational leadership and leading change Earlier in this chapter, Bass's (1985) *Leadership Performance Beyond Expectations* and Kotter's (1996) *Leading Change* were analysed using frame analysis (Fairhurst, 2011; Fairhurst and Sarr, 1996). This was motivated by their disproportionate influence upon the sub-field of leadership and organizational change, with the Matthew Effect (Merton, 1968, 1988) acknowledged as potentially being at work. In the light of their influence upon the sub-field of leadership and organizational change, in this sub-section, the focus shifts to critiques of transformational leadership and leading change.

Bass and Riggio's (2006) *Transformational Leadership* was identified as the most-cited transformational leadership publication (see Appendix One). This book commenced with a preface from James McGregor Burns and Georgia Sorenson explicitly acknowledging their endorsement of *Transformational Leadership*. However, commentators critically questioned if the transformational leadership that Burns (1978) envisaged in *Leadership* was really being realised within Bernard Bass's conceptualisations. Carey (1992) critically questioned the shift from change towards higher values that Burns (1978) encouraged as opposed to the change leadership that Bass encouraged. Carey (1992) differentiated Burns's (1978) view of transforming leadership from Bass (1985) in three ways. Firstly, for Burns, the transforming leader raises followers' needs levels, whereas for Bass, the leader expands the needs and wants of followers. Secondly, Burns regarded moral leadership as essential to transforming leadership, whereas 'Bass removes the variables of moral good and evil and simply views transformational leadership as producing change (Bass, 1990)' (Carey, 1992: 220). Thirdly, there is divergence regarding how transactional and transformational leadership are related. Carey (1992:225) subsequently delved deeper into the differences between Burns and Bass:

> While moral leadership does imply change in both leaders and followers as Burns (1978) states, change per se is not always moral, since it does not invariably result in a "relationship of mutual stimulation and elevation" (Burns, 1978: 4) for both leader and follower.

There also appears to be confusion around the treatment of charisma within transformational leadership theories. Beyer (1999) was particularly prominent in criticising an emphasis on psychological explanations at the expense of sociological explanations (such as Weber, 1947). Beyer (1999) wanted a clear differentiation between charismatic leadership and transformational leadership, which would have been beneficial, but which Bass was unable to provide (Diaz-Saenz, 2011).

Yukl's (1999) influential critique of transformational leadership acknowledged Burns's (1978) emphasis upon the importance of collective leadership within transforming leadership, but added that other accounts of transformational leadership neglected the importance of distributed and shared leadership. In identifying the conceptual weaknesses of transformational leadership, Yukl (1999) regarded Bass (1985, 1996) as generating the most research at the time of his critique (see Figure 5.7).

In reviewing 30 years of transformational leadership theorising, Yukl (1999) offered a focused critique of conceptual weaknesses (see Figure 5.7) that merits further elaboration. The numbers in the text refer to the numbering in Figure 5.7.

Yukl (1999) found the underlying influence process of transformational and transactional leadership to be vague (1) and not having been studied systematically. He believed that the theory would be stronger if the way each type of behaviour affects mediating variables and outcomes was explained.

---

1. Ambiguity about underlying influence processes
2. Overemphasis on dyadic processes
3. Ambiguity about transformational behaviours
4. Ambiguity about transactional leadership
5. Omission of important behaviours
6. Insufficient specification of situational variables
7. Insufficient identification of negative effects
8. Heroic leadership bias

Figure 5.7 Conceptual weaknesses of transformational leadership (Yukl, 1999)

Transformational leadership tended to be conceptualised at the dyadic level (2) in preferring to explain a leader's direct influence over individual followers and not paying sufficient attention to organizational processes. Transformational behaviours tended to be identified through inductive processes (3). Transactional leadership included diverse and largely ineffective behaviours, with a failure to link the process of leader-subordinate exchange with transactional behaviours (4). Yukl (1999) identified the transformational behaviours missing (5) within Bass's (1996) account of transformational leadership at the dyadic level, inspiring and empowering, at the group level, facilitating agreement, mutual trust and co-operation, and building group identification and collective identity, and at the organizational level, articulating a vision and strategy, guiding and facilitating change and promoting organizational learning. There was an assumption within the theories of transformational leadership that leadership processes and outcomes remain the same in all situations (6). Transformational leadership theories did not recognise or identify situations where transformational leadership had a detrimental outcome (7). Transformational leadership theories worked with the implicit assumption of a heroic leader (8).

> Effective performance by an individual, group, or organization is assumed to depend on leadership by an individual with the skills to find the right path and motivate others to take it. In most versions of transformational leadership theory, it is a basic postulate that an effective leader will influence followers to make self-sacrifices and exert exceptional effort. Influence is unidirectional, and it flows from the leader to the follower.
>
> (Yukl, 1999:292)

In their critical review, Tourish and Pinnington (2002) highlighted transformational leadership potentially encouraging authoritarian forms of organization, which may be related back to Yukl's (1999) concerns about transformational leadership working with a historic stereotype of a leader. Tourish and Pinnington's (2002) critique was not with leadership per se, but that the dominant transformation leadership models were fundamentally flawed. Instead, they offered an alternative model which emphasised key elements of transactional leadership. They acknowledged the ubiquity of workplace power differentials and the need to look again to democratic and stakeholder perspectives for organizational restructuring. Currie and Lockett's (2007) critique narrowed the focus to questioning the applicability of transformational leadership to English public services, noting that transformational leadership as promoted through government policy diverged from its academic conception (Bryman, 1992). However, in reviewing transformational leadership literature, they found it to be strong on rhetoric and advocacy, yet weak on evidence. For Tourish (2013), transformational leadership as traditionally envisaged had become part of the problem, rather than the solution.

The treatment of transformational leadership in this section has been deliberately critical as a counterbalance to the acritical treatment in Chapter Two. In Diaz-Saenz's (2011:307) more balanced review, he concluded that 'most of the empirical research has supported the notion that transformational leadership has a favourable influence upon follower's performance, often arguing strongly in favour of the practice and development of transformational leadership behaviours.' Certainly, the research into transformational leadership looks impressive when compared to Kotter's (1995, 1996) conceptualisation of leading change. The following critique draws upon the critique within Hughes (forthcoming).

Kotter (1996:x) admitted in his preface that 'I have neither drawn examples or major ideas from any published source except my own writing nor tried to cite evidence from other sources to bolster my conclusions.' It is consequently strange that this book has subsequently been cited 6000+ times (see Appendix Two). A revised edition of *Leading Change* appeared in 2012; it was substantially the same book, but with a new preface. Kotter (2012:vii) claimed that 'the material in this book is not only still relevant now, sixteen years after it was published, but I believe it is more relevant, and for one reason the speed of change continues to increase.' Kotter's text maintains its stability, despite stability being espoused as no longer the norm. In critically reviewing Kotter's (1996/2012) enduring and highly cited account of leading change, seven failings of Kotter's transformation explanation of leadership are apparent (see Figure 5.8).

The following discussion expands upon the failings identified in Figure 5.8, with the numbers in the text referring back to Figure 5.8. Employees are depicted as resistors (1), for example, 'the key lies in understanding why organizations resist needed change. . .' (Kotter, 1996:16), 'Colin was typical of the foot draggers' (Kotter, 1996:104), 'these blockers stop needed action' (Kotter, 1996:114), 'an unwillingness to confront managers like Frank is common in change efforts' (Kotter, 1996:114), '. . .quick

---

1) Employees depicted as change resistors

2) Ethics, power and politics underplayed

3) Overemphasis upon a sequence of linear steps

4) Disparaging history limits learning and an appreciation of incremental change

5) Leaders and their communications are overemphasised

6) Underemphasis of unique cultural contexts

7) Rhetorical treatment of organizational success/failure

Figure 5.8 Why Kotter's (1996/2012) transformation explanations of leadership fail

performance improvements undermine the efforts of cynics and major league resisters'(Kotter, 1996:123). This type of simplistic/individual-based explanation has been critically questioned (Ford et al, 2002). The depiction of people as for/against a particular change is believed to neglect the multidimensional attitudes of employees towards change (Piderit, 2000). Even the pejorative language of resistance to change is questionable (Collins, 1998). The influence of ethics, power and politics is underplayed (2). Kotter (1996:61) lamented that 'trust is often absent in many organizations,' yet he appeared to prescribe dishonest actions that would potentially breach trust.

> Visible crises can be enormously helpful in catching people's attention and pushing up urgency levels. Conducting business as usual is very difficult if the building seems to be on fire. But in an increasingly fast-moving world, waiting for a fire to break out is a dubious strategy. And in addition to catching people's attention a sudden fire can cause a lot of damage.
>
> (Kotter, 1996:45)

Dishonestly claiming that '. . .the building seems to be on fire' to catch people's attention appears to contradict Kotter's espousal of trust. Kotter favours creating short-term wins that enhance the power and authority of leaders and reaffirm their centrality/authority in leading change. However, for Grint (2005a), the antithesis was required through an atmosphere of greater trust, in which poor leadership could be seen to fail and leaders helped to understand why they failed. The implication would be that through encouraging short-term defeats, everyone would collectively take responsibility for achieving the transformation effort. Despite developments between 1996 and 2012, such as the global financial recession, Kotter did not revise his coverage of ethics in the 2012 edition of his book, which was disappointing, given Harvard Business School's explicit and public engagement with the MBA Oath (see mbaoath.org).

There is an overemphasis upon a sequence of linear steps (3), with the dust cover of *Leading Change* (Kotter, 1996) stating that 'the book identifies an eight-step process that every company must go through to achieve its goal. . .' It is questionable if the eight-step process was a new process, as claimed (see dust cover), to bring organizations into the twenty-first century (see Figure 5.9).

Lewin (1947) identified three steps required for planned change in the middle of the last century (see Figure 5.9), which now appear very similar in their consequences to what Kotter (1996) was prescribing. The problem with step-based approaches is that they offer a rational analysis, a sequential approach to the planning and management of change, couched in a generally upbeat and prescriptive tone (Collins, 1998).

Change depicted as three steps	Kotter explains his eight steps
A successful change includes three aspects: unfreezing (if necessary) the present level L^1, moving to the new level L^2 and freezing group life on the new level. (Lewin, 1947:35)	The first four steps in the transformation process help defrost a hardened status quo. If change were easy, you wouldn't need all that effort. Phases five to seven then introduce many new practices. The last stage grounds the changes in the corporate culture and helps them stick. (Kotter, 1996:22)

Figure 5.9   Lewin's (1947) three steps and Kotter's (1996) eight steps

Disparaging history limits learning and appreciation of incremental change (4). Kotter (1996:142) was irritated with corporate history, writing that 'cleaning up historical artefacts does create an even longer change agenda, which an exhausted organization will not like. But purging of unnecessary interconnections can ultimately make transformation much easier.' However, the corporate transformations that Kotter was interested in and working on required a culturally sensitive approach mindful of corporate history. For example, Stadler and Hinterhuber (2005) offered a culturally sensitive and historically grounded longitudinal analysis of the leadership of transformations within Shell, Siemens and Daimler Chrysler. Kotter was sceptical (see Kotter, 1996:173) about incremental change, yet incremental change may be part of the paradox that senior managers encounter with regards to the oscillations between evolutionary and revolutionary change (see Burke, 2009; De Wit and Meyer, 2004; Dunphy and Stace, 1988; Johnson et al, 2010).

The leader and leader communications are overemphasised (5). Critical leadership literature (Grint, 2005a; Tourish, 2013; Yukl, 1999) challenges the popular societal belief in heroic leaders. Kotter's (1996:26) central thesis was that companies have too much change management and not enough change leadership. He wrote that '. . . successful transformation is 70 per cent to 90 per cent leadership and only 10 to 30 per cent management.' However, within *Leading Change*, he warned against leadership alone, writing that 'transformation is not a process involving leadership alone; good management is also essential' (Kotter, 1996:129). This emphasis upon leadership may be related back to the discussions in Chapter Four about the American Dream.

There is an underemphasis upon unique cultural contexts (6). In *Leading Change*, Kotter (1996) did not reveal the names of the companies, their operating contexts or the names of the featured leaders, making it impossible to locate these case studies within their own unique cultural and sector contexts. Instead, Kotter (1996) invoked the threat of a vague and rapidly changing environment (see Eccles and Nohria, 1992; Sorge and Van Witteloostuijn, 2004 for a critique), giving leaders the rationale to lead change through decisive action (in essence, strong leadership). Grint (2005b) has drawn attention to the potential for the context or situation to be actively constructed by the leader (or in this case, the leadership writer).

Organizational success/failure is treated rhetorically (7). The title of Kotter's (1995) paper, *Leading Change: Why Transformation Efforts Fail*, framed (Fairhurst, 2005) the notion that transformation efforts fail. However, Kotter (1995:59) never claimed that all transformation efforts fail or succeed, instead writing that '. . .most fall somewhere in between. . .' Kotter's eight leadership errors explained transformation failure in terms of internal factors rather than external environments, which is perverse given Kotter's preoccupation with his rapidly changing external environment. *Leading Change* switches from focusing upon errors and failure to successful transformation, although Kotter neither explains how to evaluate success/failure, nor encourages undertaking such an evaluation.

This critique has focused upon Kotter's (1996) prescription for leading change, but as Tourish (2013:7) has stated, 'leadership theory also needs to change.' Whereas *Leading Change* remains a landmark of leadership studies, as evidenced by 6000+ citations, it is stuck in the past and may even discourage the change Tourish (2013) encourages. In Chapter Two, Parry (2011) and Ford and Ford's (2012) reviews of the interrelationships between leadership and organizational change were featured. Parry (2011) discussed leadership and organizational change within his contribution to *The SAGE Handbook of Leadership*, concluding that:

> Leadership and organizational change are inextricably intertwined. However, 'organizational change' has become an interest for organizational consultants more so than for empirical researchers. There are many more books and articles on practitioner or conceptual scholarship than on theoretical or empirical scholarship. Much of the practitioner work is case study-based, and anecdotal and not rigorous in its conduct.
> (Parry, 2011:57)

Parry (2011) was not alone in his characterisation of the state of accumulated leadership and organizational change literature as being largely anecdotal and lacking rigour. Ford and Ford's (2012) review focused upon empirical evidence between 1990 and 2010, identifying weaknesses within the literature:

- An overemphasis upon individual leaders
- Subjective assessments of successful change
- Prevalence of single-point data collection research designs and
- A vocabulary which confused and added to the vagueness of leadership and organizational change understanding.

They conceded that based upon the evidence they had reviewed, they could not determine the leader's influence upon organizational change, or '... what leader actions and interactions are responsible for it, or whether the influence is only on the subjective perceptions of people affected by the change or also impacts the objective outcomes of change' (Ford and Ford, 2012:33).

DISCUSSION—THE ACCUMULATED STATE OF LEADERSHIP AND ORGANIZATIONAL CHANGE KNOWLEDGE?

In this chapter, the IJMR key principles offered a structure for this evaluation, in particular asking if there is a synthesis and accumulation of knowledge. In answering this question, Chapters Two, Three and Four have been revisited (see Figure 5.10).

The synthesis and evaluation of the accumulated state of leadership knowledge as reported in Chapter Two (see Figure 5.10) could best be described as disappointing. The most-cited literature was found to have a distinctly practitioner, rather than an empirical, orientation (compatible with the findings of Parry, 2011 and Ford and Ford, 2012). In looking creatively (optimistically) towards how leadership and organizational change knowledge was being advanced through refereed journals, *The Leadership Quarterly* contributions focused upon transformational leadership, potentially at the expense of competing explanations, and the *Journal of Change Management* contributions tended to focus upon the development, capabilities and competencies of change leaders as opposed to the relationships between leadership and organizational change. These findings beg the question: If our knowledge of leadership and organizational change was so limited, how is leadership and organizational change depicted in academic handbooks and university textbooks? The analysis reported in Chapter Two suggested very limited coverage in either leadership studies handbooks or organizational change studies handbooks, potentially reflecting the lack of accumulated knowledge to report upon or a lack of interest in the sub-field within the wider fields of study. This was mirrored in textbook treatments, which tended to feature generic and chronological accounts of leadership studies with inevitably little specifically to report upon with regards to leadership and organizational change.

Any understanding of leadership and organizational change has to draw upon the fields of both organizational change studies and leadership studies. In Chapters Three and Four, the fields of study were reviewed with specific reference to advancing understanding about leadership and organizational change, with key chapter themes highlighted in Figure 5.10. Organizational change as a field is informed by different disciplines, as is leadership studies, with the implication that these fields will be characterised by divergence and dissensus, reflecting the competing philosophies, paradigms

Chapter Two
'Leadership and
  Organizational Change:
  A 35-Year Review'
	The literature has a strong practitioner emphasis, stronger on prescription than analysis.
	The Leadership Quarterly emphasised transformational leadership and the *Journal of Change Management* emphasised leadership development, competencies and capabilities.
	Insights were not evident within academic handbooks, with apparent interest very limited within both fields of study.
	Textbooks confirmed the limitations of what was known about leadership and organizational change.

Chapter Three 'Understanding Organizational Change'	Organizational change as a field is informed by different disciplines. Organizational change understanding is a product of historiographical processes. Competing and ongoing explanations for organizational change exist. Philosophies and dualities of organizational change offer a pragmatic way forward. Leadership and organizational change requires rethinking (see REPLACE). Acknowledgement of the critical and contested nature of organizational change studies.
Chapter Four 'Leadership Studies'	Acknowledgement of a requirement to transform twenty-first century leadership studies. The critical leadership studies writings of Rost (1993) offered a way forward. Leadership studies regarded as mythical and socially constructed, employing persuasive discourses and frames. Followers denigrated within leadership studies and opportunities for collaboration largely avoided. The perceived differentiation between managers and leaders is cultural rather than empirically informed. Alternative and critical conceptualisations of leadership studies exist as a counterpoint to leadership studies orthodoxy.

Figure 5.10 Key findings, themes and insights from Chapters Two, Three and Four

and perspective of the different disciplines. The apparently fixed histories of the development of knowledge within these fields may be questioned in terms of historiographies favouring orthodox and mainstream accounts of historical development. Fields are characterised by competing explanations, with Smith and Graetz's (2011) emphasis upon the philosophies and dualities of organizational change favoured as being particularly applicable to leadership and organizational change. The requirement to rethink leadership and organizational change was illustrated through the discussion of the REPLACE framework.

In parallel to organizational change, leadership studies were characterised by a rational and mainstream orthodoxy, which Rost (1993) challenged through his *Leadership for the Twenty-First Century*. Leadership studies were depicted as mythical and socially constructed, employing persuasive discourses and frames, with social construction and discourse equally applicable to organizational change. An understanding of leadership in which followers were denigrated and opportunities for collaboration were largely avoided had been socially constructed. The differentiation between management and leadership integral to a perceived shift from change management to change leadership was found to be more cultural than empirically informed.

In addressing the chapter aim of evaluating the synthesis of accumulated leadership and organizational change knowledge, Figure 5.11 revisits a key design principle of this critical review that was introduced in Chapter One, as well as summarising major themes from this chapter. Orthodox accounts of leadership studies and orthodox accounts of organizational change studies as depicted in Figure 5.11 are the norm and, by definition, are likely to remain the norm. They depict the progress of the fields of study as rational and linear, with their progressive tone implying that eventually, a synthesis of accumulated knowledge will be achieved. The only limitation with such progressive notions is that very little progress has been made over the last 35 years, since Burns accused leadership studies of suffering from intellectual mediocrity. However, a theme running throughout this critical review has been that the orthodoxies of both leadership studies and organizational change studies maintain a problematic status quo, rather than facilitating change with regards to the dominant assumptions, attitudes and beliefs.

The editors of the *International Journal of Management Reviews* acknowledged that 'in summary, the majority of MOS scholars operate within what Kuhn (1962) describes as 'normal science', in which the field moves forward by incremental steps rather than as a result of paradigm shifting breakthroughs' (Jones and Gatrell, 2014:260). Jones and Gatrell (2014) did acknowledge Shepherd and Challenger (2013) and the different paradigm assumptions which underpin management and organization studies literature. However, in working with the IJMR key principles, Kuhn's (1962) profound insights into natural sciences informed by his background

Chapter One
'Introduction'

Orthodox Leadership Studies/Orthodox Organizational Change Studies
- Consensus, Convergence, Synthesis and the Accumulation of Knowledge

Critical Leadership Studies/Critical Organizational Change Studies
- Dissensus, Divergence, Discourses
- Knowledge Construction, not Accumulation

Chapter Five
'A Critical Evaluation of Leadership and Organizational Change'

Boundaries of Leadership and Organizational Change as a Sub-field
- Boundary spanning is problematic as two fields draw upon different disciplines, paradigms and philosophies.
- There is an absence of a tightly delineated boundary.
- Definitions and meanings of key terminology are vague and inconsistent.

Maturity of leadership and organizational change as a sub-field
- Mature in terms of lineage with 'Great Men' accounts of leadership.
- Many problematic background assumptions embedded within this sub-field.
- Only certain elements of the sub-field have been nurtured and developed.
- Emphasis upon self-will of individual leaders suggests immaturity.

Categories of leadership and organizational change as a sub-field
- Theories and practices within the sub-field framed through the writings of Bernard Bass and John Kotter.
- Metaphors influence thought processes within the sub-field such as transformational leader as a pedagogue, physician, architect, commander and saint.

Leadership and organizational change—methodologies contrasted
- *Philosophies of Organizational Change* (Smith and Graetz, 2011) offered a means of contrasting leadership and organizational change methodologies in terms of philosophies: Rational, biological, institutional, resource, psychological, systems, cultural, critical, and dualities.

Challenges and critiques of leadership and organizational change
- Research design challenges exist: Ambiguity, contexts, dynamism and evaluation.
- Criticisms of transformational leadership and leading change.
- Previous reviews found a lack of empirical insights into leadership and organizational change.

Figure 5.11 Chapter One revisited and Chapter Five summarised

as a physicist fifty years ago may now obscure rather than illuminate the advance of social science. The following discussion is organised around the four interrelated themes of divergence, dissensus, discourse and disappearance applicable to leadership studies and organizational change studies separately, as well as specifically to the sub-field of leadership and organizational change.

Divergence The diversity of the separate fields of leadership studies and organizational change studies discussed earlier has implications for understanding leadership and organizational change. Kuhn's (1962) famous mapping of scientific revolutions was concerned primarily with academic communities at the disciplinary level, rather than their specialisms/fields. The applicability of Kuhn's (1962) analysis to management and organization studies characterised by fields and sub-fields may be questioned. Kuhn (1962) believed that paradigms provided scientists not only with a map, but also provided directions essential for map-making. The unified science aspirations of convergent natural sciences encouraged by Kuhn (1962) were mirrored in the early expectations about a potential science of management. Convergence similar to natural sciences was never realised; instead, we witnessed the divergence of many fields, with sub-fields developing and continuing to develop (McKinley et al, 1999; Whitley, 1984, 2000).

In seeking to understand the boundaries of leadership and organizational change as a sub-field, the sub-field would be located at the overlap/intersection between the permeable fields of leadership studies and organizational change. The complicating factor in terms of bounding these debates is that both of these fields and their respective sub-fields are characterised by divergence, in contrast with Kuhn's (1962) belief in convergence. In terms of a unified science belief in convergence, divergence would be perceived as a weakness. However, in terms of Smith and Graetz's (2011) philosophies-based approach (see Figure 5.6) and their advocacy of a dualities-aware approach to leadership and organizational change (Sutherland and Smith, 2013:220), this divergence may prove fruitful in advancing understanding. In reviewing the leadership and organizational change literature, divergence was apparent in the different background assumptions (Gouldner, 1971), metaphors (see, for example, Amernic et al, 2007) and philosophies (Smith and Graetz, 2011) that have been featured in this chapter. The writings of Bernard Bass and John Kotter have been influential in framing thinking in this sub-field, as evidenced by citation rankings. Both have been subject to critique, as discussed in this chapter, but in offering two completely different explanations of leadership and organizational change, they offer another illustration of the divergence characterising this sub-field.

Dissensus Deetz (1996) revisited Burrell and Morgan's (1979) famous four-paradigm grid and was particularly interested in the linguistic turn, arguing for a move away from the grid's reification. Deetz encouraged focusing upon discourses rather than paradigms within management and organization studies (see also Hassard and Kelemen, 2002), which has been a major theme of this critical review. He contrasted research orientation differences in terms of 'local/emergent,' 'elite/a priori' and 'consensus/dissensus.' The final dimension is particularly pertinent to this critical review, as Deetz was not concerned with agreement versus disagreement, but rather presentations of unity or difference. Deetz's characterisation of consensus as unified science, triangulation and science as neutral contrasted with dissensus, which was characterised by positional complementarity and science as political. In terms of the consensus pole, 'random events and deviance are downplayed in significance when looking at norms and the normal, and attention is usually to processes reducing deviance, uncertainty, and dissonance' whereas, the dissensus pole '. . .draws attention to research programs which consider struggle, conflict, and tensions to be the natural state' (Deetz, 1996:197).

The implication of Deetz's (1996) reasoning is that mainstream writers within fields such as leadership studies and organizational change studies will strive for consensus whilst consciously avoiding uncertainty and dissonance. By association, the evaluation of the status of leadership and organizational change will be subjected to similar consensus-based criteria. Dissensus, such as critical philosophy (Smith and Graetz, 2011), is actively discouraged when the goal is to reduce deviance, uncertainty and dissonance. A rereading of the postscript to Kuhn's (2012:179) classic 1962 work from the perspective of power/knowledge is informative here: '[A] paradigm governs, in the first instance, not a subject matter, but rather a group of practitioners.' Consensus is likely to be encouraged through IJMR key principles, yet this may limit the considerable potential contribution dissensus could make to advancing understanding about leadership and organizational change. The divergence featured in the previous sub-section viewed as dissensus becomes a strength of the sub-field of leadership and organizational change.

As previously invoked, '. . .the more things change, the more they remain the same' (Calas and Smircich, 1991:568). Rost (1993) was highlighted in Chapter Four because he regarded the consensus orthodoxy of the leadership studies that he encountered as the greatest impediment to rethinking leadership studies. Burns (1978), whose work offered the critical milestone commencing this review, explicitly advocated dissensus in the context of leadership (as discussed in Chapter Four), yet it has been unitarist and consensus-based orthodoxy which has prevailed. In reviewing the sub-field of leadership and organizational change over 35 years, there has been a strong temptation to follow the consensus norms of reducing deviance, uncertainty and dissonance. This would result in assembling insights from the literature cited in order to produce a general theory of leadership and organizational change. This temptation has been resisted.

Discourse The disciplinary privileging of convergence over divergence and consensus over dissensus is likely to discourage discourse-based approaches that highlight contradictions, power/knowledge and conflict within language. However, the linguistic turn within management and organization studies (Deetz, 1996) is likely to be integral to advancing knowledge about leadership and organizational change. Belief in leadership as managing meaning has been central to the critical conceptualisations of leadership (Pondy, 1978) drawing upon social constructionism (Berger and Luckmann, 1966). These approaches have been very influential, growing rapidly over the past 15 years with no signs of stopping (Fairhurst and Grant, 2010). Fairhurst (2008), citing Bryman (2004:755), illustrates an 'alternating lenses' view of leadership practice:

> What is important is for leaders at the very apex of a hierarchy to be managers of meaning, especially in relation to the change process, but also to ensure that the more unexciting aspects of instrumental leadership get done.

In parallel to leadership studies, critical organizational change commentators such as Tsoukas (2005) have encouraged more sophisticated engagement with discourse, differentiating between behaviourist, cognitivist and discourse analytical approaches (see Phillips and Oswick, 2011 for a comprehensive overview of organizational discourse developments). The dilemma here is that such critical insights in disrupting the convergence-based consensus of the accumulated leadership and organizational knowledge lessen the case for leadership and organizational change as a sub-field. However, dependent upon your favoured paradigm, philosophy and perspective, understanding the socially constructed nature of leadership and organizational change as a discourse may prove to be informative.

Disappearance The empirically informed insight that the more closely you examine leadership, the more it seems to disappear (Alvesson and Sveningsson, 2003), is equally applicable to examining organizational change and its facilitation. Alvesson and Sveningsson (2003) recommended that leadership studies possess openness for, without privileging incoherence, variation, and fragmentation. The dilemma with the application of the IJMR key principles is that establishing boundaries and the full development (maturity) of the sub-field towards the accumulation of knowledge, rather than reifying the sub-field, results in the disappearance of this sub-field. Alvesson and Sveningsson (2003) wanted to open up debate around the paradigmatic assumptions, methodologies and ideological commitments characterising the majority of leadership studies. However, management and organization studies remain constrained within Kuhn's (1962) 'normal science' boundaries. Unintentionally, literature reviewing best practice maintains the status quo of orthodoxy, at the expense of alternative paradigms, philosophies and perspectives and, more specifically, limits opportunities for the development of this important and socially relevant sub-field. The 'hierarchy of sciences' (Cole, 1983), which assumed that natural sciences are the model of scientific progress that social science should emulate, may still be at work (see Hassard et al, 2008; Hughes, 2013 for further discussion).

Parry's (2011) critical summary of the accumulated state of leadership and organizational change knowledge was that it is of more interest to organizational consultants than empirical researchers, resulting in case study-based practitioner work that was anecdotal and not rigorous in its conduct. This is the antithesis of research-informed and evidence-based field studies informing practice. The greatest contribution the acknowledgement of the sub-field of leadership and organizational change could make would be encouraging empirically informed leadership practices in the context of organizational transformation and change. The belief that '. . .leaders "make change happen" is a belief core to many assumptions about how organizational change works' (Ladkin et al, 2010:127). However, to date, this belief has been largely supported by practitioner-based evidence (Parry, 2011). What if the empirical evidence was unable to support the belief that leadership makes change happen? That would have considerable implications for leadership studies and the leadership development industry, and more generally, organizations and policy makers. Practitioners require research-informed and evidence-based accounts of leadership and organizational change. In the absence of such literature, case study-based, anecdotal and not rigorous practitioner work (Parry, 2011) is likely to remain the orthodoxy, supported through the dominant paradigmatic assumptions which ensure this orthodoxy is self-sustaining. As this chapter has emphasized, the dissensus Burns (1978) highlighted as integral to transforming leadership is marginalised in favour of dubious convergence and consensus. Against this problematic and contested knowledge landscape, how do we explain leadership and organizational change?

REFERENCES

Abrahamson, E., and G. Fairchild. 1999. "Management Fashion: Lifecycles, Triggers, and Collective Learning Processes". *Administrative Science Quarterly* 44 (4): 708–740.

Alvesson, M., and A. Spicer, eds. 2011. *Metaphors We Lead By: Understanding Leadership in the Real World*. Abingdon: Routledge.

Alvesson, M., and S. Sveningsson. 2003. "The Great Disappearing Act: Difficulties in Doing 'Leadership'." *The Leadership Quarterly* 14 (3): 359–381.

Amernic, J., R. Craig and D. Tourish. 2007. The Transformational Leader as Pedagogue, Physician, Architect, Commander, and Saint: Five Root Metaphors in Jack Welch's Letters to Stockholders of General Electric. *Human Relations* 60 (12): 1839–1872.

Avolio. B.J., J.J. Sosik, S.S. Kahai and B. Baker. 2014. "E-Leadership: Re-Examining Transformations in Leadership Source and Transmission". *The Leadership Quarterly* 25 (1): 105–131.

Barker, R. 1997. "How Can We Train Leaders If We Don't Know What Leadership Is?" *Human Relations* 50 (3): 343–362.

Bass, B.M. 1981. *Stogdill's Handbook of Leadership*, rev. ed. New York: The Free Press.

Bass, B.M. 1985. *Leadership and Performance Beyond Expectations*. New York: Free Press.

Bass, B.M. 1990. "Editorial: Transformational Leaders Are Not Necessarily Participative". *The Leadership Quarterly* 1 (4): 219–272.

Bass, B.M. 1996. "A New Paradigm of Leadership: An Inquiry into Transformational Leadership". Alexandria, VA: US Army Research Institute for the Behavioral and Social Sciences.

Bass, B.M., and R.E. Riggio. 2006. *Transformational Leadership*. Mahwah, NJ: Lawrence Erlbaum Associates Inc/Psychology Press.

Beer, M., and N. Nohria, eds. 2000. *Breaking the Code of Change*. Boston: Harvard Business School Press.

Beer, M., R.A. Eisenstat and B. Spector. 1990. "Why Change Programs Don't Produce Change". *Harvard Business Review* 68 (6): 158–166.

Berger, P.L., and T. Luckmann. 1966. *The Social Construction of Reality: A Treatise in the Sociology of Knowledge*. Garden City, NY: Anchor Books.

Berson, Y., and B.J. Avolio. 2004. "Transformational Leadership and the Dissemination of Organizational Goals: A Case Study of a Telecommunication Firm". *The Leadership Quarterly* 15 (5): 625–646.

Beyer, J.M. 1999. "Taming and Promoting Charisma to Change Organizations". *The Leadership Quarterly* 10 (2): 307–330.

Boje, D.M., and C. Rhodes. 2006. "The Leadership of Ronald McDonald: Double Narration and Stylistic Lines of Transformation". *The Leadership Quarterly* 17 (1): 94–103.

Bryman, A. 1992. *Charisma and Leadership in Organizations*. Newbury Park, CA: Sage Publications Inc.

Bryman, A. 2004. "Qualitative Research on Leadership: A Critical But Appreciative Review". *The Leadership Quarterly* 15 (6): 729–770.

Burke, W.W. 2009. "Leading Organization Change". In *Organization Change: A Comprehensive Reader*, eds. W.W. Burke, D.G. Lake and J.W. Paine, 737–761. San Francisco: Jossey Bass.

Burnes, B. 1992. *Managing Change*, 1st ed. Harlow: FT Prentice Hall.

Burns, J.M. 1978. *Leadership*. New York: Harper Row Publishers.

Burrell, G., and G. Morgan. 1979. *Sociological Paradigms and Organizational Analysis*. London: Heinemann.

Calas, M.B., and L. Smircich. 1991. "Voicing Seduction to Silence Leadership". *Organization Studies* 12 (4): 567–602.

Carey, M.R. 1992. "Transformational Leadership and Fundamental Option for Self—Transcendence". *The Leadership Quarterly* 3 (3): 217–236.

Carnall, C.A. 1990. *Managing Change in Organizations*, 1st ed. Hemel Hempstead: Prentice Hall International (UK) Ltd.

Cole, S. 1983. "The Hierarchy of the Sciences?" *American Journal of Sociology* 89 (1): 111–139.

Collins, D. 1998. *Organizational Change: Sociological Perspectives*. London: Routledge.

Collins, D. 2000. *Management Fads and Buzzwords: Critical—Practical Perspectives*. London: Routledge.

Collinson, D. 2011. "Critical Leadership Studies". In *The SAGE Handbook of Leadership*, eds. A. Bryman, D. Collinson, K. Grint, B. Jackson and M. Uhl-Bien, 181–194. London: Sage Publications Ltd.

Collinson, D. 2012. "Prozac Leadership and the Limits of Positive Thinking". *Leadership* 8 (2): 87–107.

Cornelissen, J.P., R. Holt and M. Zundel. 2011. "The Role of Analogy and Metaphor in the Framing and Legitimization of Strategic Change". *Organization Studies* 32 (12): 1701–1716.

Currie, G., A. Lockett and O. Suhomlinova. 2009. "Leadership and Institutional Change in the Public Sector: The Case of Secondary Schools in England". *The Leadership Quarterly* 20 (5): 664–679.

Currie, G., and O. Lockett. 2007. "A Critique of Transformational Leadership: Moral, Professional and Contingent Dimensions of Leadership Within Public Service Organizations". *Human Relations* 60 (2): 341–370.

Dawson, P. 2003. *Understanding Organizational Change: The Contemporary Experience of People at Work*. London: Sage Publications Ltd.

Dawson, P. 2014. "Reflections: On Time, Temporality and Change in Organizations". *Journal of Change Management* 14 (3): 285–308.

De Caluwe, L., and H. Vermaak. 2003. *Learning to Change: A Guide for Organization Change Agents*. London: Sage Publications Ltd.

De Wit, B., and R. Meyer. 2004. *Strategy: Process, Content and Context*. London: Thomson Learning.

Deetz, S. 1996. "Crossroads—Describing Differences in Approaches to Organization Science: Rethinking Burrell and Morgan and Their Legacy". *Organization Science* 7 (2): 191–207.

Demers, C. 2007. *Organizational Change Theories: A Synthesis*. Los Angeles: Sage Publications.

Diaz-Saenz, H.R. 2011. "Transformational Leadership". In *The SAGE Handbook of Leadership*, eds. A. Bryman, D. Collinson, K. Grint, B. Jackson and M. Uhl-Bien, 299–310. London: Sage Publications Ltd.

Docherty, T. 2014. "Hostile Takeover". *Times Higher Education* 4th–10th December 2 (181): 40–43.

Dunphy, D., and D. Stace. 1988. "Transformational and Coercive Strategies for Planned Organizational Change: Beyond the O.D. Model". *Organization Studies* 9 (3): 317–334.

Eccles, R.G., and N. Nohria. 1992. *Beyond the Hype: Rediscovering the Essence of Management*. Boston: Harvard Business School Press.

Eisenhardt, K.M. 2000. "Paradox, Spirals and Ambivalence: The New Language of Change and Pluralism". *Academy of Management Review* 25 (4): 703–705.

Fairhurst, G.T. 2005. "Reframing the Art of Framing: Problems and Prospects for Leadership". *Leadership* 1 (2): 165–185.

Fairhurst, G.T. 2008. "Discursive Leadership: A Communication Alternative to Leadership Psychology". *Management Communication Quarterly* 21 (4): 510–521.

Fairhurst, G.T. 2011. *The Power of Framing: Creating the Language of Leadership*. San Francisco: Jossey Bass, Wiley Imprint.

Fairhurst, G.T., and D. Grant. 2010. "The Social Construction of Leadership: A Sailing Guide". *Management Communication Quarterly* 24 (2): 171–210.

Fairhurst, G.T., and R.A. Sarr. 1996. *The Art of Framing: Managing the Language of Leadership*. San Francisco: Jossey Bass Inc.

Ford, J.D. and L.W. Ford. 2012. "The Leadership of Organization Change: A View from Recent Empirical Evidence". In *Research in Organizational Change and Development (Research in Organizational Change and Development, Volume 20)*, eds. In Abraham B. (Rami) Shani, William A. Pasmore, Richard W. Woodman (eds.) 1–36. Emerald Group Publishing Limited.

Ford J.D., L.W. Ford and R.T. McNamara. 2002. "Resistance and the Background Conversations of Change". *Journal of Organizational Change Management* 15 (2): 105–121.

Frahm, J. 2007. "Organizational Change: Approaching the Frontier, Some Faster than Others (combined review of five books)". *Organization* 14 (6): 945–955.

Gouldner, A.W. 1971. *The Coming Crisis of Western Sociology*. London: Heinemann.

Grint, K. 2000. *The Arts of Leadership*. Oxford: Oxford University Press.

Grint, K. 2005a. *Leadership: Limits and Possibilities*. Houndmills: Palgrave Macmillan.

Grint, K. 2005b. "Problems, Problems, Problems: The Social Construction of 'Leadership' ". *Human Relations* 58 (11): 1467–1494.

Grint, K. 2008. "Forward to the Past or Back to the Future? Leadership, 1965–2006". In *Mapping the Management Journey: Practice, Theory and Context*, eds. S, Dopson, M. Earl and P. Snow, 104–118. Oxford: Oxford University Press.

Haslam, S.A., S.D. Reicher and M.J. Platlow. 2011. *The New Psychology of Leadership: Identity Influence and Power*. Hove: Psychology Press.

Hassard, J., and M. Kelemen. 2002. "Production and Consumption in Organizational Knowledge: The Case of the 'Paradigms debate' ". *Organization* 9 (2): 331–355.

Hassard, J., M. Kelemen and J. Wolfram Cox. 2008. *Disorganization Theory: Explorations in Alternative Organizational Analysis*. London: Routledge.

Hatch, M.J., M. Kostera and A. Kozminski. 2006. "The Three Faces of Leadership: Manager, Artist and Priest". *Organizational Dynamics* 35 (1): 49–68.

Huczynski, A. 2006. *Management Gurus*, rev. ed. Abingdon: Routledge.

Hughes. M. 2011. "Do 70% of Organizational Change Initiatives Really Fail?" *Journal of Change Management* 11 (4): 451–464.

Hughes, M. 2013. Book Review Essay: The Territorial Nature of Organizational Studies. *Culture and Organization* 19 (3): 261–274.

Hughes, M. forthcoming. "Leading Changes: Why Transformation Explanations Fail". *Leadership*.

Johnson, G., R. Whittington and K. Scholes. 2010. *Exploring Strategy: Texts and Cases*, 9th ed. Harlow: Financial Times/ Prentice Hall.

Jones, O., and C. Gatrell. 2014. "Editorial: The Future of Writing and Reviewing for IJMR". *International Journal of Management Reviews* 16 (3): 249–264.

Kanter, R.M. 1999. "The Enduring Skills of Change Leaders". *Leader to Leader* Summer, 13: 15–22.

Katz, D., and R.L. Kahn. 1978. *The Social Psychology of Organizations*. Chichester: John Wiley and Sons.

Kelly, S. 2014. "Towards a Negative Ontology of Leadership". *Human Relations* 67 (8): 905–922.

Kotter J.P. 1988. *The Leadership Factor*. New York: The Free Press.

Kotter J.P. 1990. *A Force for Change: How Leadership Differs from Management*. New York: Free Press.

Kotter, J.P. 1995. "Leading Change: Why Transformation Efforts Fail". *Harvard Business Review* 73 (2): 259–267.

Kotter, J.P. 1996 and 2012. *Leading Change*. Boston: Harvard Business School Press.

Kuhn, T.S. 1962 and 2012. *The Structure of Scientific Revolutions*. Chicago: The University of Chicago Press.

Ladkin, D., M. Wood and J. Pillay. 2010. "How Do Leaders Lead Change?" In *Rethinking Leadership: A New Look at Old Leadership Questions*, ed. D. Ladkin, 127–152. Cheltenham: Edward Elgar.

Lakoff, G., and M. Johnson. 1980. *Metaphors We Live By*. Chicago: The University of Chicago Press.

Langley, A., C. Smallman, H. Tsoukas and A.H. Van de Ven. 2013. "Process Studies of Change in Organization and Management: Unveiling Temporality, Activity and Flow". *Academy of Management Journal* 56 (1): 1–13.

Lewin, K. 1947. "Frontiers in Group Dynamics: Concept, Method and Reality in Social Science; Social Equilibria and Social Change". *Human Relations* 1 (1): 5–41.

March, J.G. 1981. "Footnotes to Organizational Change". *Administrative Science Quarterly* 26 (4): 563–577

Marshak, R. 1993. "Managing the Metaphors of Change". *Organizational Dynamics* 22 (1): 44–56.

Mckinley, W., M.A. Mone and G. Moon. 1999. "Determinants and Development of Schools in Organization Theory". *Academy of Management Review* 24 (4): 634–648.

Merton, R. 1968. "The Matthew Effect in Science". *Science* 159: 56–63.

Merton, R. 1988. "The Matthew Effect in Science, II: Cumulative Advantage and the Symbolism of Intellectual Property". *ISIS* 79: 606–623.

Menges, J.I., F. Walter, B. Vogel and H. Bruch. 2011. "Transformational Leadership Climate: Performance Linkages, Mechanisms, and Boundary Conditions at the Organizational Level". *The Leadership Quarterly* 22 (5): 893–909.

Morgan, G. 1986. *Images of Organization*. Thousand Oaks, CA: Sage Publications Inc.

O'Reilly, D., and M. Reed. (2010) "'Leaderism': An Evolution of Managerialism in UK Public Service Reform". *Public Administration* 88 (4): 960–978.

Oswick, C., and R.J. Marshak. 2011. "Images of Organization Development: The Role of Metaphor in Processes of Change". In *The Routledge Companion to Organizational Change*, eds. D.M. Boje, B. Burnes and J. Hassard, 104–114. London: Routledge.

O'Toole, J. 1995. *Leading Change: Overcoming the Ideology of Comfort and the Tyranny of Custom*. San Francisco: Jossey Bass—An Imprint of Wiley.

Palmer, I., and R. Dunford. 1996. "Conflicting Use of Metaphors: Reconceptualizing Their Use in the Field of Organizational Change". *The Academy of Management Review* 21 (3): 691–717.

Parry, K.W. 2011. "Leadership and Organization Theory". In *The SAGE Handbook of Leadership*, eds. A. Bryman, D. Collinson, K. Grint, B. Jackson and M. Uhl-Bien, 53–70. London: Sage Publications Ltd.

Peters, T.J., and R.H. Waterman. 1982. *In Search of Excellence: Lessons from America's Best Run Companies*. New York: Harper Row.

Pettigrew, A.M., R.W. Woodman and K.S. Cameron. 2001. "Studying Organizational Change and Development: Challenges for Future Research". *Academy of Management Journal* 44 (4): 697–713.

Piderit, S.K. 2000. "Rethinking Resistance and Recognizing Ambivalence: A Multidimensional View of Attitudes Towards an Organizational Change". *Academy of Management Review* 25 (4): 783–794.

Pinder, C.C., and V.W. Bourgeios. 1982. "Controlling Tropes in Administrative Science". *Administrative Science Quarterly* 27 (4): 641–652.

Phillips, N., and C. Oswick. 2011. "Organizational Discourse: Domains, Debates, and Directions". *The Academy of Management Annals* 6 (1): 435–481.

Podsakoff, P.M., S.B. Mackenzie, N.P. Podsakoff and D.G. Bachrach. 2008. "Scholarly Influence in the Field of Management: A Bibliometric Analysis of the Determinants of University and Author Impact in the Management Literature of the Past Quarter of a Century". *Journal of Management* 34 (4): 641–720.

Pollitt, C. 1993. *Managerialism and the Public Services*. 2nd ed. Blackwell: Oxford.

Pondy, L.R. 1978. "Leadership Is a Language Game". In *Readings in Managerial Psychology*, eds. H.J. Leavitt, L.R. Pondy, and D.M. Boje, 224–233, 1989. Chicago: University of Chicago Press.

Reichard, R.J., R.E. Riggio, D.W. Guerin, P.H. Oliver, A.W. Gottfried and A. Eskeles. 2011. "A Longitudinal Analysis of Relationships Between Adolescent Personality and Intelligence with Adult Leader Emergence and Transformational Leadership". *The Leadership Quarterly* 22 (3): 471–481.

Rost, J.C. 1993. *Leadership for the Twenty-First Century*. Westport: Praeger Publishers.

Rost, J.C. 1997. "Moving from Individual to Relationship: A Post-industrial Paradigm of Leadership". *The Journal of Leadership Studies* 4 (4): 3–16.

Rubin, R.S., E.C. Dierdorff, W.H. Bommer and T.T. Baldwin. 2009. "Do Leaders Reap What They Sow? Leader and Employee Outcomes of Leader Organizational Cynicism About Change". *The Leadership Quarterly* 20 (5): 680–688.

Shepherd, C., and R. Challenger. 2013. "Revisiting Paradigm(s) in Management Research: A Rhetorical Analysis of the Paradigm Wars". *International Journal of Management Reviews* 15 (2): 225–244.

Smircich, L., and G. Morgan. 1982. "Leadership: The Management of Meaning". *The Journal of Applied Behavioural Science* 18 (3): 257–273.

Smith, A.C.T., and F.M. Graetz. 2011. *Philosophies of Organizational Change*. Cheltenham: Edward Elgar Publishing Ltd.

Sorge, A., and A. Van Witteloostuijn. 2004. "The (Non) Sense of Organizational Change: An Essai About Universal Management Hypes, Sick Consultancy Metaphors and Healthy Organization Theories". *Organization Studies* 25 (7): 1205–1231.

Spicer, A., and M. Alvesson. 2011. "Metaphors for Leadership". In *Metaphors We Lead By: Understanding Leadership in the Real World*, eds. M. Alvesson and A. Spicer, 31–50. Abingdon: Routledge.

Stadler, C., and H.H. Hinterhuber. 2005. "Shell, Siemens and Daimler Chrysler: Leading Change in Companies with Strong Values". *Long Range Planning* 38 (5): 467–484.

Stickland, F. 1998. *The Dynamics of Change*. London: Routledge.

Sutherland, F., and A.C.T. Smith. 2013. "Leadership for the Age of Sustainability: A Dualities Approach to Organizational Change". In *Organizational Change, Leadership and Ethics: Leading Organizations Towards Sustainability*, eds. R.T. By and B. Burnes, 216–239. London: Routledge.

Tichy, N.M., and M.A. Devanna. 1986. *The Transformational Leader: The Key to Global Competitiveness*. New York: John Wiley and Sons.

TIME. (2014). *The 25 Most Influential Business Management Books*. http://content.time.com/time/specials/packages/completelist/0,29569,2086680,00.html Accessed 13/10/14.

Tourish, D. 2013. *The Dark Side of Transformational Leadership*. London: Routledge.

Tourish, D., and Pinnington, A. 2002. "Transformational Leadership, Corporate Cultism and the Spirituality Paradigm: An Unholy Trinity in the Workplace". *Human Relations* 55 (2): 147–172.

Tsoukas, H. 2005. "Afterword: Why Language Matters in the Analysis of Organizational Change". *Journal of Organizational Change Management* 18 (1): 96–104.

Van de Ven, A.H., and M.S. Poole. 1995. "Explaining Development and Change in Organizations". *Academy of Management Review* 20 (3): 510–540.

Van de Ven, A.H., and M.S. Poole. 2005. "Alternative Approaches for Studying Organizational Change". *Organization Studies* 26 (9): 1377–1404.

Wagner, T., R. Kegan, L.L. Lahey, R.W. Lemons, J. Garnier, D. Helsing, A. Howell and H.T. Rasmussen. (2010). *Change Leadership: A Practical Guide to Transforming Our Schools*. San Francisco, CA: Jossey Bass—An Imprint of Wiley.

Weber, M. 1947. *The Theory of Social and Economic Organization (trans)*. Glencoe, Il: Free Press.

Western, S. 2013. *Leadership: A Critical Text*, 2nd ed. Los Angeles: Sage Publications.

Whitley, R. 1984. "The Fragmented State of Management Studies: Reasons and Consequences". *Journal of Management Studies* 21 (3): 331–348.

Whitley, R. 2000. *The Intellectual and Social Organization of the Sciences*. Oxford: Oxford University Press.

Yukl, G. 1999. "An Evaluation of Conceptual Weaknesses in Transformational and Charismatic Leadership Theories". *The Leadership Quarterly* 10 (2): 285–305.

Zhu, W., I.K.H. Chew and W.D. Spangler. 2005. "CEO Transformational Leadership and Organizational Outcomes: The Mediating Role of Human-Capital-Enhancing Human Resource Management". *The Leadership Quarterly* 16 (1): 39–52.

6 Towards the Leadership of Organizational Change

INTRODUCTION

> If a man will begin with certainties, he shall end in doubts; but if he will
> be content to begin with doubts, he shall end in certainties.
>   Francis Bacon (1561–1626) "Of Great Place"

In *Developing Change Leaders*, Aitken and Higgs (2010:119) thoughtfully
invoked Francis Bacon. In this critical review, a waltz has featured between
the promise and seduction of leadership of organizational change discourses that suggest organizational change and transformation certainties
and academic doubt about the intangible and socially constructed nature of
leadership and organizational change. Far more practitioner or conceptual
scholarship than theoretical or empirical scholarship currently informs our
understanding of leadership and organizational change (Parry, 2011). Consultants understandably gravitate towards certainties in their prescriptions,
and practitioners by definition undertake practices, rather than introspec-
tively reflecting upon what all of this means. It is not part of consultants',
developers' or practitioners' primary remit to empirically advance understanding; the responsibility to inform understanding resides with academics,
through their research, scholarship and teaching.

The existence of large volumes of leadership literature (Grint, 2005a)
and organizational change literature (Thomas and Hardy, 2011) implies
the existence of an extensive and informative leadership and organizational
change literature that is successfully informing practice. Whilst outwardly,
the extensive fields of organizational change studies (Chapter Three) and
leadership studies (Chapter Four) appear convincing, looking inwards, these
chapters highlighted fields characterised by dissensus and divergence, rather
than the rational and functional orthodoxies that scholars in these fields
reassuringly imply to external audiences. The major finding of this critical
review was that the existence of a significant body of research that informed
leadership and organizational change literature was largely a chimera. There
were empirical insights, which were highlighted in Chapter Two, but these
were exceptions rather than the rule.

In previous overviews of leadership and organizational change, Parry (2011) largely encountered practitioner work that was case study-based, anecdotal and lacking rigour. Ford and Ford (2012) identified weaknesses in this literature as an over-emphasis on the role of individual leaders, subjective assessments of change implementation and leadership, single-point data collection and a vocabulary that added to the confusion about and vagueness of both the research and conclusions. Based upon the evidence they reviewed, Ford and Ford (2012) could not conclude what a leader's influence upon organizational change was, what leader actions and interactions were responsible for change, or whether the influence was only on subjective perceptions of people affected by the change or actually impacted objective outcomes of change. The preliminary conclusions reported in Chapter Two confirmed these earlier findings. These conclusions are a disappointing indictment of the progress made within the fields of organizational change studies and leadership studies in terms of establishing what is known, let alone critically questioning what is known about leadership and organizational change. However, hope resides within Bacon's wise encouragement cited earlier. The sub-field of leadership and organizational change does need to embrace doubt, rather than the spurious certainties currently characterising this sub-field. If these depressing conclusions are perceived as reasons to doubt what we know, in Bacon's terms, they may eventually lead towards the certainties that we seek and that practitioners deserve. The large caveat, which this critical review has highlighted, relates to the ability of the status quo to endure, supported through mainstream and orthodox theories and academic moments for change being 'lost in translation' (discussed further in this chapter). In Chapter One, Grint's (2008) insight into the tendency of leadership studies to go forward to the past, rather than going back to the future, was highlighted. The sub-field of leadership and organizational change appears to be at such a crossroads, and only time will tell if this sub-field over the next few years is characterised by forward-to-the-past certainties or back-to-the-future uncertainties. The hope here is that this critical review will encourage colleagues to go back to the future and question dominant paradigms and assumptions which hamper learning, but in reviewing this literature, the capacity of the orthodox/mainstream literature for self-preservation has been very prevalent.

In this concluding chapter, eight very different explanations of leadership and organizational change informed by the previous five chapters are presented, with a final concluding section that draws upon these explanations. Those who favour convergence and the natural science aspirations of a unified management science might prefer a single, universal consensus explanation, with two or three pithy conclusions, yet such a consensus would misrepresent the divergent sub-field that has been encountered. Instead, alternative explanations reflect and draw upon the diversity and dissensus of both the fields of leadership studies and organizational change studies and their different background assumptions of competing philosophies, paradigms and perspectives. In this spirit, the review favoured a broadly critical/questioning approach, with pluralist understanding reflected within these eight explanations (see Figure 6.1).

Before elaborating on these eight explanations, it is necessary to take stock of the review process reported here, which is 'a complex mixture of appreciation, wariness, anticipation, regret and pride, all fused into thoughts of renewal' (Weick, 1996:301). Weick's poetic rendition of taking stock offers a means to undertake self-inventory with regards to this critical review. Appreciation relates to having an opportunity to undertake this 35-year historic review and having the necessary tools and resources. Wariness relates to the volume of leadership literature and organizational change literature that now exists. There is a liberating certainty in wariness, knowing that publications offering insights will have been missed and some of those that have been cited should have received greater attention. Anticipation relates to the high, unfulfilled expectations about the leadership and organizational change literature, superseded by the anticipation

Explaining leadership and organizational change as:	Reflected in mainstream orthodoxy	Explanation orientation/ level	Informed by this chapter, as well as, these chapters
1. Problematic assumptions	Chapter Two	Paradigm	Chapters One, Three and Five
2. The gap between literatures	Chapter Two	Paradigm	Chapters Three, Four and Five
3. A socially constructed mythology	Chapters Two and Four	Paradigm	Chapter Four
4. Leading change rather than managing stability	Chapters Two and Four	Culture	Chapter Four
5. Opportunities lost in translation	Chapters Two, Three and Four	Past	Chapters Three and Four
6. The show that never ends	Chapter Two	Past	Chapter Five
7. The practice of leading organizational change	Chapter Two	Future	Chapters Three, Four and Five
8. Collaborative change leadership	Chapter Four	Future	Chapters Three, Four and Five

Figure 6.1 Emerging explanations of leadership and organizational change

that this critical review might potentially provoke colleagues to doubt the current leadership of organizational change discourses. Regret that there was never going to be enough time to complete this labour of love; even a lifetime would not be quite enough time to comprehensively review this divergent and contradictory literature. Pride relates to at least attempting the review regardless of the outcome. Every journey begins with the smallest step, and this journey really did begin with unease about Kotter's (1996) eight steps and their influence upon the sub-field. Most important, though, is the relevance of thoughts of renewal, regardless of if you are an enthusiastic structural-functionalist preoccupied with the practicalities of leading change or a weary Critical Theorist challenging painful structural inequalities. Leadership and organizational change as a sub-field has potential for renewal, and it would be a tragedy if the defining characteristic of the sub-field remained as the sub-field's inability to change.

Two final questions based upon the *International Journal of Management Reviews* key literature reviewing principles were carried over from Chapter Five:

- Is there a clear statement about what contribution the review makes to theory, practice and/or research?
- Are there reasoned and authoritative conclusions as to where the literature is, or perhaps should be going, and what important questions, or gaps, still exist in the field?

The following eight explanations of leadership and organizational change each conclude with a succinct and clear signalling of the implications of the explanation for theory, research and practice (signposted by bold and italicised sub-headings). The nature of the eight explanations addresses where the literature should be going, questions raised and identifies gaps in the field. These explanations should be read in conjunction with the evaluation of the status of the sub-field of leadership and organizational change, which was the focus of Chapter Five. After the eight explanations, a final concluding commentary drawing upon the eight explanations is offered.

1. LEADERSHIP AND ORGANIZATIONAL CHANGE AS PROBLEMATIC ASSUMPTIONS

In Chapter Five, interest in background assumptions (Gouldner, 1971) within social theory was revisited, prompted by the background assumptions encountered when reviewing leadership and organizational change literature, the assumed existence of consensus understandings of leadership and of organizational change, assumptions that leadership and management can/should be differentiated and the assumption that leadership combined with organizational change results in successful change. As cited in Chapter Five, changes derive not so much from the invention of new research techniques, but from new ways of looking at data, and they may neither refer to nor be occasioned by 'data,' old or new (Gouldner, 1971). In seeking to understand leadership and organizational change, it is difficult to disrupt the background assumption that leadership results in successful organizational change. More broadly, societies feature stories about the role of great leaders making history and initiating change going back a long way (Haslam et al, 2011). For Barker (1997:346), the influence of a feudal paradigm of leadership was still at work, characterised by '. . .an image of a powerful male who sits atop a hierarchical structure directing and controlling the activities of subjects toward the achievement of the leader's goals.' In many ways, the assumptions around leadership and organizational change are continuations of such societal beliefs, with discussions about research and theories as inconvenient sideshows that distract from the main event. In this critical review, attempts have been made to disrupt the assumption that leadership results in successful organizational change. In Chapter Three, this was accomplished by highlighting the influence of competing historiographies, paradigms and philosophies upon fields. In Chapter Four, this was achieved by highlighting the socially constructed nature of leadership mythologies, as well as questioning the differentiating and privileging of leadership over management. In Chapter Five, the ways leadership and organizational change had been framed (Fairhurst, 2005) in terms of transformational leadership (Bass, 1985) and leading change (Kotter, 1996) and the weaknesses within these explanations were presented.

Alvesson and Sandberg (2011) highlighted a tendency of researchers to creatively construct gaps in the literature without significantly challenging the literature's underlying assumptions. In encouraging the problematisation of assumptions, they offer a healthy warning:

> Challenging assumptions that underlie existing studies is often risky, since it means questioning existing power relations in a scientific field, which may result in upsetting colleagues, reviewers, and editors.
> (Alvesson and Sandberg, 2011:250)

Alvesson and Sandberg (2011) identified five broad sets of assumption open for problematisation: In-house, root metaphor, paradigm, ideology and field assumptions. This typology informs the first explanation of leadership and organizational change as problematic assumptions. In-house assumptions with regards to transformational leadership (Bass, 1985) and leading change (Kotter, 1996) were very apparent. For example, Bass (1985) regarded transformational leadership as an extension of Burns's (1978) work, whereas Carey (1992) questioned this assumption. Kotter (2012) believed that his revised edition of *Leading Change* (1996) was still relevant and required no changes to the main text (see Hughes, forthcoming, for a critique of this assumption). In terms of root metaphor assumptions, Chapter Five highlighted many metaphors apparent both within leadership studies and organizational change studies. In reviewing this literature, the root metaphor of the leader as a messiah critically depicted by Western (2013) was apparent over many decades, perversely undiminished by the 2008 global financial recession and the failures of leaders. Paradigmatic assumptions as highlighted by Alvesson and Sandberg (2011) have been central to this critical review. The functionalist paradigm accounted for by far the largest proportion of theory and research in the field of organization studies (Burrell and Morgan, 1979). It was this paradigm that appears to have so annoyed Rost (1993) when he conducted his leadership studies literature review. In both the fields of leadership studies and organizational change studies, rational/functionalist paradigms dominated the knowledge landscape, and it was no surprise that their offspring (leadership and organizational change) should grow up the way that it did. Smith and Graetz (2011:45) argued that there is a belief that 'change can be controlled because everything in an organization should be subservient to the will, vision and action of leaders.' At times, the will of the leader even seems to extend to preferred paradigmatic assumptions. Ideological assumptions again ripple through the leadership and organizational change literature and were particularly evident with regards to gender-related assumptions about leadership (discussed in Chapter Four). Organizational scholarship was critically depicted as being primarily a literature written by men, for men and about men (Calas and Smircich, 1996). Unfortunately within leadership studies a specific set of practices and discourses have been in place through which 'leadership' has been constituted and re-constituted (Calas and Smircich, 1991). Finally, field assumptions are part of the problem of leadership and organizational change. Rost (1993:8) beautifully parodied leadership as a mythological narrative generating '. . . a mythological story of leadership that has been told over and over again and that almost everyone believes.' This mythology suggested that the work is ongoing, progress is being made and explanations are getting more and more sophisticated, with such a mythology equally applicable to organizational change studies. However, it is the riskiest of the assumptions to challenge (Alvesson and Sandberg, 2011), as for those working in a field, it means questioning their (my) identity. As far back as 1997, Barker offered the following paradigmatic warning:

> If we limit ourselves to rational or scientific approaches to understanding leadership that presume cause-effect relationships, then we will exclude much of the experience of leadership.
>
> (Barker, 1997:361)

Studies of leadership and organizational change have largely resisted this challenge to underlying assumptions, whereas this critical review has consciously challenged such assumptions and thus does not reflect the orthodoxy.

Theory Implications This explanation has highlighted the prevalence of background assumptions (Gouldner, 1971) and a typology of problema-tising assumptions (Alvesson and Sandberg, 2011) relevant to leadership and organizational change. They inform an innovative critique of leadership and organizational change. *Research Implications* Problematic assumptions of leadership and organizational change proactively offer a theory-testing research agenda and reactively, they help to explain research findings, their analysis and their reception. *Practice Implications* The cautionary note for practitioners is that if leadership and organizational change is only under-pinned by a set of problematic assumptions, practice is little more than an optimistic self-fulfilling prophecy at work.

2. LEADERSHIP AND ORGANIZATIONAL CHANGE AS THE GAP BETWEEN LITERATURES

This critical review is part of a monograph series themed around under-standing organizational change and development. The review required seri-ous engagement with the field of leadership studies as well as the field of organizational change studies. It would have been impossible to conduct this review from the perspective of one field, looking over towards the other field. However, it has to be acknowledged that this review was undertaken by an organizational change scholar. Beyer's (1999) strong critique of the treatment of the sociological concept of charisma within transformational leadership was cited in earlier chapters. She began her contribution to a special issue by acknowledging that she was apparently an outsider to lead-ership research. It is easy to empathise with her position, and this notion of being located inside or outside a field (such as leadership studies) is very informative.

The impossible dream of this critical review was that leadership scholars and organizational change scholars, or scholars from other fields, would transcend their field boundaries and undertake boundary-spanning research into leadership and organizational change. As Chapter Two acknowledged this dream was not realised. There was plenty of evidence of scholars pas-sionate about their own fields and doing excellent work to advance their fields. However, the intersection between the two fields appeared to be under-researched despite the high levels of interest in the leadership of orga-nizational change in organizations and societies and amongst policy makers. This paradox is integral to furthering understanding about leadership and organizational change. It wasn't that there was a gap in the literature, but that the literature can best be explained as the gap between literatures.

In previous chapters, the influence of Kuhn (1962) and his natural sci-ence belief in disciplines was acknowledged. The focus here has been upon fields, rather than disciplines, but the experience of interdisciplinary management studies (Knights and Willmott, 1997) is informative. In revisiting Knights and Willmott (1997), they takes us back to the nineties emphasis upon interdisciplinary management studies as encouraged by universities and funding councils. They acknowledged the hype and hope of interdisciplinarity, but that it didn't really happen. Their paper offered insights into the problematic nature of interdisciplinary management studies relevant to the problematic intersection of two fields—the sub-field of leadership and organizational change. Knights and Willmott (1997) warned that despite the espoused values of open-mindedness and being self-critical, the culture and career ladders of academia endorse a defensive kind of disciplinary closure that inhibits critical self-reflection (Knights and Willmott, 1997:10). Leadership scholars and organizational change scholars may pay lip service to other fields, but in terms of career progression, they maintain allegiance to a particular field of study. The implication of this is that cross fertilisation between fields of study will be limited. Where there was a requirement for interdisciplinary management studies, Knights and Willmott (1997) detected two responses.

Firstly, the selective borrowing of concepts or ideas with little attempt to fully integrate such borrowed information was apparent. And secondly, the sphere over which expertise is claimed has been extended. In terms of leadership and organizational change, the norm was for either leadership scholars to borrow concepts and ideas from organizational change or vice versa. At the time of writing, scholars in both fields were not extending their sphere to include leadership and organizational change; if anything, the opposite was happening. This was confirmed through an analysis of the academic handbooks of both fields. The preliminary conclusions of Chapter Two with regards to academic handbooks are repeated here. In leadership handbooks (Bryman et al, 2011, Day, 2014; Rumsey, 2012; Nohria and Khurana, 2010) and organizational change handbooks (Beer and Nohria, 2000, Burke et al, 2009; Boje et al, 2011; By and Burnes, 2013), the anticipated coverage of leadership and organizational change was missing. This may have been a reflection of the lack of empirical work to report upon, or subject experts focusing on their own fields of leadership studies and organizational change studies, rather than engaging in the messy intersection between these two fields.

This gap between literatures raises issues of loyalty for scholars who have been socialised and schooled in a particular field, for whom cooperating and cohabiting with members of a different field can be regarded as a kind of defection (Knights and Willmott, 1997). In the literature reviewed, it is impossible to gauge such emotions, but this insight appears to be highly applicable to anybody straddling leadership and organizational change.

> By becoming a disciplinary specialist, we learn to interpret the world through the frames of reference provided by this specialism. In becoming

'disciplined' by the specialism, we routinely become identified with, and attached to, its distinctive frame of reference.

(Knights and Willmott, 1997:18)

Again, this insight is pertinent when seeking to understand the intersection between leadership and organizational change. A leadership specialist will have been disciplined to see the intersection from a leadership frame of reference, and an organizational change specialist will see the relationship from an organizational change frame of reference. Knights and Willmott (1997) subsequently highlight quite unsavoury colonisation strategies that have been evident, and also acknowledge institutional blocks to interdisciplinarity. They conclude optimistically that for 'defectors,' challenging and extending the limits of boundaries becomes important for their identity, which brings us full circle to Beyer (1999) as a sociologist doing leadership studies and feeling like an outsider.

Theory Implications Theory development suffers from the boundaries of a field disciplining academics, and this is likely to apply to other intersecting fields of study. Theoretical explanations are likely to privilege one field over the other, potentially reflecting a loyalty to a particular field reflected in selective borrowings. *Research Implications* Research can be informed by, rather than constrained by, competing bodies of knowledge and their favoured methods and methodologies (see Chapter Five for the application of Smith and Graetz's (2011) organizational change-based approach to leadership studies). The implication for data gathering is that those being researched may be more influenced by either leadership or organizational change, even if they do not use the language of fields and disciplines. *Practice Implications* In practice, the gap between literatures does not exist, but there may still be imbalances of emphasis between leadership and organizational change, potentially resulting in, for example, leadership development or action research.

3. LEADERSHIP AND ORGANIZATIONAL CHANGE AS A SOCIALLY CONSTRUCTED MYTHOLOGY

As far back as the 1950s, Selznick (1957) innovatively depicted leadership as a socially integrating myth. As an alternative conceptualisation, understanding leadership as the management of meaning (Pondy, 1978) has been favoured over many decades, and in this review, is believed to be particularly pertinent to leadership and organizational change. Leaders actively manipulate symbols in order to instill visions, manage change and achieve support for new directions (Bryman, 2004). However, mythology is not exclusively the preserve of leaders, with leadership studies perceived as a mythological narrative (Rost, 1993) (see Chapter Four). The mythological leadership narrative suggested that research was working, that leadership scholars were increasing understanding of leadership, which was increasingly sophisticated and which would help organizations become more productive. In parallel to Rost's (1993) critique, Gemmill and Oakley (1992) depicted leadership as an alienating social myth that limited alternative conceptualisations of leadership, as well as limiting participation in alternative organizational processes. Social beliefs and structures reinforced the need for both hierarchy and leaders within organizations at the expense of more collaborative conceptualisations; leadership perversely existed to maintain the status quo, rather than facilitate change (Gemmill and Oakley, 1992). The false hope of better leadership definitions, research designs, methodologies, and theoretical frameworks is maintained to this day by the proponents of mainstream orthodoxy (Kelly, 2014).

Social construction offers an alternative and informative perspective on leadership, with this literature growing rapidly over the past 15 years (Fairhurst and Grant, 2010). Social constructionist leadership approaches move attention away from leader-centric approaches emphasising the leader's personality, style, and/or behaviour, towards leadership as a co-constructed reality. According to Grint (2005b), leaders may even be engaged in socially constructing the contexts for their leadership. Leadership thinking is framed by both leadership writers and leaders themselves framing thinking within organizations (see discussion in Chapters Four and Five). Framing is an important manifestation of social constructionism that enables leaders as managers of meaning to determine the meaning of subjects, to make sense of them, and to judge their character and significance (Fairhurst and Sarr, 1996). For Huczynski (2006), leadership became the way people understood the cause of important organizational events and outcomes; leadership was sanctified and given a central role in our construction of organized activities and their outcomes.

This perspective regards the leadership of organizational change discourses as socially constructing what is happening. For example, a sense of urgency may intentionally be manipulated in order to assist leaders in leading change, as Kotter (1996: 45) encouraged: '[V]isible crises can be enormously helpful in catching people's attention and pushing up urgency levels. Conducting business as usual is very difficult if the building seems to be on fire.' However, reality can also be more honourably co-constructed in tandem with stakeholders with the mutual purpose of bringing about real, intended change, often evident with regards to campaigning social movements, such as the suffragettes seeking the vote for women in the UK, or a new social enterprise seeking to galvanise effort and enthusiasm with regards to providing new services for the disadvantaged. Even within the rational/functional paradigm change, leader communications socially construct visions of futures arising out of organizational change. Social constructionism here offers explanations for how these imagined realities might influence organizational members. This explanation in focusing on the intangible element of leadership and organizational change may clarify why empirical advances have been so disappointing, but also why there has been so much interest in analysing socially constructed leadership discourses.

Theory Implications There is a need for caution with regards to the seductive nature of leadership studies (Calas and Smircich, 1991) and the potential mythical narrative of leadership. Theories may be part of this seduction, rather than explanations of something real. *Research Implications* Reimagining leadership and organizational change as socially constructed offers an explanation for the paucity of research into the sub-field, but also offers a research agenda. A discursive approach to leadership (Fairhurst, 2008) was discussed in Chapter Four, emphasising communication as the primary focus of the research with the object of study discourse and the analytical focus as textual and contextual. *Practice Implications* If leaders are managers of meaning, this has implications for their practices and development. Academic interest in discourses and framing also has practical relevance to activities of leading and leadership.

4. LEADERSHIP AND ORGANIZATIONAL CHANGE AS LEADING CHANGE RATHER THAN MANAGING STABILITY

There has been a shift within management and organization studies, and 'leadership rather than management is currently advocated in the mainstream management literature and organizational policies as the key to effective organizational performance' (Ford and Harding, 2007:475). Leadership is privileged through disparaging management, as typified by Riggio (2011:120), 'when the field of management began to make the shift from viewing those in positions of power and control as mere "managers" to viewing them as taking on higher-level "leadership" activities. . .' This shift raised the questions addressed in Chapter Four: What were the cultural aspects of this shift, what were the perceived deficiencies within change management, what theoretical milestones marked the rise of leadership? The shift authored in America was consequently traced back to the American Dream (Guest, 1990), with roles such as leader and manager ascribing meaning to organizational events (Czarniawska-Joerges and Wolff, 1991) and reflecting shifts in the culture of the seventies and eighties. Influential scholars very publically began to declare that change management was failing (see Hughes, 2011 for further discussion) and given that the primary goal was successful change, they created the requirement for a new approach (leadership).

Spector (2014) revisited Lee Iacocca as the personification and embodiment of transformational leadership, offering an intriguing historical perspective on leadership and management differentiations that acknowledged the difficulties of the seventies for America and the lack of leadership believed to be behind this malaise. As Spector (2014: 364) observed, referring back to Zaleznik's (1977) article, '. . .[A] new hypothesis had emerged:

American industry was suffering from an overabundance of managers and a paucity of leaders.' The mandate to develop more leaders and fewer managers was popularised through Kotter's (1988, 1990) writings. Chapter Four featured key milestones in differentiating leadership from management (Selznick, 1957; Zaleznik, 1977 and Kotter, 1988, 1990, 1995, 1996). This literature largely offered informed opinions rather than empirical evidence, with the shift appearing to be more cultural than evidence-based.

The consequence of these developments that is particularly pertinent to this critical review was that management was increasingly associated with stability and leadership with change (Barker, 1997). Dubious dualisms between management and leadership and change and stability have endured, possibly due to their deep cultural roots. However, Sutherland and Smith (2013:220) were cited in previous chapters as a critical counterpoint, as they encouraged an appreciation of how dualistic forces shape and enable change, writing that 'by adopting a dualities aware perspective, leaders can come to terms with the intuitive desire to resolve contradiction by instead managing the complementarities within contradictory forces.' This currently is not the orthodoxy, with contradiction still resolved through simplistic depictions of leaders leading change and managers managing stability. Embedded within any explanation of the leadership of organizational change are assumptions about the desirability and efficacy of leadership. This critical review suggests that regardless of your favoured perspective, the anticipated empirical evidence underpinning societal and organizational shifts from management towards leadership was missing. Instead, American billionaires encouraged this shift in the best interests of America (see the discussion in Chapter Four). An absence of empirical evidence supporting profound cultural shifts towards an emphasis upon leadership does not necessarily mean that such shifts have not been beneficial. However, the only certainty is that such shifts have been highly lucrative for elite business schools and other providers of leadership development.

Theory Implications Mainstream management literature now emphasises leadership over management. The theoretical implication is that there is a need for caution in theorising what might merely be a cultural shift. Barker's (1997) and Kotter's (1990 and 1996) belief in leaders leading change and managers managing stability appears to be a false dichotomy. *Research Implications* Research into leader/manager differentiations/dualities appears fruitful and relevant to current interests in practice/process research (see Langley et al, 2013). Research could potentially clarify the involvement of leaders and managers within organizational change, or potentially the same role at different stages in a process of organizational change. *Practice Implications* Does the perceived shift from management to leadership really serve organizations and practitioners? There is practical merit in revisiting the role of management within organizational change. For example, in terms of management control being overwhelmed by leadership, the case of

Enron is a salutary warning for practitioners (see Tourish and Vatcha, 2005 for further discussion).

5. LEADERSHIP AND ORGANIZATIONAL CHANGE AS OPPORTUNITIES LOST IN TRANSLATION

An advantage of looking back over earlier explanations is that patterns and preferences become apparent that are less apparent when considering leadership and organizational change in the context of today. Although this review has focused on the last 35 years, the literature going back to the forties and fifties informed featured debates. What becomes apparent are moments lost in translation, when the development of leadership and organizational change theories and practices could have taken a very different turn (see Figure 6.2).

The literature in this review has been interpreted in a particular way and will continue to be interpreted in different ways (see the discussion of the historiography of organizational change in Chapter Three). There is no single, fixed interpretation, however mainstream/orthodox explanations have framed understanding in ways that limit alternative explanations. It is troubling that over many decades the key milestones (Figure 6.2) offering directions for development were either misrepresented, misunderstood or mislaid.

Rost's (1993) critical review of leadership studies featured prominently in Chapter Four; in summary, he believed that the industrial leadership paradigm of the previous two centuries was no longer appropriate for the challenges and complexities faced in the twenty-first century, arguing passionately for a new leadership studies paradigm. Two decades later, the mainstream leadership studies orthodoxy that troubled him so much has not really changed. It is perverse that despite the unrelenting backdrop of leadership of organizational change discourses, certain institutional beliefs and practices repeatedly resist change. Rost's (1997:11) innovative definition of leadership as 'an influence relationship among leaders and collaborators who intend real changes that reflect their mutual purposes' (Rost, 1997:11) has been adopted here as offering a way forward, yet remains largely ignored within leadership studies. Even Rost's (1993) book had to be acquired as a print-on-demand publication, in an era when leadership books apparently proliferate. Sixty years earlier, Lewin (1947) offered America a vision of participative and democratic organizational change that would enable America to productively respond to the large-scale demands being placed upon businesses arising out of the end of World War II in a fair and egalitarian manner. This vision was too radical and fifty years later, when Rost proposed something similar from a leadership perspective, the vision was still too radical.

Year & Author	Title	Potential Implication	Interpreted as. . .
1947 Weber	*The Theory of Social and Economic Organization* Account of sociology, economics and types of authority	Extraordinarily gifted person A social crisis or situation of desperation A set of ideas providing a radical solution to the crisis A set of followers who are attracted to the exceptional person Validation through repeated success (Trice and Beyer, 1986)	Charismatic Leadership
1947 Lewin	*Frontiers in Group Dynamics* Account of a new stage of development of social sciences	Successful behavioural change could be achieved through democratic-participative learning process, initiated by a person's own volition	Unfreeze, change and refreeze simplifications Planned change superseded by emergent change
1948 Coch and French	*Overcoming Resistance to Change* Account of pioneering research into organizational change	Involvement of factory workers as participants in organizational change processes resulted in more successful change	The need to overcome employee resistance to change
1951 Selznick	*Leadership in Administration: A Sociological Interpretation* Inspiration for institutional theory	Institutional leader as primarily an expert in the promotion and protection of values	Founding father of institutional theory. Encouragement to differentiate leadership and management
1978 Burns	*Leadership* Account of the potential of leadership to transform institutions and societies	The potential of moral and egalitarian leadership to transform societies and institutions	Differentiating transformational from transactional leadership
1993 Rost	*Leadership in the 21st Century* Critical leadership studies literature review informing a new leadership studies paradigm	Industrial paradigm leadership is no longer appropriate, there is a need for a new paradigm	Largely ignored by management and organization studies—business as usual

Figure 6.2 Leadership of organizational change moments lost in translation

Approaches to leading organizational change existed and have existed for many decades. The dilemma is that they are not acted upon if they do not fit within and reinforce the assumptions of the dominant rational/functional paradigm (see earlier discussion of assumptions in this chapter). Those moments lost in translation (as featured in Figure 6.2) may be a consequence of the exercise of power, both in terms of what explanations are accepted and promoted and an unwillingness of the most powerful within organizations to relinquish power. These discussions highlight a very particular historiography at work. For Diaz-Saenz (2011), transformational leadership had been the single most-studied and debated idea within the field of leadership studies, and Kotter's (1996) *Leading Change* was by far the most cited publication within this critical review. These solutions were made in America and shaped by American businesses' desire to respond to international competition, particularly in the eighties (Conger, 1999). Both transformational leadership (Bass, 1985) and leading change (Kotter, 1996) were primarily solutions to perceived problems, rather than serious attempts to understand the problem.

Cooke (1999) has demonstrated how the left has been written out of change management history, and this was an enduring pattern within all of these lost-in-translation moments. In essence, Figure 6.2 highlights ways forward in terms of combining leadership and organizational change, but this would require significant shifts in employee relations, work organization and the exercise of power and politics within organizations. These attitudes, values and beliefs are deeply entangled with selfish and self-serving Western beliefs in individualised cultures and the benefits of materialistic societies (see Guest, 1990 for further discussion of the influence of the American Dream).

Theory Implications Historiography has shaped what we know separately about leadership and about organizational change; consequently, theories of leadership and organizational change are shared and constrained by such historiographies. Theoretical insights from history remain on the 'cutting room floor.' For example, Burnes (2004) re-evaluated the contribution of Kurt Lewin (1947), highlighting how his writing had been misrepresented. *Research Implications* There may be merit in going back to the future (Grint, 2008) and in revisiting earlier theories and implications for research today. Whilst opportunities may have been lost in translation, they remain opportunities for further research. *Practice Implications* Today's best practices and benchmarking against competitors may neglect alternative/innovative historic ways of working which could be fruitful.

6. LEADERSHIP AND ORGANIZATIONAL CHANGE AS THE SHOW THAT NEVER ENDS

In the 1700s, an appetite for transformation within societies was awakened. Prior to this, societies had been sceptical about future progress, even believing that they were experiencing decline when compared to an earlier golden age. '. . .[T]he fluid state of constant change and improvement was not an easy idea to grasp' (Keller, 1966:469). Schaffer (1995) believed that perpetuum mobiles (perpetual-motion machines) offered a metaphor then and now for the encouragement of constant change and progress within societies. Battilana et al (2010:422) cited Lippitt et al (1958), highlighting the dilemma of persuading stakeholders that future changes were going to happen, that they will follow a plan and that they will be successful. Comparison between the leadership of organizational change and perpetuum mobiles is pertinent in terms of five themes: Functional, linear and mechanistic machines, machine development driven by financial benefit, a common quest for more output through less input, the invisibility of machine mechanisms and encouraging the quest for perpetual motion (constant change). Each of these five themes is elaborated upon with specific reference to historical accounts of perpetuum mobiles (for a fuller exposition of these ideas, see Hughes, 2015) and illustrated with particular reference to Kotter's (1996) *Leading Change*.

Perpetuum mobiles were functional rather than merely conceptual; they were linear in that their operation involved inputs transformed into a potential output of motion, and they were mechanical, employing often-complicated (although hidden) mechanics. However, despite these inputs, '. . .the ineluctable laws of motion and energy conservation, of which they could have had no knowledge, systematically denied them success' (Ord-Hume, 1977:16). *Leading change* (Kotter, 1996) involved clearly defined functions (eight steps) undertaken in a linear manner with successful transformation achieved through following the eight steps of leading change. As with most machinery, *Leading Change* (Kotter, 1996) came with user manuals and operating guides; *The Heart of Change* (Kotter and Cohen, 2002) helped people to more deeply understand the eight-step formula, along with *The Heart of Change Field Guide: Tools and Tactics for Leading Change in your Organization* (Cohen, 2005).

The development of the perpetuum mobiles was driven by financial benefit. Schaffer (1995) highlighted projects for perpetual motion promising automatic profits and it was this promise that drove interest. Ord-Hume (1977:17) highlighted ordinary people, industrialists, financiers and politicians investing in perpetuum mobiles in the belief that in the future, they would give them untold wealth. In the case of Kotter's (1996) recipe for successfully leading change, the financial driver was that previous transformation efforts in corporations had failed due to leadership (Kotter, 1995), and that with the right leadership, they would now be successful.

Perpetuum mobiles promised more output for less input. Ord-Hume (1977:19) succinctly caught the essence of perpetuum mobiles as 'find something that does more work than the energy you put into it—and you have solved perpetual motion!' In terms of what was and what is now known about physics and mechanics this was impossible; however, the laws of thermodynamics did not dampen enthusiasm for perpetual-motion machines (Ord-Hume, 1977). *Leading Change* (Kotter, 1996) promised greater employee output with less management/leader input. This input/output exchange is also evident within transformational leadership: '[T]o achieve follower performance beyond the ordinary limits, leadership must be transformational' (Bass, 1985: xiii).

The mechanics of the perpetuum mobiles remained invisible despite the hype. Schaffer (1995:159) highlighted how the mechanisms of perpetuum mobiles remained hidden as illustrated through the Orffyreus Wheel: '[I]t was not possible, regrettably, to inspect the inside of the wooden wheel though the witnesses could hear a number of weights gently falling when it turned. . .He reassured his guests that there was no deception involved, no hidden moving parts.' Ord-Hume (1977:16) highlighted the different motivations at work amongst the promoters of the perpetuum mobiles; those who embarked upon fraud from the outset, and those who '. . .finding their labours frustrated, employed some form of trickery to make out to the public at large that they had succeeded.' In a similar manner, the elements of the leadership of organizational change have remained invisible, 'black boxes' integral to operations, yet intangible and out of sight. Kotter's (1996) eight steps emphasise cultural and communication intangibles, particularly with regards to visionary aspects of leadership, with the outcomes of organizational change remaining equally intangible (see Pettigrew et al, 2001 for further discussion about the intangibles of organizational change).

Perpetuum mobiles encouraged the quest for perpetual motion (constant change). Inventors of perpetuum mobiles were caught within an impossible obsession to achieve perpetual motion, similar to today's management fads and buzzwords (Collins, 2000). Qualified and respected scientists, charlatans, as well as ordinary people clamoured to invest their life savings. The objective of discovering something that did more work than the energy you put into it (Ord-Hume, 1977) proved elusive. If anything, the opposite was achieved—there was far less output than the input into the quest. One of Kotter's (1996) eight steps even encouraged 'consolidating gains and producing more change.' As Child (2005) ironically warned, change had become the organizational norm.

Theory Implications Leadership theories and organizational change theories appear to work with an erroneous background assumption (Gouldner, 1971) that we know what is going on inside the 'black box.' Parallels between perpetuum mobiles seeking perpetual motion and contemporary interest in constant organizational change have implications for theorising constant change. ***Research Implications*** Research needs to target more explicitly what is going on inside the 'black box.' Instead of researching how we develop transformational or change leaders, we need to do research inside the 'black box' to understand how/if leadership influences organizational change. ***Practice Implications*** Practice does not have to be research informed, but if a practitioner favours a research-informed approach, it must be acknowledged that we do not know what is going on inside the 'black box.' The contrast made here with the hype and promotion of perpetuum mobiles offers a cautionary note from history: Research may subsequently reveal that the leadership of organizational change 'black boxes' are largely empty.

7. LEADERSHIP AND ORGANIZATIONAL CHANGE AND THE PRACTICE OF LEADING ORGANIZATIONAL CHANGE

Theories and practices of management are inextricably intertwined (Knights and Willmott, 1997). This critical review has avoided practical debate in favour of academic debate as there are already too many prescriptions, tool kits, recipes and anecdotes about the best way to lead change. However, the practical challenge of how to lead organizational change offers a means of synthesising discussion in earlier chapters into a more applied explanation of leadership and organizational change. In Chapter Three, empirical/theoretical advances were drawn together relating to Resistance, Ethics, Power and politics, process thinking, Learning, Agency and discourse, Context and Evaluation using the mnemonic REPLACE. This mnemonic encouraged replacing deficiencies within leadership of organizational change discourses, but also proactively offered a way forward in terms of how to lead organizational change informed by empirical and theoretical advances.

A singular, best-practice prescription of how to lead change is not favoured. As Chapter Three highlighted, organizational change is informed by many competing philosophies, paradigms and perspectives, each of which would encourage a different practical approach to leading change. For example, Smith and Graetz's (2011) *Philosophies of Organizational Change* (rational, biological, institutional, resource, psychological, systems, cultural, critical and dualities approaches) offered different theoretical explanations. But as well as the academic framing of debates, the approaches of leaders to change are based upon their assumptions about how change works (Smith and Graetz, 2011). Smircich and Morgan's (1982) insight into leadership as realised through individuals framing and defining the reality for others highlights such competing explanations of leadership. As well as these differences, the uniqueness of every organizational change (type of change, organization, leader and context) means that there will never be a valid universal way to lead change, although practitioner literature may imply that there is one best way. Accepting these caveats, three approaches to leading change may be ventured (see Figure 6.3).

In Figure 6.3, approaches to leading change, each with strengths and weaknesses and each with more or less applicability to particular scenarios, are highlighted. Kotter (1996) and Bass and Riggio (2006) feature as the most-cited publications within the sub-field; citations are no indication of practical application, but do indicate that these publications are influential. Kotter's (1996) eight steps potentially framed leadership and

Approach	Leading Change	Transformational Leadership	Change Leadership Bricolage
Author/s Essence	Kotter (1996) Eight Steps - Establishing a sense of urgency - Forming a powerful guiding coalition - Creating a vision - Communicating the vision - Empowering others to act on the vision - Planning for and creating short term wins - Consolidating improvements and producing still more change - Institutionalising new approaches	Bass and Riggio (2006) Transformational Behaviour Components - Idealised influence - Inspirational motivation - Intellectual stimulation - Individualised consideration	Various empirical contributions: - The dynamics of collective leadership and strategic change in pluralistic organizations (Denis et al, 2001) - Leadership self-efficacy and managers' motivation for leading change (Paglis and Green, 2002) -All changes great and small: Exploring approaches to change and its leadership (Higgs and Rowland, 2005) - Process-based leadership: Fair procedures and reactions to organizational change (Tyler and De Cremer, 2005) - Leadership competencies for implementing planned organizational change (Battilana et al, 2010) - The leadership of organization change: A view from recent empirical evidence (Ford and Ford, 2012)
Strengths	Enduring popularity, practitioner accessibility and applicability	Extensive research undertaken into transformational leadership	Encourages flexibility and enables improvisation Empirically informed
Weaknesses	Lack of empirical and scholarship evidence informing the eight steps	Transformation focus is primarily upon followers, rather than organizational change	Sources may be contradictory, potentially a lack and unity of strategic direction

Figure 6.3 Three approaches to leading organizational change

organizational change thinking (as discussed in Chapter Five) as offering an accessible methodology for leading change that emphasised leaders operating within a guiding coalition (see Chapter Five for a critique). Bass and Riggio's (2006) *Transformational Leadership* was advanced through research, testing and conceptual development, and has featured prominently within this critical review. Bernard Bass regarded transformational leadership as a development of Burns's (1978) work on leadership (see Chapter Five for a critique).

The final answer to the question of how one leads an organizational change is through change leadership bricolage, which requires more explanation. According to Weick (1990), the map is not the territory; he reasoned persuasively that maps were abstractions of reality, providing a simplified frame within which experiences could be understood. They provide reassurance by relating current steps to previous steps taken on previously completed projects. In this way, *Leading Change* (Kotter, 1996) and *Transformational Leadership* (Bass and Riggio, 2006) may be regarded as maps offering reassurance. In terms of the earlier Francis Bacon quotation, they begin with certainties, but the critical implication is that they may end in doubts. Weick's (1993) writings about improvisation offer an alternative potential starting point that instead embraces uncertainty. Weick (1993) favoured more fluid recipes as opposed to static blueprints, attention rather than intention and bricolage with its acknowledgement of the flexible use of repertoires and resources.

This spirit of bricolage offers a way forward for leadership and organizational change that is respectful of the philosophies, paradigms and perspectives characterising the fields of leadership studies and organizational change studies. Change leadership bricolage also respects the uniqueness of every leader, collaborator, organization and organizational change with an implication that there is no singular/universal approach to leading change. Instead, reflexive leaders aware of their own unique context improvise approaches to lead change, which may still be informed by empirical evidence, but are drawn upon more flexibly and creatively rather than prescriptively.

The final column (Figure 6.3) revisits publications cited in Chapter Two. Empirically based publications have been chosen, primarily for how, in combination, they could inform an improvised approach towards leading organizational change. The choice of publications reflects personally favoured philosophies, paradigms and perspectives, rather than judgements about quality. In the following discussion they are featured in order of publication, again in order to avoid implied rankings, and they are discussed specifically in terms of their potential to inform leading change practices.

Denis et al (2001) addressed a practice-orientated research question: How can leaders achieve deliberate strategic change in organizations where strategic leadership roles are shared, objectives are divergent and power is diffuse? They were particularly interested in leading change in pluralistic organizations characterised by '. . .fragmented power and multiple objectives, were reconciliation by fiat is not an option, these opposing forces are in constant dynamic tension' (Denis et al, 2001:826). In developing their process theory of strategic change, they developed five case studies in health care settings. Their research informed the development of an emerging process theory of leadership and strategic change in pluralistic settings that is comprised of six components:

1) Major change in a pluralistic organization is likely to be achieved under unified collective leadership.
2) Unified collective leadership is necessary yet also fragile in the context of diffuse power and multiple objectives.
3) Change in pluralistic organizations tends to occur in a cyclical manner.
4) The effect of leaders' actions on their political positions drives cycles of change.
5) Four factors can contribute to the stabilization of change in pluralistic settings: Slack; social embeddedness; creative opportunism; and time, inattention and formal position.
6) Extreme pluralism adds to the difficulty of forming unified leadership constellations.

Paglis and Green's (2002) research focused on managers' motivations for attempting the leadership of change. They drew on Bandura's (1986) social cognitive theory in developing their construct of leadership self-efficacy (LSE). Their '. . .central hypothesis was that high LSE managers would engage in more leadership attempts, compared to self-doubters' (Paglis and Green, 2002:230). Their findings were mostly supportive of this hypothesis. They concluded with three surprises from their findings. Firstly, although mastery experiences are traditionally viewed as one of the most important influences on self-efficacy, this was not supported by their findings. Secondly, they were surprised about the lack of influence of superiors' behaviour on managers' LSE. Finally, managers' crisis perceptions did not moderate the relationship between LSE and proposed leadership attempts.

> In this study, a manager's characterization of the work environment as being in a reactive 'crisis mode' was related to diminished self-efficacy, for initiating change efforts.
>
> (Paglis and Green, 2002: 232)

All Changes Great and Small: Exploring Approaches to Change and its Leadership (Higgs and Rowland, 2005) is very compatible with the debates featured in this critical review. In terms of how one leads organizational change, they offered readers guidance through the competing approaches and by relating approaches to leader behaviours. Their paper was informed by literature reviewing and case studies of 70 change stories, drawn from 40 informants in seven organizations. They focused their inquiries on three pertinent research questions, which are restated here with summary answers.

1) What approach to change management is likely to be most effective in today's business environment?

Approaches based upon an acknowledgement of complexity and emergence were found to be the most successful, whereas those based upon linearity were least successful, although this was found to be very contingent upon the change approach and the change context.

2) What leadership behaviours tend to be associated with effective change management?

They identified three leadership behaviours associated with change management. *Shaping behaviour* was comprised of what leaders say and do, making others accountable, thinking about change and using an individual focus. *Framing change* was comprised of establishing points for change, designing and managing the change journey and communicating guiding principles. *Creating capacity* was comprised of creating individual and organizational capabilities and communicating and creating connections. In most contexts, *shaping behaviour* appeared to be negatively related to success (Higgs and Rowland, 2005:137).

3) Are leadership behaviours related to an underlying assumption within different approaches to change?

Through literature reviewing, they were able to identify four approaches to change: Directive (simple), master (sophisticated), self-assembly (DIY) and emergence. They found that the same range of leadership behaviours were exhibited within each of the change approaches examined, although the dominance of behaviours varied within each approach.

> . . .[S]haping behaviour is the most frequently used leadership in directive change thus indicating the impact of underlying assumptions on leadership behaviours.
>
> (Higgs and Rowland, 2005:147)

Tyler and De Cremer's (2005) *Process-based Leadership: Fair Procedures and Reactions to Organizational Change* is included in the change leadership bricolage as a reminder to employ fair leadership procedures. Tyler and De Cremer (2005:529) hypothesised '. . .that those who are more strongly identified with their company will be more influenced by procedural justice information.' They tested their hypothesis in a merger in which the unit being studied was completely taken over and incorporated into another company—this was a hostile takeover. They focused on the actions of lead-ers leading the company, with the study examining the employees' accep-tance of the merger. As cited in Chapter Two, leaders acting fairly becomes a factor that motivates employees to buy into changes. Leaders can lead via the procedures they use to implement change.

In *Leadership Competencies for Implementing Planned Organizational Change*, Battilana et al (2010) focused on 89 clinical managers in the UK National Health Service who were implementing change projects between 2003 and 2004. They identified relationships between effectiveness at task-oriented and person-oriented leadership behaviours and the change implementation activities of communicating, mobilising and evaluating. Two of their findings speak to how one leads organizational change:

1) Those leaders more effective at task-oriented behaviours were more likely to focus on mobilising and evaluating activities.
2) Those leaders more effective at person-oriented behaviours were more likely to focus on communicating activities.

The final change leadership bricolage resource would be Ford and Ford's (2012) review of the empirical evidence. This review has been cited previ-ously in support of the conclusion that currently, there is a lack of empirical evidence informing leadership and organizational change understanding. However, the review may also be used by anyone seeking guidance about how to lead change. The following is illustrative of the practical insights that Ford and Ford (2012:22) offer. The authors offer caveats and limita-tions, which is why, overall, they remained sceptical, but within their review, the themes in the following quotation are expanded upon:

> The research reviewed here indicates that the leadership of change, in all forms and through all ways of leading, has an impact on both the leaders and the led. But the nature and extent of that impact depends on the form of leadership considered as well as the way approaches to change, leader behaviours, and change activities are measured.

The seven studies cited here as change leadership bricolage are far less reassuring than Kotter's (1996) and Bass and Riggio's (2006) approaches. Change leadership bricolage as depicted here is far more discursive, com-plicated and even at times contradictory. But despite these limitations, it is favoured as a response to the question of how to lead organizational change for the following reasons. The approach encourages creativity and improvisation. Seven studies have been used but they could be replaced with other studies from this review. Even if these seven studies appeal, they could still be drawn upon selectively—one might be very influential, whereas another is supplementary. Creative choices about favoured change leader-ship approaches are informed by a change leader's understanding of his/her own unique context, competencies and capabilities. Change leadership bricolage encourages the development of change leaders and collaborators as self-managed and independent learners. It is telling that both Kotter (1996) and Bass and Riggio (2006) did not emphasise learning within their leadership approaches (see Yukl, 1999 and Hughes, forthcoming, for critiques of the coverage of learning within these approaches). This is an alternative to the dependency of the addictive quick fixes certain consultants and business school developers may offer that require change leaders to return to their 'dealer' for repeat prescriptions. Unfortunately, some things never change.

Theory Implications The leadership studies' search for a general theory of leadership to date has been unsuccessful. There is a danger in replicating this quest and searching for a general theory of leadership and organizational change as an attempt to resolve contradictions (Sutherland and Smith, 2013). Theory development may be better served through bricolage, as encouraged by Weick (1993). *Research Implications* In the spirit of Higgs and Rowland's (2005) identification of four approaches to change (directive (simple), master (sophisticated), self-assembly (DIY) and emergence), there is merit in inductive research, which gathers and analyses evidence about how leaders lead change and then builds a theory from this starting point. *Practice Implications* Whilst benchmarking appears to be in vogue, many choices for practitioners still exist, and the discussion here encourages bricolage, although in mitigation, this might be what practitioners are already doing.

8. LEADERSHIP AND ORGANIZATIONAL CHANGE AS COLLABORATIVE CHANGE LEADERSHIP

The leadership of organizational change as a sub-field may be imagined for a moment as a green field site, never before studied, with no accumulated background assumptions, nothing yet preconceived or prescribed. In beginning to study, research and develop theories with regards to this sub-field, collaborators in processes of organizational change in relation with leaders would be the central focus of investigation, research and theory development. Collaborators numerically constitute the vast majority of people involved in any organizational change process. If they do not change their attitudes, values and behaviours either for good or bad reasons, there will be no organizational change, only empty leadership rhetoric that an organization is one day going to change. The potential of collaboration and participation has been emphasised previously, both with regards to leadership studies and with regards to organizational change studies (see Figure 6.2). However, as Chapter Four highlighted, collaborators (followers) did not feature prominently in either leadership studies research or within leadership studies theories.

This perplexing omission may be explained in terms of the historiography of leadership studies. The early 'Great Men' theories by definition were not interested in anything other than the exceptional qualities, competencies and capabilities of individual leaders and unfortunately, the early preoccupations with individual leaders appear to have endured amongst societies, institutions and individuals. Rost (1993), in his critical review of leadership studies, encountered a field that remained individualistic and male orientated. A shortcoming of the leadership studies tendency to celebrate the field's historic foundations was implying that finally the gap in leadership knowledge was about to be closed, paraphrased as 'just a little more research funding and we are there.' This perversely maintains continuities with earlier preoccupations, emphasising the agency of individual leaders at the expense of any refocusing on or engagement with the potential contribution of collaborators.

In reflecting back upon the state of knowledge, even the 'follower' label favoured by leadership studies scholars disparages, disempowers and marginalises non-leaders both within leadership theories and within organizations. Consequently, in this review, the more positive and proactive label of 'collaborator' used by Rost (1997) has been adopted as a celebration of such collaborative agency. In defining leadership, Rost recognised the centrality of collaborators within leadership relations, identifying the importance of real, intended change and mutual purpose facilitating collaboration within organizational change. This aligned Rost with earlier organizational change scholars (Coch and French, 1948; Lewin, 1947) and leadership scholars (Burns, 1978; O'Toole, 1995) who imagined democratic, moral and egalitarian futures.

If leadership studies do suffer from the semantics of 'followers' and lack of engagement with collaborators (followers), then this is magnified when leadership and organizational change are combined. Leadership does not occur through big new ideas and visions of sweeping change, but instead by convincing others to contribute and turn these ideas and visions into reality (Haslam et al, 2011). This will never happen whilst those collaborating in the real, intended change are conceived of as unable to act intelligently and without the guidance, control and direction of leaders (Rost, 1993). Rost's vision of post-industrial leadership focused on influence relationships and related to real, intended changes that reflected mutual purposes. Two decades later, Rost's vision is still intuitively appealing, yet still contrary to leadership fetishes with individualistic celebrations of strong and heroic leaders.

It has been intriguing revisiting leadership and organizational change studies with the benefit of what we know today. In literary studies, there is a concept referred to as 'histories of the future' (Sandison and Dingley, 2010), in which science fiction is revisited from the vantage point of today. These can be stories set in the past, or stories set in the past where a time traveller arrives to change the future, or stories of the present that we now live, which have been altered by a change in the past. In this way, as space cadets, we travel through time, disrupting traditional, linear and rational histories. The global financial recession, which centred upon financial sector leadership, may now be viewed from the perspective of a history of the future. Rost (1993, 1995, 1997) was concerned that the old industrial paradigm of leadership practice and studies was no longer fit for its purpose. The developments that Rost was witnessing within economies, societies and institutions urgently required a new paradigm of leadership. The complexities and ethical challenges that were beginning to occur demanded a new leadership paradigm, and for Rost, this was not an aspiration, this was an imperative. As we know, whereas leadership of organizational change discourses have become very prevalent, the old leadership paradigm that troubled Rost remained intact, more resistant to change and even more pronounced than when Rost encountered it. Over the past decade, banks, hedge funds and financial institutions embarked upon considerable innovation and change in terms of what they did and how they did it; these changes were initially very lucrative for shareholders and other stakeholders. They were the real beneficiaries of the shifts from the stabilising influence of management and management controls towards change enabling leadership. Subsequently, innovations in sub-prime lending and futures trading were found to be at the heart of the collapse of the financial markets (see the case studies from Tourish, 2013 for further discussion).

Looking back today at what Rost (1993) was writing about, having now experienced the global financial recession, he passionately and assertively warned that the industrial leadership paradigm of previous centuries would not serve the challenges of the twenty-first century. However, the danger is that learning may still not have been extracted. In looking back over 35 years, Bernard Bass and John Kotter featured prominently and repeatedly, particularly when gauged through citation rankings. They creatively invoked discourses of transformational leadership and leading change without ever altering, questioning or challenging the old leadership paradigm that so troubled Rost (1993). Rost's emphasis upon real, intended change through influence relationships and based upon mutual purposes offered safeguards that today's conceptualisation of the leadership of organizational change lacks. We may not have suffered the very real suffering arising out of the global financial recession if Rost's post-industrial paradigm had been adopted. We will never know. The collaborators that Rost envisaged were never just tokenistic additions, they were integral to ensuring that change was for the greater good, rather than the narrow self-interest of an individual leader or those vested financial interests they represent as leaders. Leaders may frown upon the imposition of such a 'hand brake' upon their unrestrained will. However, this 'hand brake' potentially serves as an integral control mechanism both for themselves and others.

It is very unlikely that Rost's vision of leadership will ever be realised, given the storyline of this critical review. The beneficiaries of today's inequalities have far too much to lose. Critical scholars after the global financial recession encourage a reappraisal of leadership (Alvesson and Spicer, 2011; Collinson, 2011, 2012; O'Reilly and Reed, 2010), but nothing really changes. Kotter's (1996) *Leading Change* featured prominently in this critical review and in 2012, Kotter brought out a new edition of his book (as discussed in Chapter Five), which was substantially the same book, but with refreshed penguin imagery and a new preface. In his new preface to *Leading Change*, Kotter (2012:vii) wrote,

> The material in this book is not only still relevant now, sixteen years after it was published, but I believe it is more relevant, and for one reason the speed of change continues to increase.

Paradoxically, those who espouse leading change favour stability when it comes to their own leadership orthodoxy preferences. The concept of relating influence relationships and mutual purposes to the leadership of real, intended change is challenging for leaders, mainstream leadership studies and the lucrative income streams of elite business schools. Organizations and societies maintain a considerable appetite for leadership and organizational change, which begs the awkward question: What would ethical leadership of organizational change look like?

Even an emphasis upon leader-collaborator influence relationships based upon mutual purpose rather than narrow self-interest may not fully resolve the ethical challenges that are raised by achieving real, intended change. Rost's (1995) concern was that the nature of changes was increasingly troublesome and complex. Existing ethical/moral conceptual frameworks provided only minimal guidance, and Rost believed they were inadequate for leaders and collaborators who wanted to resolve the ethical dilemmas inherent within complex organizational changes. Once again, Rost was prescient in anticipating the ethical challenges of combining leadership and organizational change (see By and Burnes, 2013 for further discussion of ethics, leadership and change). In the following quotation cited in Chapter Four, Rost's more radical intent becomes evident as he wearily reflects back over 200 years of leadership studies: '[T]he liberal philosophy has bred a society that feeds on materialism and individualism and eschews spirituality and the common good' (Rost, 1995:138). The radicalism of what Rost was beginning to articulate still remains challenging twenty years later.

We can involve collaborators in organizational change, rather than imposing it upon them, we can complain when they resist the imposition of a leader's will, labelling it pejoratively as 'resistance to change.' We can highlight the deficiencies of the industrial leadership paradigm studies that served us for 200 years, and even pay lip service to an alternative vision of leadership for the twenty-first century (Rost, 1993). However, what Rost (1995, 1997) pessimistically implied was that without radical economic, structural change, the neo-classical economic models so favoured by Western governments and the inequalities they seek to maintain would negate the efforts of even the most inspired and visionary leader. The notion of transforming leadership that drove Burns (1978) to political science polemic and was subsequently taken up by Rost (1993) as a student of Burns was never realised. Both Burns and Rost romantically reimagined transforming leadership as facilitating movement towards fairer, more democratic and egalitarian societies. Inevitably, such a transformation would require structural economic change, which to date has neither been open to negotiation or even meaningful debate.

Theory Implications Belief in the democratic, egalitarian and collaborative leadership of organizational change is a value judgement. However, in terms of developing collaborative leadership and organizational change theories, there are many theories within this critical review that could be drawn upon by those sharing such values. **Research Implications** It would be good to test the efficacy of collaborative leadership of organizational change against non-collaborative leadership of organizational change, although given the paucity of theory, this may be difficult. In the interim, action research around the collaborative leadership of organizational change as a methodology would closely align with practice. *Practice Implications* In conducting this review, the potential of collaborative change leadership has surfaced many times. It was the conclusion that Rost (1993) appeared to reach, and it really does offer benefits to leaders, collaborators and organizations, even if it is unorthodox.

IN CONCLUSION

In reviewing leadership studies, Grint (2008) detected a strong tendency to go forward to the past, and in this critical review, there was normative pressure to adopt the prevalent orthodoxy about what is 'known' about leadership and organizational change. The agenda then becomes filling in gaps in the literature or making recommendations for further research, in the process solidifying the spurious orthodoxy encountered. This critical review has presented an opportunity to challenge this orthodoxy and encourage change within conceptualisations of leadership and organizational change.

Leaders making change happen predates the 35 years featured here, and as long as we do not look inside the 'black box,' the show never ends. The mythologies and social constructions featured in Chapter Four discourage looking inside the 'black box.' However, in the eighties and nineties, American corporations struggled to compete, particularly with Japanese corporations. The imperative of leaders leading change required cultural reinforcement. Historical milestones informing belief in leaders leading change and managers managing stability were revisited and found to be largely informed by opinions, rather than the outcome of rigorous empirical studies.

This critical review has intentionally crossed the boundaries of the fields of leadership studies and organizational change studies, and it became apparent over decades that opportunities both to lead and to change in more democratic, egalitarian and collaborative ways were lost in the translation into orthodoxy. A conscious choice was made to go back to the future in order to understand how such futures were being constructed (Grint, 2008). Choices determined the literature reviewed (and not reviewed) and how it was reviewed. Kuhn's (1962) notion of academic disciplines converging and encouraging synthesis and knowledge accumulation was persuasive, yet rejected. These notions dictate literature reviewing best practice (featured in Chapter Five), but result in gap filling or what Rost (1993) mischievously labelled as the mythical leadership narrative (see Figure 4.2) without any challenging of background assumptions (Gouldner, 1971) or problematising of assumptions (Alvesson and Sandberg, 2011). Instead of characterising the fields of organization change studies (Chapter Three) and leadership studies (Chapter Four) by consensus and convergence, the divergence and dissensus of these fields have featured prominently. Burns (1978) argued for dissensus to be built into the structures of organizations, but again, this emphasis upon dissensus was lost in the translation into transformational leadership as imagined by Bass (1985).

In focusing on leadership and organizational change, despite the volume of literature, it really did not have that much to say about leadership and organizational change (see Ford and Ford, 2012; Parry, 2011). As long as we are haunted and governed by the paradigmatic assumptions of the natural sciences, which encourage convergence and consensus, resulting in gap filling, paraphrased as the 'we are almost there' type thinking, nothing will change. That is really how 'the smoke and mirrors' of leadership and organizational change works. This critical review has strived to highlight the potential within divergence and dissensus. A potential uncomfortable outcome that Chapter Five highlighted was even the disappearance of what was being studied, which is compatible with Grint's (2000:13) position that '. . .leadership is primarily rooted in, and a product of, the imagination.' However, ending on a slightly more hopeful note, this critical review has offered grounds for optimism, which may be couched in terms of theory, research and practice.

In terms of leadership and organizational change theories, the philosophies of organizational change (Smith and Graetz, 2011) introduced in Chapter Three and applied to leadership studies in Chapter Five offer a means to creatively work with the divergence and dissensus characterising the sub-field of leadership and organizational change. Theories of leadership and organizational change have been framed in particular ways (see discussion in Chapter Four and application in Chapter Five). The findings from Chapter Two were that when gauged against citation counts, the transformational leadership writings of Bernard Bass and the leading change writings of John Kotter had been particularly influential. These writings may have framed how leadership and organizational change is now understood (see Chapter Five), but the sub-field still could potentially be theoretically framed in very different ways.

In terms of leadership and organizational change research, the anticipated research-informed advances were not evident. In Chapter Five, this was explained in terms of the research design and methodological challenges of researching the intersection of two separate and divergent fields. The major research question, which remains unanswered, is, Do leaders influence the success of organizational change and if they do, how do they?

> . . .[W]e find the available research equivocal and incomplete regarding both what constitutes effective leadership and the impact of change leader approaches, behaviors and activities on change outcomes of any type.
>
> (Ford and Ford, 2012:22)

The normal recommendations for further research may prove fruitful, but this critical review has favoured the need for a more fundamental rethink of the assumptions and paradigms influencing leadership and organizational change understanding.

In terms of leadership of organizational change practices, the REPLACE framework introduced in Chapter Three highlighted empirical advances pertinent to the practicalities of leading change. The framework does not have the same persuasive practitioner appeal as Kotter's (1996) *Leading Change*, but offers a way forward for those practitioners favouring a research-informed/evidence-based approach. In a similar manner, a bricolage (Weick, 1993) approach to change leadership has practical merit; it encourages practitioners to develop their own frameworks/models selectively by drawing upon elements from the literature featured in this review in response to their own unique situation, instead of placing faith in off-the-shelf/one best way solutions. Finally, Rost (1997), through his own immersion in the leadership studies literature, came to the realisation that leadership was an influence relationship amongst leaders and collaborators with the intention of real changes reflecting mutual purposes. Dominant mindsets and their embedded assumptions currently maintain the status quo of neglecting collaborators in processes of changing and avoiding the ethical safeguards of mutual purpose. There are very real reasons why such certainties have been maintained over many decades. However, it is never too late to question such orthodoxy and the inequalities it perpetuates.

REFERENCES

Aitken, P., and M. Higgs. 2010. *Developing Change Leaders: The Principles and Practices of Change Leadership Development*. London: Butterworth—Heinemann.
Alvesson, M., and A. Spicer, eds. 2011. *Metaphors We Lead By: Understanding Leadership in the Real World*. London: Routledge.
Alvesson, M., and J. Sandberg. 2011. "Generating Research Questions Through Problematization". *Academy of Management Review* 36 (2): 247–271.

Bandura, A. 1986. *Social Foundations of Thought and Action: A Social Cognitive Theory*. Englewood Cliffs: Prentice Hall.

Barker, R. 1997. "How Can We Train Leaders If We Don't Know What Leadership Is?" *Human Relations* 50 (4): 343–362.

Bass, B.M. 1985. *Leadership and Performance Beyond Expectations*. New York: Free Press.

Bass, B.M., and R.E. Riggio. 2006. *Transformational Leadership*, 2nd ed. Mahwah, NJ: Lawrence Erlbaum Associates Inc/Psychology Press.

Battilana, J., M. Gilmartin, M. Sengul, A.C. Pache, and J.A. Alexander. 2010. "Leadership Competencies for Implementing Planned Organizational Change". *The Leadership Quarterly* 21 (3): 422–438.

Beer, M., and N.Nohria, eds. 2000. *Breaking the Code of Change*. Boston: Harvard Business School Press.

Beyer, J.M. 1999. "Taming and Promoting Charisma to Change Organizations". *The Leadership Quarterly* 10 (2): 307–330.

Boje, D.M., B. Burnes and J. Hassard, eds. 2011. *The Routledge Companion to Organizational Change*. London: Routledge.

Bryman, A. 2004. "Qualitative Research on Leadership: A Critical but Appreciative Review". *The Leadership Quarterly* 15 (6): 729–769.

Bryman, A., D. Collinson, K. Grint, B. Jackson and M. Uhl-Bien, eds. 2011. *The SAGE Handbook of Leadership*. London: Sage Publications Ltd.

Burke, W.W., D.G. Lake and J.W. Paine, eds. 2009. *Organization Change: A Comprehensive Reader*. San Francisco: Jossey Bass.

Burnes, B. 2004. "Kurt Lewin and the Planned Approach to Change: A Re-appraisal". *Journal of Management Studies* 41 (6): 977–1002.

Burns, J.M. 1978. *Leadership*. New York: Harper Row Publishers.

Burrell, G., and G. Morgan. 1979. *Sociological Paradigms and Organizational Analysis*. London: Heinemann.

By, R.T., and B. Burnes, eds. 2013. *Organizational Change, Leadership and Ethics: Leading Organizations Towards Sustainability*. London: Routledge.

Calas, M.B., and L. Smircich. 1991. "Voicing Seduction to Silence Leadership". *Organization Studies* 12 (4): 567–602.

Calas, M.B., and L. Smircich. 1996. "From the 'Womans' Point of View: Feminist Approaches to Organization Studies". In *Handbook on Organizations*, eds. S. Clegg and C. Hardy, 212–251. London: Sage Publications Ltd.

Carey, M.R. 1992. "Transformational Leadership and Fundamental Option for Self—Transcendence". *The Leadership Quarterly* 3 (3): 217–236.

Child, J. 2005. *Organization: Contemporary Principles and Practices*. Oxford: Blackwell Publishing.

Coch, L., and French, J.R.P (jnr). 1948. "Overcoming Resistance to Change". *Human Relations* 1 (4): 512–532.

Cohen, D.S. 2005. *The Heart of Change Field Guide: Tools and Tactics for Leading Change in Your Organization*. Boston: Harvard Business School Press.

Collins, D. 2000. *Management Fads and Buzzwords: Critical-Practical Perspectives*. London: Routledge.

Collinson, D. 2011. "Critical Leadership Studies". In *The SAGE Handbook of Leadership*, eds. A. Bryman, D. Collinson, K.Grint, B. Jackson and M. Uhl-Bien, 181–194. London: Sage Publications Ltd.

Collinson, D. 2012. "Prozac Leadership and the Limits of Positive Thinking". *Leadership* 8 (2): 87–107.

Conger, J.A. 1999. "Charismatic and Transformational Leadership in Organizations: An Insider's Perspective of These Developing Streams of Research". *The Leadership Quarterly* 10 (2): 145–179.

Cooke, B. 1999. "Writing the Left Out of Management Theory: The Historiography of the Management of Change". *Organization* 6 (1): 81–105.

Czarniawska-Joerges, B., and R. Wolff. 1991. "Leaders, Managers, Entrepreneurs on and off the Organizational Stage". *Organization Studies* 12 (2): 529–546.

Day, D. 2014. *The Oxford Handbook of Leadership and Organizations (Oxford Library of Psychology)*. Oxford University Press: New York.

Denis, J. L., L. Lamothe and A. Langley. 2001. "The Dynamics of Collective Leadership and Strategic Change in Pluralistic Organizations". *Academy of Management Journal* 44 (4): 809–837.

Diaz-Saenz, H.R. 2011. "Transformational Leadership". In *The SAGE Handbook of Leadership*, eds. A. Bryman, D. Collinson, K. Grint, B. Jackson and M. Uhl-Bien, 299–310. Sage Publications Ltd, London.

Fairhurst, G.T. 2005. "Reframing the Art of Framing: Problems and Prospects for Leadership". *Leadership* 1 (2):165–185.

Fairhurst, G.T. 2008. "Discursive Leadership: A Communication Alternative to Leadership Psychology". *Management Communication Quarterly* 21 (4): 510–521.

Fairhurst, G.T., and D. Grant. 2010. "The Social Construction of Leadership: A Sailing Guide". *Management Communication Quarterly* 24 (2): 171–210.

Fairhurst, G.T., and R.A. Sarr. 1996. *The Art of Framing: Managing the Language of Leadership*. San Francisco: Jossey Bass Inc.

Ford, J.D. and L.W. Ford. 2012. "The Leadership of Organization Change: A View from Recent Empirical Evidence". In *Research in Organizational Change and Development (Research in Organizational Change and Development, Volume 20)*, eds. In Abraham B. (Rami) Shani, William A. Pasmore, Richard W. Woodman (eds.) 1–36. Emerald Group Publishing Limited.

Ford, J.D., and N. Harding. 2007. "Move Over Management: We Are All Leaders Now". *Management Learning* 38 (5): 475–493.

Gemmil, G., and G. Oakley. 1992. "Leadership: An Alienating Social Myth". *Human Relations* 45 (2): 113–129.

Grint, K. 2000. *The Arts of Leadership*. Oxford: Oxford University Press.

Grint, K. 2005a. *Leadership: Limits and Possibilities*. Houndmills: Palgrave Macmillan.

Grint, K. 2005b. "Problems, Problems, Problems: The Social Construction of 'Leadership' ". *Human Relations* 58 (11): 1467–1494.

Grint, K. 2008. "Forward to the Past or Back to the Future? Leadership, 1965–2006". In *Mapping the Management Journey: Practice, Theory and Context*, eds. S. Dopson, M. Earl, and P. Snow, 104–118. Oxford: Oxford University Press.

Gouldner, A.W. 1971. *The Coming Crisis of Western Sociology*. London: Heinemann.

Guest, D. 1990. "Human Resource Management and the American dream". *Journal of Management Studies* 27 (4): 377–397.

Haslam, S.A., S.D. Reicher and M.J. Platlow. 2011. *The New Psychology of Leadership: Identity Influence and Power*. Hove: Psychology Press.

Higgs, M., and D. Rowland. 2005. "All Changes Great and Small: Exploring Approaches to Change and Its Leadership". *Journal of Change Management* 5 (2): 121–151.

Huczynski, A. 2006. *Management Gurus*, rev. ed. Abingdon: Routledge.

Hughes, M. 2011. "Do 70 Per Cent of All Organizational Change Initiatives Really Fail?" *Journal of Change Management* 11 (4): 451–464.

Hughes, M. forthcoming. "Leading Changes: Why Transformation Explanations Fail". *Leadership*.

Hughes, M. 2015. "The Perpetual Motion of the Change Machines". *British Academy of Management Conference*, University of Portsmouth, 9th–11th September.

Keller, A. 1966. "The Age of the Projectors". *History Today* 16 (7): 467–474.
Kelly, S. 2014. "Towards a Negative Ontology of Leadership". *Human Relations* 67 (8): 905–922.
Knights, D., and H. Willmott. 1997. "The Hype and Hope of Interdisciplinary Management Studies". *British Journal of Management* 8 (1): 9–22.
Kotter, J.P. 1988. *The Leadership Factor*. New York: Free Press.
Kotter, J.P. 1990. *A Force for Change: How Leadership Differs from Management*. New York: Free Press.
Kotter, J.P. 1995. "Leading Change: Why Transformation Efforts Fail". *Harvard Business Review* 73 (2): 59–67.
Kotter, J.P. 1996 and 2012. *Leading Change*. Boston, MA: Harvard Business School Press.
Kotter, J.P., and D.S. Cohen. 2002. *The Heart of Change: Real-Life Stories of How People Change Their Organizations*. Boston: Harvard Business School Press.
Kuhn, T.S. 1962. *The Structure of Scientific Revolutions*. Chicago: The University of Chicago Press.
Langley, A., C. Smallman, H. Tsoukas and A.H. Van de Ven. 2013. "Process Studies of Change in Organization and Management: Unveiling Temporality, Activity and Flow". *Academy of Management Journal* 56 (1): 1–13.
Lewin, K. 1947. "Frontiers in Group Dynamics: Concept, Method and Reality in Social Science; Social Equilibria and Social Change". *Human Relations* 1 (1): 5–41.
Lippitt, R., J. Watson and B. Westley. 1958. *The Dynamics of Planned Change*. New York: Harcourt, Brace and Company.
Nohria, N., and R. Khurana, eds. 2010. *Handbook of Leadership Theory and Practice: A Harvard Business School Centennial Colloquium*. Harvard: Boston: Harvard Business Press.
Ord-Hume, A.W.J.G. 1977. *Perpetual Motion: The History of an Obsession*. Kempton Illinois: Adventures Unlimited Press.
O'Reilly, D., and M. Reed. 2010. " 'Leaderism': An Evolution of Managerialism in UK public Service Reform". *Public Administration* 88 (4): 960–978.
O'Toole, J. 1995. *Leading Change: Overcoming the Ideology of Comfort and the Tyranny of Custom*. San Francisco: Jossey Bass—An Imprint of Wiley.
Paglis, L.L., and Green, S.G. 2002. "Leadership Self Efficacy and Managers' Motivation for Leading Change". *Journal of Organizational Behavior* 23 (2): 215–35.
Parry, K.W. 2011. "Leadership and Organization Theory". In *The SAGE Handbook of Leadership*. eds. A. Bryman, D. Collinson, K. Grint, B. Jackson and M. Uhl-Bien, 53–70. London: Sage Publications Ltd.
Pettigrew A.M., R.W. Woodman and K.S. Cameron. 2001. "Studying Organizational Change and Development: Challenges for Future Research". *Academy of Management Journal* 44 (4): 697–713.
Pondy, L.R. 1978. "Leadership Is a Language Game". In *Readings in Managerial Psychology*, eds. H.J. Leavitt, L.R. Pondy, and D.M. Boje, 224–233, 1989. Chicago: University of Chicago Press.
Riggio, R.E. 2011. "The Management Perspective: Engineering Effective Leadership in Organizations". In *Leadership Studies: The Dialogue of Disciplines*, eds. M. Harvey and R.E. Riggio, 119–128. Cheltenham: Edward Elgar.
Rost, J.C. 1993. *Leadership for the Twenty-First Century*. Westport: Praeger Publishers.
Rost, J.C. 1995. "Leadership: A Discussion about Ethics". *Business Ethics Quarterly* 5 (1): 129–142.
Rost, J.C. 1997. "Moving from Individual to Relationship: A Post-Industrial Paradigm of Leadership". *The Journal of Leadership Studies* 4 (4): 3–16.

Rumsey, M.G. 2012. *The Oxford Handbook of Leadership (Oxford Library of Psychology)*. New York: Oxford University Press.

Sandison, A., and R. Dingley, eds. 2010. *Histories of the Future: Studies in Fact, Fantasy and Science Fiction*. Houndmills: Palgrave.

Schaffer, S. 1995. "The Show That Never Ends: Perpetual Motion in the Early Eighteenth Century". *British Journal of the History of Science* 28 (2):157–189.

Selznick, P. 1957. *Leadership in Administration: A Sociological Interpretation*. Berkeley: University of California Press.

Smircich, L., and G. Morgan. 1982. "Leadership: The Management of Meaning". *The Journal of Applied Behavioural Science* 18 (3): 257–273.

Smith, A.C.T., and F.M. Graetz. 2011. *Philosophies of Organizational Change*. Cheltenham: Edward Elgar Publishing Ltd.

Spector, B. 2014. "Flawed from the 'Get-Go': Lee Iacocca and the Origins of Transformational Leadership". *Leadership* 10 (3): 361–379.

Sutherland, F., and A.C.T. Smith. 2013. "Leadership for the Age of Sustainability: A Dualities Approach to Organizational Change". In *Organizational Change, Leadership and Ethics: Leading Organizations Towards Sustainability*, eds. R.T. By and B. Burnes, 216–239. London: Routledge.

Thomas, R., and C. Hardy. 2011. "Reframing Resistance to Organizational Change". *Scandinavian Journal of Management* 27 (3): 322–331.

Tourish, D. 2013. *The Dark Side of Transformational Leadership*. Hove: Routledge.

Tourish, D., and N. Vatcha. 2005. "Charismatic Leadership and Corporate Cultism at Enron: The Elimination of Dissent, the Promotion of Conformity and Organizational Collapse". *Leadership* 1 (4): 455–480.

Trice, H.M., and J.M. Beyer. 1986. "Charisma and Its Routinization in Two Social Movement Organizations". *Research in Organizational Behavior* 8: 113–164.

Tyler, T.R., and D. De Cremer. 2005. "Process-Based Leadership: Fair Procedures and Reactions to Organizational Change". *The Leadership Quarterly* 16 (4): 529–545.

Weber, M. 1947. *The Theory of Social and Economic Organization*. Glencoe, IL: Free Press.

Weick, K.E. 1990. "Cartographic Myths in Organisations". In *New Thinking in Organizational Behaviour*, ed. H. Tsoukas, 211–220. Oxford: Butterworth Heinemann.

Weick, K.E. 1993. "Organizational Redesign as Improvisation". In *Making Sense of the Organization*, ed. K.E. Weick, 57–91. Oxford: Blackwell Publishing.

Weick, K. 1996. "Drop your Tools: An Allegory for Organization Studies". *Administrative Science Quarterly* 41 (2): 301–313.

Western, S. 2013. *Leadership: A Critical Text*, 2nd ed. Los Angeles: Sage Publications.

Yukl, G. 1999. "An Evaluation of Conceptual Weaknesses in Transformational and Charismatic Leadership Theories". *The Leadership Quarterly* 10 (2): 285–305.

Zaleznik, A. 1977. "Managers and Leaders: Are they Different?" *Harvard Business Review* 15 (3): 67–84.

Appendices

Appendix One

The Most-Cited Transformational Leadership Publications (1978–2014)

	Citations	Book/Paper	Title	Author/s
1.	3539	Book	Transformational leadership	Bass and Riggio (2006)
2.	3240	Paper	Transformational leader behaviors and their effects on followers' trust in leader, satisfaction, and organizational citizenship behaviors	Podsakoff et al (1990)
3.	2846	Paper	From transactional to transformational leadership: Learning to share the vision	Bass (1990)
4.	2284	Book	The transformational leader: The key to global competitiveness	(Tichy and Devanna, 1986a)
5.	2225	Paper	Effectiveness correlates of transformational and transactional leadership: A meta-analytic review of the MLQ literature	Lowe et al (1996)
6.	1783	Paper	Ethics, character, and authentic transformational leadership behavior	Bass and Steidlmeier (1999)
7.	1704	Paper	Does the transactional–transformational leadership paradigm transcend organizational and national boundaries?	Bass (1997)
8.	1599	Paper	Transformational leadership, transactional leadership, locus of control, and support for innovation: Key predictors of consolidated-business-unit performance	Howell and Avolio (1993)

(Continued)

Citations	Book/Paper	Title	Author/s
9. 1429	Paper	Two decades of research and development in transformational leadership	Bass (1999)
10. 1318	Paper	Transformational leadership development: Manual for the multifactor leadership questionnaire	Bass and Avolio (1990)

Notes on Appendix One

1. Books and journal papers published between the 1st of January 1978 and the 31st of December 2014 that referred to 'transformational leader/s,' 'transformational leadership,' 'leadership of transformation' and 'leading transformation' within their titles, as identified on the 2nd of April 2015 were ranked in terms of their number of citations. One thousand publication listings were generated and in some instances, the Google-based citations featured a publication more than once in these instances only the highest ranking was included.

2. Please see reference list at the end of Chapter Two for full references.

Appendix Two

The Most-Cited Leadership of Change Publications (1978–2014)

No	Citations	Book/Paper	Title	Author/Year
1.	6638	Book	Leading change	Kotter (1996)
2.	4340	Paper	Leading change: Why transformation efforts fail	Kotter (1995)
3.	471	Book	Leading change: Overcoming the ideology of comfort and the tyranny of custom	O'Toole (1995)
4.	438	Book	Beyond change management: How to achieve breakthrough results through conscious change leadership (1st and 2nd Editions)	Anderson and Ackerman Anderson (2010)
5.	360	Book	Leading change toward sustainability	Doppelt (2009)
6.	263	Paper	The effects of transformational and change leadership on employees' commitment to a change: A multilevel study	Herold et al (2008)
7.	257	Book	Change leadership: A practical guide to changing our schools	Wagner et al (2010)
8.	238	Book	Building the bridge as you walk on it: A guide for leading change	Quinn (2011)
9.	237	Paper	Change management—or change leadership?	Gill (2003)
10.	233	Paper	Leadership self efficacy and managers' motivation for leading change	Paglis and Green (2002)

Notes on Appendix Two

1. Books and journal papers published between the 1st of January 1978 and the 31st of December 2014 that referred to 'change leader/s,' 'change leadership,' 'leadership of change' and 'leading change' within their titles as identified on the 2nd of April 2015 were ranked in terms of the number of citations. One thousand publication listings were generated and in some instances, the Google-based citations featured a publication more than once. In these instances, only the highest ranking has been included.

2. Please see reference list at the end of Chapter Two for full references.

Appendix Three

The Leadership Quarterly Papers

Year	Vol/Issue	Author/s	Paper Title	Change Theme	Original Research
1990	1(2)	Podsakoff, MacKenzie, Moorman and Fetter	Transformational Leader Behaviors and Their Effects on Followers' Trust in Leader, Satisfaction, and Organizational Citizenship Behaviors	Transformational Leader	Yes
1990	1(4)	Bass	Editorial: Transformational Leaders Are Not Necessarily Participative	Transformational Leaders	No
1990	1(4)	Ehrlich, Meindl and Viellieu	The Charismatic Appeal of a Transformational Leader: An Empirical Case Study of a Small, High-Technology Contractor	Transformational Leader	Yes
1992	3(3)	Carey	Transformational Leadership and Fundamental Option for Self—Transcendence	Transformational Leadership	No
1993	4(1)	Yammarino, Spangler and Bass	Transformational Leadership and Performance: A Longitudinal Investigation	Transformational Leadership	Yes
1994	5(2)	Druskat	Gender and Leadership Style: Transformational and Transactional Leadership in the Roman Catholic Church	Transformational Leadership	Yes
1994	5(2)	Wofford and Goodwin	A Cognitive Interpretation of Transactional and Transformational Leadership Theories	Transformational Leadership	Yes

Year	Vol(Issue)	Author	Title	Category	
1995	6(2)	Avolio and Bass	Individual Consideration Viewed at Multiple Levels of Analysis: A Multi-Level Framework for Examining the Diffusion of Transformational Leadership	Transformational Leadership	No
1995	6(4)	Bass	Theory of Transformational Leadership Redux	Transformational Leadership	Yes
1998	9(1)	Brown and Lord	The Utility of Experimental Research in the Study of Transformational/Charismatic Leadership	Transformational Leadership	Yes
1998	9(1)	Wofford, Goodwin and Whittington	A Field Study of a Cognitive Approach to Understanding Transformational and Transactional Leadership	Transformational Leadership	Yes
1998	9(1)	Yammarino, Spangler and Dubinsky	Transformational and Contingent Reward Leadership: Individual, Dyad and Group Levels of Analysis	Transformational Leadership	Yes
1999	10(2)	Bass and Steidlmeier	Ethics, Character, and Authentic Transformational Leadership Behavior	Transformational Leadership	No
1999	10(2)	Beyer	Taming and Promoting Charisma to Change Organizations	Charisma and Organizational Change	No
1999	10(2)	Conger	Charismatic and Transformational Leadership in Organizations: An Insider's Perspective of These Developing Streams of Research	Transformational Leadership	No
1999	10(2)	Conger and Hunt	Charismatic and Transformational Leadership: Taking Stock of the Present and the Future (Part 1)	Transformational Leadership	No
1999	10(2)	Hartog	Culture Specific and Cross-Culturally Generalizable Implicit Leadership Theories: Are Attributes of Charismatic/Transformational Leadership Universally Endorsed?	Transformational Leadership	Yes
1999	10(2)	Hunt	Transformational/Charismatic Leadership's Transformation of the Field: An Historical Essay	Transformational Leadership	No

(Continued)

Year	Vol/Issue	Author/s	Paper Title	Change Theme	Original Research
1999	10 (2)	Yukl	An Evaluation of Conceptual Weaknesses in Transformational and Charismatic Leadership Theories	Transformational Leadership	No
2000	11 (2)	Zacharatos, Barling and Kelloway	Development and Effects of Transformational Leadership in Adolescents	Transformational Leadership	Yes
2000	11 (2)	Popper, Mayseless and Castelnovo	Transformational Leadership and Attachment	Transformational Leadership	Yes
2000	11 (2)	Hooijberg and Choi	From Selling Peanuts and Beer in Yankee Stadium to Creating a Theory of Transformational Leadership: An Interview with Bernie Bass	Transformational Leadership	No
2003	14 (1)	Popper and Mayseless	Back to Basics: Applying a Parenting Perspective to Transformational Leadership	Transformational Leadership	No
2003	14 (1)	Price	The Ethics of Authentic Transformational Leadership	Transformational Leadership	No
2003	14 (2)	Pillai, Williams, Lowe and Jung	Personality, Transformational Leadership, Trust, and the 2000 U.S. Presidential Vote	Transformational Leadership	Yes
2003	14 (3)	Dvir and Shamir	Follower Developmental Characteristics as Predicting Transformational Leadership: A Longitudinal Field Study	Transformational Leadership	Yes
2003	14 (4–5)	Jung, Chow and Wu	The Role of Transformational Leadership in Enhancing Organizational Innovation: Hypotheses and Some Preliminary Findings	Transformational Leadership	Yes
2004	15 (2)	Sosik, Godshalk and Yammarino	Transformational Leadership, Learning Goal Orientation, and Expectations for Career Success in Mentor-Protégé Relationships: A Multiple Levels of Analysis Perspective	Transformational Leadership	Yes

2004	15 (2)	Bommer, Rubin and Baldwin	Setting the Stage for Effective Leadership: Antecedents of Transformational Leadership Behavior	Transformational Leadership	Yes
2004	15 (3)	Rafferty and Griffin	Dimensions of Transformational Leadership: Conceptual and Empirical Extensions	Transformational Leadership	Yes
2004	15 (5)	Kan and Parry	Identifying Paradox: A Grounded Theory of Leadership in Overcoming Resistance to Change	Leadership and Resistance to Change	Yes
2004	15 (5)	Berson and Avolio	Transformational Leadership and the Dissemination of Organizational Goals: A Case Study of a Telecommunication Firm	Transformational Leadership	Yes
2004	15 (5)	Fletcher	The Paradox of Postheroic Leadership: An Essay in Gender, Power, and Transformational Change	Transformational Change	No
2004	15 (5)	Whittington, Goodwin and Murray	Transformational Leadership, Goal Difficulty, and Job Design: Independent and Interactive Effects on Employee Outcomes	Transformational Leadership	Yes
2005	16 (1)	Zhu, Chew and Spangler	CEO Transformational Leadership and Organizational Outcomes: The Mediating Role of Human-Capital-Enhancing Human Resource Management	Transformational Leadership	Yes
2005	16 (2)	Brown and Keeping	Elaborating the Construct of Transformational Leadership: The Role of Affect	Transformational Leadership	Yes
2005	16 (4)	Epitropaki and Martin	The Moderating Role of Individual Differences in the Relation between Transformational/Transactional Leadership Perceptions and Organizational Identification	Transformational Leadership	Yes
2005	16 (4)	Tyler and De Cremer	Process-Based Leadership: Fair Procedures and Reactions to Organizational Change	Process-Based Leadership and Organizational Change	Yes

(Continued)

Year	Vol/Issue	Author/s	Paper Title	Change Theme	Original Research
2005	16 (5)	Benefiel	The Second Half of the Journey: Spiritual Leadership for Organizational Transformation	Spiritual Leadership and Organizational Transformation	No
2006	17 (1)	Boje and Rhodes	The Leadership of Ronald McDonald: Double Narration and Stylistic Lines of Transformation	Leadership and Organizational Transformation	Yes
2006	17 (1)	Schriesheim, Castro, Zhou and DeChurch	An Investigation of Path-Goal and Transformational Leadership Theory Predictions at the Individual Level of Analysis	Transformational Leadership	Yes
2007	18 (1)	Nemanich, and Keller	Transformational Leadership in an Acquisition: A Field Study of Employees	Transformational Leadership	Yes
2007	18 (2)	Rowold and Heinitz	Transformational and Charismatic Leadership: Assessing the Convergent, Divergent an Criterion Validity of the MLQ and the CKS	Transformational Leadership	Yes
2007	18 (5)	Maslin-Wicks	Forsaking Transformational Leadership: Roscoe Conkling, the Great Senator from New York	Transformational Leadership	Yes
2008	19 (5)	Jung, Wu and Chow	Towards Understanding the Direct and Indirect Effects of CEOs' Transformational Leadership of Firm Innovation	Transformational Leadership	Yes
2009	20 (1)	Nemanich and Vera	Transformational Leadership and Ambidexterity in the Context of an Acquisition	Transformational Leadership	Yes
2009	20 (5)	Balthazard, Waldman and Warren	Predictors of the Emergence of Transformational Leadership in Virtual Decision Teams	Transformational Leadership	Yes

Year	Vol(Issue)	Authors	Title	Theme	
2009	20 (5)	Currie, Lockett and Suhomlinova	Leadership and Institutional Change in the Public Sector: The Case of Secondary Schools in England	Leadership and Institutional Change	Yes
2009	20 (5)	Ndofor, Priem, Rathburn and Dhir	What Does the New Boss Think?: How New Leaders' Cognitive Communities and Recent "Top-Job" Success Affect Organizational Change and Performance	Leadership Succession and Organizational Change	Yes
2009	20 (5)	Osborn and Marion	Contextual Leadership, Transformational Leadership and the Performance of International Innovation Seeking Alliances	Transformational Leadership	Yes
2009	20 (5)	Purvanova and Bono	Transformational Leadership in Context: Face-to-Face and Virtual Teams	Transformational Leadership	Yes
2009	20 (5)	Rubin, Dierdorff, Bommer and Baldwin	Do Leaders Reap What They Sow? Leader and Employee Outcomes of Leader Organizational Cynicism about Change	Organizational Cynicism and Change	Yes
2010	21 (1)	Simola, Barling and Turner	Transformational Leadership and Leader Moral Orientation: Contrasting an Ethic of Justice and an Ethic of Care	Transformational Leadership	Yes
2010	21 (1)	Levay	Charismatic Leadership in Resistance to Change	Charismatic Leadership and Resistance to Change	Yes
2010	21 (1)	Liu, Zhu and Yang	I Warn You Because I like You: Voice Behaviour, Employee Identifications, and Transformational Leadership	Transformational Leadership	Yes

(*Continued*)

Year	Vol/ Issue	Author/s	Paper Title	Change Theme	Original Research
2010	21 (2)	Ospina and Foldy	Building Bridges from the Margins: The Work of Leadership in Social Change Organizations	Leadership in Social Change Organizations	Yes
2010	21 (3)	Tucker, Turner, Barling and McEvoy	Transformational Leadership and Children's Aggression in Team Settings: A Short-Term Longitudinal Study	Transformational Leadership	Yes
2010	21 (3)	Battilana, Gilmartin, Sengul, Pache and Alexander	Leadership Competencies for Implementing Planned Organizational Change	Leadership Competencies and Organizational Change	Yes
2011	22 (1)	Tims, Bakker and Xanthopoulou	Do Transformational Leaders Enhance Their Followers' Daily Work Engagement?	Transformational Leaders	Yes
2011	22 (1)	Vinkenburg, Van Engen, Eagly and Johannessen-Schmidt	An Exploration of Stereotypical Beliefs about Leadership Styles: Is Transformational Leadership a Route to Women's Promotion?	Transformational Leadership	Yes
2011	22 (2)	Nielsen and Cleal	Under Which Conditions Do Middle Managers Exhibit Transformational Leadership Behaviors? —An Experience Sampling Method Study on the Predictors of Transformational Leadership Behaviors	Transformational Leadership	Yes
2011	22 (3)	Reichard, Riggio, Guerin, Oliver, Gottfried and Eskeles	A Longitudinal Analysis of Relationships between Adolescent Personality and Intelligence with Adult Leader Emergence and Transformational Leadership	Transformational Leadership	Yes
2011	22 (4)	Hur, Van den Berg and Wilderom	Transformational Leadership as a Mediator between Emotional Intelligence and Team Outcomes	Transformational Leadership	Yes

Year	Vol (Issue)	Authors	Title	Construct	
2011	22 (5)	Menges, Walter, Vogel and Bruch	Transformational Leadership Climate: Performance Linkages, Mechanisms, and Boundary Conditions at the Organizational Level	Transformational Leadership	Yes
2011	22 (5)	Zhu, Avolio, Riggio and Sosik	The Effect of Unauthentic Transformational Leadership on Follower and Group Ethics	Transformational Leadership	No
2012	23 (2)	Balthazard, Waldman, Thatcher and Hannah	Differentiating Transformational and Non-Transformational Leaders on the Basis of Neurological Imaging	Transformational Leadership	Yes
2012	23 (3)	Williams, Pillai, Deptula and Lowe	The Effects of Crisis, Cynicism about Change, and Value Congruence on Perceptions of Authentic Leadership and Attributed Charisma in the 2008 Presidential Election	Cynicism about Change and Authentic Leadership	Yes
2012	23 (3)	Cavazotte, Moreno and Hickmann	Effects of Leader Intelligence, Personality and Emotional Intelligence on Transformational Leadership and Managerial Performance	Transformational Leadership	Yes
2012	23 (3)	Nielsen and Daniels	Does Shared and Differentiated Transformational Leadership Predict Followers' Working Conditions and Well-Being?	Transformational Leadership	Yes
2012	23 (3)	Stoker, Grutterink and Kolk	Do Transformational CEOs Always Make the Difference? The Role of TMT Feedback Seeking Behavior	Transformational CEOs	Yes
2012	23 (5)	Hu, Wang, Liden and Sun	The Influence of Leader Core Self-Evaluation on Follower Reports of Transformational Leadership	Transformational Leadership	Yes
2012	23 (5)	Hutzschenreuter, Kleindienst and Greger	How New Leaders Affect Strategic Change Following a Succession Event: A Critical Review of the Literature	Leadership Succession and Strategic Change	No
2012	23 (5)	Wang and Howell	A Multilevel Study of Transformational Leadership, Identification, and Follower Outcomes	Transformational Leadership	Yes

(Continued)

Year	Vol/Issue	Author/s	Paper Title	Change Theme	Original Research
2012	23 (6)	Dionne, Chun, Hao, Serban, Yammarino and Spangler	Article Quality and Publication Impact via Levels of Analysis Incorporation: An Illustration with Transformational/Charismatic Leadership	Transformational Leadership	Yes
2013	24 (1)	Zhu, Newman, Miao and Hooke	Revisiting the Mediating Role of Trust in Transformational Leadership Effects: Do Different Types of Trust Make a Difference?	Transformational Leadership	Yes
2013	24 (1)	Braun, Peus, Weisweiler and Frey	Transformational Leadership, Job Satisfaction, and Team Performance: A Multilevel Mediation Model of Trust	Transformational Leadership	Yes
2013	24 (2)	Epitropaki and Martin	Transformational—Transactional Leadership and Upward Influence: The Role of Relative Leader Member Exchanges (RLMX) and Perceived Organizational Support (POS)	Transformational Leadership	Yes
2013	24 (2)	Nohe, Michaelis, Menges, Zhang and Sonntag	Charisma and Organizational Change: A Mutilevel Study of Perceived Charisma, Commitment to Change, and Team Performance	Charisma and Organizational Change	Yes
2013	24 (4)	Ewen, Wihler, Blickle, Oerder and Ellen	Further Specification of the Leader Political Skill-Leadership Effectiveness Relationships: Transformational and Transactional Leader Behavior as Mediators	Transformational Leadership	Yes
2013	24 (4)	Koivisto, Lipponen and Platow	Organizational and Supervisory Justice Effects on Experienced Threat During Change: The Moderating Role of Leader In-Group Representativeness	Leaders, Organizational Justice and Change	Yes

Year	Vol (Issue)	Authors	Title	Leadership Focus	Original Research
2013	24 (4)	Parr, Hunter and Ligon	Questioning Universal Applicability of Transformational Leadership: Examining Employees with Autism Spectrum Disorder	Transformational Leadership	Yes
2013	24 (5)	Tse, Huang, and Lam	Why Does Transformational Leadership Matter for Employee Turnover? A Multi-Foci Social Exchange Perspective	Transformational Leadership	Yes
2014	25 (1)	Avolio, Sosik, Kahai and Baker	E-Leadership: Re-Examining Transformations in Leadership Source and Transmission	Transformations in Leadership	No
2014	25 (2)	Zhang, Wang and Pearce	Consideration for Future Consequences as an Antecedent of Transformational Leadership Behavior: The Moderating Effects of Perceived Dynamic Work Environment	Transformational Leadership	Yes
2014	25 (3)	Van Dierendonck, Stam and Boersma	Same Difference? Exploring the Differential Mechanisms Linking Servant Leadership and Transformational Leadership to Follower Outcomes	Transformational Leadership	Yes
2014	25 (4)	Antonakis and House	Instrumental Leadership: Measurement and Extension of Transformational-Transactional Leadership Theory	Instrumental Leadership	Yes
2014	25 (5)	Spisak, Grabo, Arvey and van Vugt	The Age of Exploration and Exploitation: Younger-Looking Leaders Endorsed for Change and Older-Looking Leaders Endorsed for Stability	Age and Endorsement for Change or Stability Leadership	Yes

Notes on Appendix Three

1. Back issues were reviewed to identify all papers published between 1990 and the end of 2014 that referred to 'organizational change' and/or 'transformation' in their titles.

2. Papers that reported on primary data gathering were coded as original research (yes); it is acknowledged that some of those coded (no) extensively reported research. The intention was to gauge the original research being undertaken into leadership and organizational change.

3. Please see reference list at the end of Chapter Two for full references.

Appendix Four

The Journal of Change Management Papers

Year	Vol/Issue	Author/s	Paper Title	Leadership Theme	Original Research
2000	1 (2)	Higgs and Rowland	Building change leadership capability: 'The quest for change competence'	Competency and Capability	Yes
2000	1 (3)	Bloch	Positive deviants and their power on transformational leadership	Positive Deviance	No
2001	2 (1)	Higgs and Rowland	Developing change leaders: Assessing the impact of a development programme	Competency and Capability	Yes
2001	2 (2)	James and Ward	Leading a multinational team of change agents at Glaxo Wellcome (now GlaxoSmithKline)	Team dynamics	No
2001	2 (3)	Hyde and Paterson	Leadership development as a vehicle for change during merger	Leadership Development	No
2001	2 (4)	Miller	Successful change leaders: What makes them? What do they do that is different?	Competency and Capability	No
2002	3 (4)	Higgs	Guest Editorial—Special issue on leadership	Editorial	N/A
2002	3(4)	Vinnicombe and Singh	Women-only management training: An essential part of women's leadership development	Leadership Development	No

Year	Code	Author	Title	Theme	Selected
2002	3 (4)	Weymes	Relationships not leadership sustain successful organisations	Leadership Relations	No
2002	3 (4)	Conger and Toegel	Action learning and multi-rater feedback as leadership development interventions: Popular but poorly deployed	Leadership Development	No
2002	3 (4)*	Gill	Change management—or change leadership?	Differentiating leadership and management	No
2002	3 (4)	Parry and Proctor-Thompson	Leadership, culture and performance: The case of the New Zealand public sector	Culture and Performance	Yes
2002	3(4)	Pepper	Leading professionals: A science, a philosophy and a way of working	Complexity Science Servant Leadership	No
2004	4 (2)	Woodward and Hendry	Leading and coping with change	Coping Processes	Yes
2005	5 (2)*	Higgs and Rowland	All changes great and small: Exploring approaches to change and its leadership	Change leadership approaches	Yes
2005	5 (2)	Kuhl, Schnelle and Tillman	Lateral leadership: An organizational approach to change	Lateral leadership	No
2005	5 (3)	Wren and Dulewicz	Leading competencies, activities and successful change in the Royal Air Force	Competency and Capability	Yes
2005	5(4)	Lakshman	Top executive knowledge leadership: Managing knowledge to lead change at General Electric	Knowledge Leadership	Yes

(Continued)

Year	Vol/ Issue	Author/s	Paper Title	Leadership Theme	Original Research
2006	6 (1)	Smid, Hout and Burger	Leadership in organisational change: Rules for successful hiring in interim management	Interim Management	Yes
2006	6 (1)	Karp	Transforming organisations for organic growth: The DNA of change leadership	Chaos Theory Organic Growth	No
2006	6 (4)	Young and Dulewicz	Leadership styles, change context and leader performance in the Royal Navy	Competency and Capability	Yes
2007	7(1)	Ferdig	Sustainability leadership: Co-creating a sustainable future	Sustainability Leadership	No
2008	8 (1)	Karp and Helgo	From change management to change leadership: Embracing chaotic change in public service organizations	Chaotic Change	No
2009	9 (2)*	Van Dijk and Van Dick	Navigating organizational change: Change leaders, employee resistance and work-based entities	Resistance to Change Social Identity	Yes
2009	9 (2)*	Higgs	The good, the bad and the ugly: Leadership and narcissism	Leadership Narcissism	No
2009	9 (3)	Hartley	Leading grassroots change in the academy: Strategic and ideological adaptation in the civic engagement movement	Grassroots Leadership	Yes

Year	Vol (Issue)	Authors	Title	Theme	Empirical
2009	9 (3)	Hawkins and Dulewicz	Relationships between leadership style, the degree of change experienced, performance and follower commitment in policing	Leadership Style	Yes
2009	9(3)	Mars	Student entrepreneurs as agents of organizational change and social transformation: A grassroots leadership perspective	Grassroots Leadership	Yes
2009	9 (4)	Lyons, Swindler and Offner	The impact of leadership on change readiness in the US military	Change Readiness	Yes
2009	9 (4)	Michaelis, Stegmaier and Sonntag	Affective commitment to change and innovation implementation behavior: The role of charismatic leadership and employees' trust in top management	Charismatic Leadership	Yes
2010	10 (2)	Good and Sharma	A little more rigidity: Firming the construct of leader flexibility	Leadership Development	No
2010	10 (4)	Higgs and Rowland	Emperors with clothes on: The role of self-awareness in developing effective change leadership	Leadership Development	Yes
2012	12 (1)	By, Burnes and Oswick	Change management: Leadership, values and ethics	Editorial	N/A
2012	12 (4)	Grover, Nadisic, and Patient	Bringing together different perspectives on ethical leadership—Ethics, Justice and Leadership (Special Issue)	Editorial	N/A
2012	12 (4)	Heres and Lasthuizen	What's the difference? Ethical leadership in public, hybrid and private sector organizations	Ethical Leadership	Yes

(Continued)

Year	Vol/ Issue	Author/s	Paper Title	Leadership Theme	Original Research
2012	12 (4)	Innocenti, Peluso, and Pilati	The interplay between HR practices and perceived behavioural integrity in determining positive employee outcomes	Behavioural Integrity	Yes
2012	12 (4)	Klaussner	Trust and leadership: Toward an interactive perspective	Trust and Mistrust	No
2012	12 (4)	Moorman, Darnold, and Priesemuth	Toward the measurement of perceived leader integrity: Introducing a multidimensional approach	Leader Integrity	Yes
2013	13(1)	By, Burnes, and Oswick	Creating a leading journal and maintaining academic freedom	Editorial	N/A
2014	14(1)	Grover	Moral identity as a lens for interpreting honesty of indirect leaders	Moral Identity	Yes
2014	14(2)	Van der Voet, Groeneveld and Kuipers	Talking the talk or walking the walk? The leadership of planned and emergent change in a public organization	Planned and Emergent Change	Yes

Notes on Appendix Four

1. Back issues were reviewed to identify all papers published between 2000 and the end of 2014 that referred to 'leader/s,' 'leading,' 'leadership' or 'lead' in their titles.

2. Papers with a * after the volume/issue number indicate that the paper was featured in the top twenty most-cited papers on the journal's home page.

3. Papers that reported on primary data gathering were coded as original research (yes); it is acknowledged that some of those coded (no) extensively reported research. The intention was to gauge the original research being undertaken into leadership and organizational change.

4. Please see reference list at the end of Chapter Two for full references.

Index

Note: Italicized page numbers indicate a figure on the corresponding page.

academic evaluations of organizational change 90–1
academic handbooks reviewed 40–6, 44
Academy of Management Journal 77
administration leadership 128–9
agency and organizational change 89
All Changes Great and Small: Exploring Approaches to Change and its Leadership (Higgs, Rowland) 209
American Dream 126, 133, 199
American Journal of Sociology 101–2
The Art of Framing: Managing the Language of Leadership (Fairhurst, Sarr) 115–16

Bethlehem Steel Company 70
Beyond Change Management (Anderson, Ackerman-Anderson) 32
biological philosophies 79
Building the Bridge as You Walk on It: A Guide for Leading Change (Quinn) 33
Burns, James MacGregor 100–3
Business Ethics Quarterly 138

cause-and-effect in leadership 114
Change Leadership: A Practical Guide to Transforming Our Schools (Wagner) 32
change management *vs.* leadership 125–33
chaos theory 39
charisma in transformational leadership 34–5, 75

Chartered Management Institute (CMI) 117
chief executive officers (CEOs) 81, 159, 164
cognitive aspects of transformational leadership 35
collaborative leadership 122, 122–5, 123, 212–16
Collier, John 71
common good 108, 137–8, 215
Conger, Jay 132
contextualisation of organizational change 90
creating capacity 210
Critical Leadership (Rost) 103
critical philosophies 82
critical review of leadership 7–14, 8, 11
Critical Theorists 74, 192
cultural discourse of leadership 157
culture-based philosophies 80

democratic leadership 4
democratic organizational change 201
Developing Change Leaders (Aitken, Higgs) 189
dialectical theory 76, 82
dictatorial transformation 75
disappearance and organizational change 89, 145, 181–2
disciplinary specialists 196–7
discourse and organizational change 89, 145, 180–1
Discursive Leadership (Fairhurst) 113
dissensus and organizational change 89, 145, 179–80
distributed leadership 50, 121

divergence and organizational change 89, 145
Docherty, Thomas 153
dualities philosophy *83*, 83–4
dynamism 84–6, 166–78

egalitarian leadership 4
emergent leadership approaches 39
EndNote software 27
ethical/moral conceptual frameworks 215
ethics and organizational change 88
evaluation of organizational change 90–1

The Fifth Discipline (Senge) 89
focused leadership 50
forced evolution 75
A Force for Change: How Leadership Differs from Management (Kotter) 131
fourfold typology of leadership *118*, 118–22
framing opportunities: of change 210; leadership and organizational studies 156–7; leadership studies 114–17, *116*, *117*, 134
From Transactional to Transformational Leadership: Learning to Share the Vision (Bass) 29
functionalism 68, 75

global financial recession 214
Google scholar citations 27
'Great Men' leadership theories 4, 5, 148, 213
grounded theory 37

The Handbook of Leadership Theory and Practice (Nohria, Khurana) 41
Harvard Business Review 50, 128, 159
Harvard Business School 6, 127
The Heart of Change Field Guide: Tools and Tactics for Leading Change in your Organization (Cohen) 204
heroic leader: distributed leadership and 48; 'Great Men' theories 136, 148, 160; mythological leadership narrative 123, 133; personalistic focus on 107;

post-heroic leadership 37; post-industrial leadership 213; revolutionary nature of 103, 130; societal belief in 173; transformational leadership and 170
humanism 68, 75, 82
human resource management (HRM) 164

Iacocca, Lee 132, 199
improvisation characteristic 86
incremental organizational change 16–17
individualism 138, 215
industrial-era leadership studies 134–7
industrial leadership paradigm *104*, 104–8
interdisciplinary leadership studies 135
International Journal of Management Review's (IJMR) 19, 145–7, *146*, 175, 177, 180, 192
interpretivism 68, 75, 82
intractable problems 144

Journal of Change Management 10, 11, 18, 33–40, 153

King, Martin Luther 113

language, landscape, boundaries and map 14–20
language and discourse in leadership studies *113*, 113–14
lateral leadership 39
leader-centric approach 111
leader-collaborator influence relationships 215
leader-follower influence relationships 102, 122–5, *123*
leaderism in managerialism 160–1
leader-member exchange 42
Leader-Member Exchange Theory (LMX) 30, 43–4
leadership: in administration 128–9; cause-and-effect in 114; change leadership bricolage 208; change management *vs.* 125–33; collaborative leadership *122*, 122–5, *123*, 212–16; critical depictions of 100; decision-making 85; defined 15, 17–18, 122; distributed leadership

50, 121; emergent leadership approaches 39; failure of 146; focused leadership 50; fourfold typology of *118*, 118–22; 'Great Men' accounts of 148; industrial leadership paradigm *104*, 104–8; interdisciplinary leadership studies 135; lateral leadership 39; leader-follower influence relationships 102, 122–5, *123*; management and 107; mythological leadership studies narrative 13, 133–4, 150; negative ontology of 110; organizational change and 42–5, *44*; post-heroic leadership 37; seduction of 136; social construction of 25; studies of 133–9, *134*; sub-field of 66; value-based leadership 37, 164; *see also* heroic leader; leadership of organizational change; leadership studies; transformational leadership

Leadership (Burns) 100–2, 154

Leadership: Limits and Possibilities (Grint) 112, 118–21

Leadership and Performance Beyond Expectations (Bass) 114, 155

Leadership Competencies for Implementing Planned Organizational Change (Battilana) 211

The Leadership Factor (Kotter) 130–1

Leadership for the Twenty-First Century (Rost) 100, 101, 103, 177

Leadership in Administration: A Sociological Interpretation (Selznick) 101, 128–9

leadership narcissism 39

leadership of organizational change: academic handbooks reviewed 40–6, *44*; background assumption *149*, 149–50; boundaries of 146–8; categories of 154–62, *159*, *161*; challenges and critiques of 166–75, *169*, *171*, *173*; as collaborative change leadership 212–16; conclusion 216–18; critical review 7–14, *8*, *11*; development implications

of 195, 197, 199, 200, 203, 205, 212, 216; development of research and scholarship within 33–40; discussion and preliminary conclusions 49–53, *51*, 175–94, *176*, *178*; future of 3–7, 203–6; as gap between literatures 195–7; introduction 24–5, 144–5, 189–92, *191*; language, landscape, boundaries and map 14–20; leading change *vs.* managing stability 199–201; maturity as a sub-field 148–54, *149*; methodologies contrasted 162–6, *163*; most-cited publications 25–33, *26*, *28*, *31*; as opportunities lost in translation 201–3; practice of leading 206–12, *207*; as problematic assumptions 192–5; as socially constructed mythology 197–9; sub-field of leadership 1–3, *2*; transformational leadership 28–30, *31*; university textbooks reviewed 46–9, *48*; *see also* organizational change; transformational leadership

The Leadership Quarterly: focus of 153; industrial leadership paradigm theory 108; introduction 10, 12, 18; leadership of organizational change 33–40, 49; philosophies-based approach to leadership 164; quantitative questionnaire surveys 167; transformational leadership contributions 175

leadership self-efficacy (LSE) 209

leadership studies: beyond orthodoxy 106–9; change management *vs.* leadership 125–33; collaborative leadership *122*, 122–5, *123*; framing in 114–17, *116*, *117*, 134, 156; industrial leadership paradigm *104*, 104–8; introduction 19, 99–101; language and discourse *113*, 113–14; limits and possibilities 117–22, *118*; mythological leadership studies narrative 13, 133–4, 150; myths and 109–11, *110*; social construction

and 111–13, *112*; twenty-first century leadership 101–5
leader *vs.* manager distinction 41–2
leading change 4, 47–8, *48*
Leading Change: Overcoming the Ideology of Comfort and the Tyranny of Custom (O'Toole) 31
Leading Change: Why Transformation Efforts Fail (Kotter) 4, 15, 28, 31, 32, 47, 75; academic citations of 93; boundary-defining note in 147; conceptual weaknesses of transformational leadership *169, 170–5, 171*; defined functions in 204; differentiation of leaders and managers 130–2; frame analysis of 157–8; guiding coalition *vs.* individual 107; impact of 155, 208; masculine tone of 108; metaphors in 159, 160–1; rethinking leadership 86–91, *87*; revised edition of 171, 193–4, 215; transformational leadership and 114–15, 151, 203
Leading Change toward Sustainability (Doppelt) 32
Leading Organizations through Transition: Communication and Cultural Change (Deetz) 115
learning and organizational change 88–9
Lewin, Kurt 70–1, 150
The Limits and Possibilities of Leadership (Grint) 19
logical incrementalism 47

male model of life 108
management: change management *vs.* leadership 125–33; gurus 149; human resource management 164; leadership 107, 130–3, 209; scientific management 70
managerial grid 70
Managers and Leaders: Are they Different? (Zaleznik) 129–30
Marxist–Leninist ideology 128
materialism 137, 138, 215
Matthew Effect 158
mental model of leadership and organizational change 155, 157
metaphors of leadership and organizational change 159
Midvale Steel Company 70

minimal threshold characteristic 85–6
morality and transformational leadership 102–3, 152
Multifactor Leadership Questionnaires (MLQ) 16, 29–30, 43
mythological leadership studies narrative 13, 133–4, 150, 194, 197–9
myths and leadership studies 109–17, *110*

National Health Service (UK) 38, 119, 211
neo-classical economic models 215
New Deal 126

Orffyreus Wheel 205
organizational change: critical and contested 91–3; dissensus and 89, 145, 179–80; explanation of 72–8, *73*; field studies 67–9; histography of 69–71; introduction 65–7; leadership and 42–5, *44*; philosophies and dualities of 78–86, *83*; as real, intended change 104; rethinking leadership 86–91, *87*; structural-functional view of 135; *see also* leadership of organizational change
Organizational Change, Leadership and Ethics: Leading Organizations towards Sustainability (By, Burnes) 45
Organization Change: A Comprehensive Reader (Burke) 44
organization development (OD) 70–1, 81
Organization Studies (Hinings) 69
The Oxford Handbook of Leadership (Rumsey) 43–4

parenting perspective in transformational leadership 35–6
participative evolution 75
Perot, H. Ross 130
perpetuum mobiles 204–5
phenomenological experiences 112
Philosophies of Organizational Change (Smith, Graetz): leadership *vs.* organizational change 148–9, 162; theoretical explanations

in 206; understanding
organizational change 66, 72,
77–9
pluralism of organizational change 91
politics and organizational change 88
positivism 138
post-heroic leadership 37
post-modernists/postmodernism 74, 82
post-positivist paradigms 45–6
post-structuralists 74
power and organizational change 88
*The Power of Framing: Creating
the Language of Leadership*
(Fairhurst) 116
practitioner-orientated writing 27
*Process-based Leadership: Fair
Procedures and Reactions to
Organizational Change* (Tyler,
De Cremer) 210
process thinking and organizational
change 88
pseudo-transformational leadership 30
psychology-based explanations of
leadership 139
Publish or Perish software 27

radical humanism 68, 75, 82
radicalism 215
radical structuralism 68, 75, 82
reality construction rules *116*
resistance, ethics, power and politics,
process thinking, learning,
agency and discourse, context
and evaluation (REPLACE):
empirical advances with 218;
in organizational change 87,
91; replacing deficiencies within
leadership of organizational
change 206; rethinking
leadership of organizational
change 19, 67, 177
resistance to organizational change 88
resource-based philosophies 79–80
Ronald McDonald (clown character)
165
*The Routledge Companion to
Organizational Change*
(Boje) 45

The SAGE Handbook of Leadership
(Bryman) 13–14, 42–3
salutary warnings 13, 201
Schein, Edgar 71
scientific management 69–71

scientism 138
shaping behavior 210
simultaneity characteristic 85
social construction of leadership:
concepts of 100; leadership
studies 111–13, *112*; mythology
of 197–9; overview 25
social science-orientated philosophies
162
*Sociological Paradigms and
Organisational Analysis* (Burrell,
Morgan) 68, 74
spirituality 138, 215
Stogdill's Handbook of Leadership
(Bass) 105
structural-functionalism 106, 135
structuralism 68, 75, 82
successful change equation 151–2
Sugar, Alan 119

*The Theory and Practice of Change
Management* (Hayes) 48
Times Higher Education 153
transactional *vs.* transformational
leadership 151, 156
transformational leadership: charisma
in 34–5, 75; cognitive aspects
of 35; conceptual weaknesses
of *169*, 170–5, *171*; critiques
of 168; emergence of 164;
historical perspective on 132;
introduction 3–4, 6, 15–17;
morality and 102–3, 152;
organizational change and 52;
overview 28–32, *31*; parenting
perspective in 35–6; studies and
debates over 154; transactional
leadership *vs.* 151, 156;
understanding 114–15
Transformational Leadership (Bass,
Riggio) 15–16, 75, 107–8, 132,
147, 208

university textbooks reviewed
46–9, *48*
urban *vs.* rural academic life 67–8
utilitarian leadership studies 137

value-based leadership 37, 164

Web of Knowledge software 27
Welch, Jack 160
Western Electric 70–1
Wild West frontier mentality 126